W. W Hibben

Rev. James Havens

one of the heroes of Indiana Methodism

W. W Hibben

Rev. James Havens
one of the heroes of Indiana Methodism

ISBN/EAN: 9783337194932

Printed in Europe, USA, Canada, Australia, Japan

Cover: Foto ©Lupo / pixelio.de

More available books at **www.hansebooks.com**

REV. JAMES HAVENS.

Rev. James Havens,

ONE OF THE HEROES

OF

Indiana Methodism.

By REV W. W. HIBBEN.

"Mr. Havens was one of the most powerful preachers I ever heard, and I have no hesitation in saying that the State of Indiana owes him a heavier debt of gratitude for the efforts of his long and valuable life, to form society upon the basis of *Morality, Education, and Religion*, than any other man living or dead."
HON. OLIVER H. SMITH.

FIRST EDITION.

INDIANAPOLIS:
SENTINEL COMPANY, PRINTERS AND BINDERS.
1872.

Entered according to Act of Congress, in the year 1872,
By REV. W. W. HIBBEN,
In the Office of the Librarian of Congress, at Washington, D. C.

PREFATORY

The venerable moral hero of this book merited a far richer monument than we have built for him; but with what material we could get, we have done the best we could, and we place our effort before the public, confident of their indulgence as we are of our own purposes and sincerity.

Our object has been to do justice to the man and to furnish to his friends some abiding evidence of his honesty and usefulness, of his goodness and greatness.

What we have said of him has been written fearlessly, and with no disposition to conceal his defects or to magnify his virtues. We have always remembered that he was but a man.

What we have said of others was forced upon us by their own relationships, and in this connection their fraternal recognition was a matter of duty as well as of justice.

To live forever in the world of example was the well earned honor of our grand old itinerant, and as we here present him, we rely more on the fame of the man, the Christian, and Gospel minister, to sustain the work, than we do, or can, on the accomplishment of our own performance.

THE AUTHOR.

CONTENTS.

	PAGE.
CHAPTER I. His Early Years	9
CHAPTER II. Christian Character	20
CHAPTER III. Domestic Habits	30
CHAPTER IV Personal Economy	39
CHAPTER V Character of his Friendships	49
CHAPTER VI. His Moral Firmness	59
CHAPTER VII. Heroic Spirit	69
CHAPTER VIII. Knowledge of Men	78
CHAPTER IX. His Opposition to Innovations	87
CHAPTER X. Devotion to Methodism	97
CHAPTER XI. Preparation for the Pulpit	107
CHAPTER XII. Style of his Preaching	116
CHAPTER XIII. Character as a Revivalist	126
CHAPTER XIV. Ministerial Success	136
CHAPTER XV Personal Popularity	146
CHAPTER XVI. His Generalship	157
CHAPTER XVII. Liberality of Sentiment	167
CHAPTER XVIII. Patriotism	177
CHAPTER XIX. His Orthodoxy	188
CHAPTER XX. Peculiar Oratory	199
CHAPTER XXI. Ohio Confreres	209
CHAPTER XXII. Indiana Cotemporaries	220

	PAGE
CHAPTER XXIII. His Local Ministry	231
CHAPTER XXIV His Circuits	242
CHAPTER XXV Stations	253
CHAPTER XXVI. Districts, and Character as Pres. Elder.	263
CHAPTER XXVII. Misconceptions of the Man	274
CHAPTER XXVIII. Itinerant Review	285
CHAPTER XXIX. Superannuated Years	296
CHAPTER XXX. Character and Death of his Wife	306
CHAPTTR XXXI. His own Demise	317
CHAPTER XXXII. Funeral Obsequies	327
CHAPTER XXXIII. His Monument	338

REV. JAMES HAVENS.

CHAPTER I.

HIS EARLY YEARS.

The log cabins of the West have been the birthplaces of many of our pioneer heroes, whose subsequent renown have placed them among the foremost of our American citizens. From many of these primitive dwelling places of the early settlers have come the distinguished orator, the eminent jurist, and many of our ablest and most useful ministers. The obscurity of their origin could not becloud their genius, as the defectiveness of their education failed to fetter their destinies. What nature had done for them was on a liberal scale, without stint or limit; and though rough and awkward, they were still the children of genius, as they were of the wilderness. Partaking of the nature of the soil on which they were born, they grew up to manhood erect and stately as their native forest trees, and felt their strength to be that of men, who should fear no danger, or shrink in the presence of the proudest foe. Deprived of the higher advantages of social and scholastic life, they yet learned, even in their youth that honor was the basis of all true manhood, and truth the foundation of substantial integrity. It was such convictions as these which gave them so frequently honor and eminence, and filled their lives so full of the lessons of instructive history. Every hill and dale of their native forests abounded with legends of Indian life, and these stories of valor and romance which were so often told them, gave to the spirits of the youthful pioneers especially, that high and noble daring, which, to a greater or less extent, marked the after years of their histories. The hardships of the hunter's life developed their muscular systems to their fullest perfection, and the bold daring of their wild adventures made them familiar with dangers, and often led them to risk their lives in perilous chases, where timidity and cowardice would have shrunk back as if shaken with terror. Every hill and valley around them had its story of their adventurous experiences; and the beautiful summer freshness of their wilderness homes gave them a love of cabin life, which could not be blotted from their memories or lost in their imagery. With such men dangers were not embarrassments, and obstacles were but seldom impediments; for no matter what might come or threaten,

> "They nobly dared the wildest storm,
> And stemmed the hardest gale;
> As brave of heart and strong of arm,
> They roamed o'er hill and dale."

To write the history of these early pioneers at this late day, we must gather fragments from a thousand battle fields, where physical action was considered life's highest virtue, and the true and the bold, the unselfish and heroic, were alone honored with the coronets of distinction.

But few of the life-stories of these foundation-builders of our western civilization have ever been written. But if they had been, their thrilling originality and grand personal achievements would, doubtless, have given them a place of prominence on the shelves of historical connoisseurs, as sacred as any of our American classics. What these men were in their simple combinations, and in the circles of their primitive society, may be gathered in part from the many broken sketches which have been gleaned, here and there, by a few of our western authors. But in thousands of instances, unfortunately, the individual hero had no historian to tell his tale, and the consequence was that his virtues were interred with his bones.

With the cabin for their birthplace and the wilderness for their college, these uncouth sons of the forest grew up to manhood, knowing nothing of book learning, and never dreaming of the important part they were playing in the grand march of our civilization.

Acute and simple, and as confiding, as they were heroic and daring, they were even in their natural virtues just such samples of our countrymen, as we who have succeeded them, should never cease to remember. For, humble and obscure as were their birthplaces, they were not disposed to forget them. Their young imaginations had pictured them in their hearts as wilderness grottos, whose beauty and finish were more complete and nearer the order of nature than any

Corinthian embellishment they ever subsequently scrutinized. The reminiscent lines of Hood—

> "I remember, I remember,
> The house where I was born;
> The little window where the sun
> Came peeping in at morn."

Were expressive of the religious reverence these cabin-born heroes of the West had for their early homes. Such impressions of childhood are indeed apt to be indelible, and with most men they are associated with life's purest, brightest and happiest pictures. In them they felt the first breath of a mother's love beat upon their bosoms, and there they learned the manly daring of a father's bravery. There they drank their first love of social life as it burst from the tender hearts of brothers and sisters, whose memories, like the dying tones of a mother's voice, lingered in their memories till life's latest hour.

It was in one of these humble tenements, in Mason county, Kentucky, where the subject of this tribute was born in the year 1791.

The whole western country, at that time, was more or less agitated with the gloomy threats of Indian depredations, and the defeats of Harmer and St. Clair had given to the scattered inhabitants a general trepidation, which made many fear a total devastation of the country. Mothers were alone with their children, while their husbands and older sons were out on the Indian path, in defence of the country. The day, indeed, was a dark one, and the clouds were ominous and fearful, for the wild tongue of rumor was uttering a thousand stories of danger, and the well known barbarities of the savage foe were dreaded by the helpless and the innocent, whose fruitful imaginations needed no exaggerations to picture out even the most threatening dangers.

Many sleepless nights were spent around their cabin fires, by these wilderness families, recounting the hair breadth escapes of the heroes of the West, which were vividly remembered by their children.

Mr. Havens' mother being the daughter of a Baptist minister, her religious confidence in the divine protection gave her assurance of safety which many others did not possess, and being a good singer she kept the candle of daylight burning in her cabin home by her cheerful spirit and pious song, and by this means quieted her children, and doubtless impressed them with sentiments of the divine protection which followed them through their future years.

The influence of such a mother can never be weighed or measured. Her impressions upon her children are those of the Divinity, and can not well be obliterated; for they are the first touches upon the heart of the types of life, and are imprinted with the ink of love which goes to the soul as with the power of an eternal covenant.

It was the misfortune of Mr. Havens, however, to lose this mother when he was yet but a little more than twelve years of age, a loss which he never ceased to mourn. For young as he was, he had learned to love her as the best friend of his life. The sunlight of her presence had made the brightest days of his youth, and when it was told him that she was dead, it seemed to him the sun itself had gone out forever. His young heart could scarcely realize that she was no more, and he fed himself with the belief that her pure spirit, though unseen, would be his angel guardian, until like her, he should give his body to the worms, and his soul to God who gave it. To a poor, ignorant boy, how sad is such a calamity! How pungent and painful the sorrow! How deep, and irretrievable the bereavement! It is like the thunder shock, and the lightning flash, which bears death on its stroke, and leaves but a single heart to feel the curse. Such a sudden exit seems to be as the burning wrath of the Omnipotent One—which none can read, but which all are compelled to bow to.

We remember, when many long years had rolled over Mr. Havens' head, on one occasion, at the house of a friend, where he was stopping, he took up the poems of Cowper, and with evident emotions, he read those inimitable lines:

> "My Mother! when I learned that thou was't dead,
> Say was't thou conscious of the tears I shed?
> Hovered thy spirit o'er thy sorrowing son,
> Wretch even then, life's journey just begun?
> Perhaps thou gav'st me, though unfelt, a kiss;
> Perhaps a tear, if soul's can weep in bliss—
> Ah, that Maternal smile! it answers, Yes."

Then closing his eyes to hide his tears, and laying down the book, he said: "If I had been capable of writing when my own dear mother died, I would have written just such sentiments as Cowper has, for no poor boy ever loved his mother better than I did."

We looked at the venerable pilgrim, as he stood before us on that occasion, moved, as he was, by the awakened love of a mother's memory, who had been in her grave for more than half a century, and we could but admire his sublimated emotions, and place a still higher estimate upon his Christian character. The feeling had in it the kindredship of the heavenly, and bore living testimony of the filial constancy of the aged veteran.

As was natural, a year or two after his mother's death, his father married again—when Mr. Havens, then a boy of fourteen, determined to make his home, for the future, with an elder brother, who lived in the State of Ohio. In a few weeks, after making some preparation, and with his father's consent, he accomplished his purpose. His brother was but an humble farmer, but, of course, could find some work for an energetic and well developed lad; and in the cultivation of the soil, which was then so primitive, he occupied his time, never once thinking for a moment but it would be the calling of his life.

The work of a farm always affords wholesome exercise and greatly favors the development of muscular strength and energy, and it was here, while yet in his teens, that he became known for his cool and calculating agility, as well as for that adventurous daring which showed he was a stranger to fear. The sports of those days were chiefly muscular; but no matter what they were, or where they led him, "our young Kentuck," as the boys frequently termed him, always evinced such spirit as showed he was · " to the manor born." Physical education, and development, were the only fashions of the times, and he that possessed them in their fullest capacity, was, as a matter of course, the hero of the hour. Intellectual culture had then but few advocates, and it was only rarely that a book of any sort was either seen or made use of. Consequently book learning was at a heavy discount, and none seemed to care to have it otherwise. Reading and laziness were considered synonymous, because but few of the inhabitants had ever realized the availability of either education or intelligence. Work was believed to be the only source of bread-making; and in that direction the whole community bent their energies. Of course, as yet, the schoolmaster was unknown among them, and therefore it will not be thought strange that Mr. Havens grew to manhood, with only the accomplishment of being a very poor reader of his own vernacular.

These misfortunes made the elements of youthful associations by which he was surrounded through all his younger years; and we here offer them as a full and honorable apology for that acknowledged deficiency in his education—but for which, he doubtless, would have made one of the most prominent stars in the galaxy of the Christian ministry in the west.

But hardy in constitution, as the oaks of his native forests, and governed as he always seemed to be by the conscientious ardor of the heroic virtues, he even in his youth had many thoughts far above his years. The teachings of his childhood had not been forgotten, and the death of his mother, at the tenderest period of his history, had kept alive the fires of a moral life, which taught him many of the lessons of his personal responsibility, and in some degree prepared him for the great work of the future.

The circumstances of the period may be somewhat comprehended when it is stated that the whole land was without churches or school houses, and even the moral status of the people was both confused and indefinite. The only religious privileges of the country were an occasional sermon by some Methodist itinerant, whose visits on a week day attracted but little attention, as most of the people were bitterly prejudiced and many believed that all such men aimed at was to get money and to tie up the people in the freedom of their privileges. It was not, therefore, strange that these Gospel pioneers often received more curses than blessings, and were frequently threatened with mob law and the dubious adornment of a coat of tar and feathers.

This moral monotony, however, was not destined to continue, for an event which occurred about this time took the entire country by surprise and resulted in such a change among the people as they had never witnessed before. A bold and stout young man, the son of a Presbyterian minister, had returned from a Kentucky camp meeting professing to be a converted sinner and a Methodist. He was full of zeal and fire, and he went through the whole neighborhood telling the story of his conversion and holding prayer meetings, where the people crowded to hear him by hundreds, and in a short time many others made a profession of their faith in Christ, and a large society was soon organized.

Such a change was indeed marvelous in the eyes of many, for the young exhorter had for years stood among the foremost in wickedness, and had even won the sobriquet of "The New Market Devil." Everybody in the land knew James B. Finley, and they could scarcely believe their own senses when they saw him and heard his exhortations Foremost in sin, he was now at the head of the little band of Christians, and he led them to victory as if he had been a veteran.

Among the converts under the exhorter ministry of Mr. Finley was James Havens, then but a boy of only fourteen summers, yet old enough to know that goodness was essential to true happiness, and that a life of honor must be a life of virtue. Young as he was, his act of joining the church was doubtless the turning point of his life—the Rubicon of all his future fortunes. This new relation gave to his youthful mind the reflections of a religious experience, while it imparted to his character the moral stamina of a fixed and decided purpose.

With his new thoughts and happy change of feeling, he was so highly elated that he wished to return to his old home in Kentucky to tell his father what God had done for him. A few months afterward he started on foot for Kentucky, little dreaming that he was going back to the place of his birth as a Christian Missionary; and yet it was so, for though the family were Baptists, they were only nominally in the church, and when the new convert related his experience, they were as much surprised as if they had never made any profession. They thought the change was too sudden to be either genuine or permanent, but yet they heard him tell his whole story without any show of doubt or irreverence, because they saw that the boy was honest and sincere, and evidently believed that the work wrought within him was none other than the witness of the Spirit that he was a child of God. But simple as his story was, it was not without its influence upon the family, and even upon others, who heard him tell it again and again, for each new comer must hear it; and thus, without any pretentions to anything more than a simple relation of his experience, the boy became the preacher of the richest theory of philosophy and of life the world of sinners has ever heard.

How often has the sentiment been uttered " that the boy is father to the man," and well it may be, for close observation will discover that the elements of character are often incorporated with the tenderest years, and that frequently genius flashes in the eyes of youth as flowers of beauty flourish in the bud. And yet, how strange is the intimation of either genius or character, particularly where it is concealed under the substratum of simplicity and ignorance, as innocent of either as if such things had never been.

What we are we make ourselves, for neither genius nor character is ever forced upon us. Nature is always lavish of her gifts, but then moral principle demands the personal improvement of each endowment, and, therefore, he alone becomes great and good who improves the gift that is within him and diligently gives his life to the happiness and welfare of others.

CHAPTER II.

CHRISTIAN CHARACTER.

"Would I describe a Preacher such as Paul,
I would express him simple, grave sincere;
In doctrine incorrupt; in language plain,
And plain in manner; decent, solemn, chaste,
And natural in gesture."

WE believe it was Richard Baxter who made the remark "that the people looked at the Preacher six days in the week to see what he meant when he preached to them on Sunday." The declaration is doubtless a true one of any age and of any people, and therefore demands serious consideration in any effort which may be made in the delineation of Christian character, and more particularly where the subject has been in the ministry.

Many thousands have heard Father Havens preach who never knew him either as a man or as a Christian, for he was emphatically the Preacher of the multitude, and of course, many never saw him except in the pulpit. Therefore, their observations were limited, as to what he was, in those delicate traits and personal developments which constitute the true man and the genuine and consistent Christian. But what he was in spirit, principle, honor, integrity and charity, was well known among his friends, for he wore no masks and assumed no pretensions, as he always scorned everything which bore even the type of hypocrisy.

Peter Cartwright was once asked if he was "sanctified?" "Yes," said he, "I think I am—in spots." Father Havens had something of the same spirit of the distinguished and venerable Cartwright, that is to say, he was a little particular who led the class where he attended, and besides this, he was not always ready to hang out "his flag of personal purity," if for no other reason, least he might cast his pearls before swine. The fact was, his religion was never gotten up for human inspection or show, or with any pharisaical purpose of building up a character of superior piety. He was willing for all men to judge him by his deeds, and, as he often used to say, "by the company he kept." He well knew that "birds of a feather would flock together." This was his own basis in his judgment of character, and of course he was willing to be judged by the same rule himself.

With Mr. Havens, principle made the man infinitely above all the tricks of pious policy, no matter how sanctimonious might be their pretensions. Indeed, he was never the friend of any sort of silk or satin piety, and he always looked with contempt and pity upon any and every effort which smacked in the least of Pharisaism. Still, his opinions of men were not usually formed hastily, and his general habit was to judge them by their spirit and intentions rather than by their professions as it was these points he aimed to guard so particularly in himself. To always mean well, he thought was a happy "leaning toward virtue's side," and went a long ways to make a good character. This virtue he well exemplified in his own life, as he ever fearlessly evinced it both in his frankness and honesty.

Simplicity was one of his prominent traits, and those who knew him best will readily accept of Webster's definition of the term as being peculiarily characteristic. The distinguished Lexicographer could not have hit the man, or comprehended his Christian character better, than he has in his definitions, "artless," "unaffected," "inartificial," "plain." Dr. Young has also defined it as well, when he says:

"In simple manners all the secret lies."

Though Mr. Havens had much about him of the stern dignity of a proud and noble manhood, his mien was never haughty or overbearing, for except when in the heat of an ardent contest, his spirit was much like that of a child; and but few men could be appealed to with better hopes of sympathy, or with stronger assurances of assistance. Though he sometimes seemed to be almost vindictively eager to have the guilty punished, no compeer he ever had was more ready or willing to extend the sympathies of forgiveness, where there were any reasonable evidence of sincere repentance. In this respect he was as honorable as he was honest, for when he once uttered his forgiveness of an error, his treatment of the delinquent was as kind and generous as if the act had never been committed. His gentle nature and tender sympathies, associated as they always were with his strong and vigorous intellect, gave him that high and benignant character which so well became his profession, and enabled him to secure the respect and veneration of religious men of all denominations. Such, indeed, was the spirit and action and decided character of the man and minister, and so firmly and sincerely did he demonstrate this in his religious profession, that he never failed to command respect in any crowd. His very presence, indeed, as well as his conversation, vindicated his Christian character on all occasions, and honored it as well as that of his ministerial office.

His religion was never put on to serve a holiday, or to display any Sabbath appearances; for what he was one day he was another, and whether at home or abroad, he seemed always to be conscientious in regard to the duties of his ministerial mission, and therefore, no matter how much of a stranger he was, he did not hesitate to bear his testimony against evil of any kind, or to admonish the erring, however prominent or distinguished. His ideas were, that the true Christian belonged to the grand army of the redeemed, and that no matter where he was, he was ever on duty, and therefore his obligations demanded that he should stand up for the right, and defend the cause of morals, even though some might think the battle-field was not a legitimate one. This peculiar disposition of his Christian character, did not grow out of any fondness he had for contention, for this was not his spirit; but it doubtless found its impulse in his personal independence, and in his fearless opposition to all the vices and practices which, in his view, drew men down to perdition. As an illustration of this trait in his Christian character, we here give the following little story, which has been furnished us by one of his friends, who vouches for its authenticity, as he was present and witnessed the scene.

In 1844, Mr. Havens attended the General Conference of his Church, which was held in the city of New York—the memorable Conference which resulted in the division of the great Methodist body, and which is so often referred to as the most eventful of any in its history. The venerable Indiana minister and delegate had participated in the exciting scenes of the long and protracted sessions of that Conference, and had witnessed its mournful adjournment. Returning home by way of Pittsburg, in company with several other ministers from the West, they took passage on board of one of the palatial steamers which plied between that city and Cincinnati. On the first evening, after supper, he and several of his brethren were seated round a table in the cabin, when some four or five gentlemen approached and requested them, in no very polite manner, to vacate their seats, as they wished to take a game of cards. Two or three of Mr. Havens' friends were inclined at once to obey the rather peremptory order and arose from their seats to seek some other quarters.

Mr. Havens was reading, and although he heard the request of the gamblers, he paid no attention to it, and did not seemingly raise his eyes from his paper. After eyeing him intently for a moment, as though he was measuring his strength and muscular abilities, one of the gamblers—himself a large and powerful man—approached Mr. Havens and requested him to get up and give them the table. The old veteran raised his head and looked at the intruder as if he was measuring him, but said nothing.

"You had better move, sir," said the impertinent intruder, with a scowling frown.

"That will depend upon circumstances," responded the brave old man.

"How so?" retorted the gambler, with a fiercer scowl, which he thought would frighten the old gentleman.

"If you are a better man than I am, sir," replied Mr. Havens, "it would probably be more prudent for me to obey your request, but it looks to me as if that was a very doubtful point; for *I do not know*," he added, "*that the Almighty has ever made a better man than I am myself.*"

This was said in so cool a manner and with so much earnest gravity, that the gambler shrank back as if he "had waked up the wrong passenger;" for he saw that though his antagonist was a minister, the old hero appeared to have the St. Peter kind of religion, and that, on this occasion at least, "discretion was the better part of valor."

The captain of the boat appearing just then, the affair was happily adjusted by his requesting the gamblers to withdraw to another part of the cabin, where he would accommodate them with another table.

"Who is that brave old codger?" asked the gambler of the captain after he had taken his seat.

"Why," said the captain, "they tell me he is an old Hoosier Methodist Preacher. They call him 'Father

Havens,' and they say he is afraid of nobody but the Almighty."

Father Havens sat and read his paper as if nothing had occurred, but the crowd of gamblers appeared to be quite evidently disturbed, and kept their eyes on the old "Hoosier Preacher" as long as he remained in the cabin.

Incidents of this character we are aware, with some do not affirm the highest Christian eminence, but then they should remember that the heroic in moral life are often the essential instruments in making aggressions, and that such spirits in many instances are found to do and dare where even the lamb-like are liable to flinch and falter. Then, it should not be forgotten that Father Havens was a western pioneer and that the fields of his ministry were often pretty well supplied with that class of men who have been termed "the baser sort." With this class, indeed, he often had to deal, and through all his eventful ministry, no instance ever occurred if it was within his power where he failed to teach them a lesson or to command their respect. Father Havens was eminently a peaceable Christian, and yet he did not believe in crying "peace! peace! when there was no peace." He well knew that there were many men who could not be held by silken cords or be quieted by the timid conservativeness of a non-combative submission, and therefore, while he hated war and despised contention, he was nevertheless of the firm conviction that the rights of all Christians were, at least, as sacred as those of any others, and hence, should be guarded with equal tenaciousness and care by every true believer.

He was not of the conviction that the good man should spend all his breath in prayer, or that he should profess by signs and sanctimonious pretensions that he was better than his neighbors. His theory of the Christian life was a practical one, for he believed that a good deal of it should be spent for the welfare of our fellow men, as well as for ourselves, personally. He did not understand the Christian character to imply either passive uselessness or cowardly conservativeness, for the one he knew would suffer Christianity to perish for the want of aggressions, while the other would hide itself amid the rocks while the wolves of a heartless infidelity would tear it to tatters.

Father Havens' faith was eminently a practical one, and as he believed, worked directly for the heart's purification. He did not embrace Christianity as a theory of moral problems merely, for he believed it was a system of living principles, which involved the true pith of all human civilizations, and was the only religious system that would, or could, lead mankind to the higher elevations of law and liberty, or to the real greatness of any intellectual progression or national renown. He therefore advocated a strict regard for all the minor virtues as well as the major, as they were essential in the building up of any sort of true and genuine character.

That he was sometimes led to doubt the religion of certain individuals was neither strange nor uncharitable, as he always believed that a Christian should be, and was, both frank and honest just in proportion as he was sincere and conscientious. These judgments were not designed by him to be harsh or even unkind, he only aimed to think of others as he thought of himself, and if, at any time, he became convinced that he had done any one injustice, he was as prompt to retract his opinions of doubt or censure, as he had been in uttering his condemnation. No man could well have a higher, or purer, or nobler charity than Father Havens, although he did not always possess the most polished way of showing it. His style was never that of the flatterer, and there was nothing he viewed with greater personal disgust than the popularity-seeking-theory of oily tongues, or the empty compliments of cringing sycophants.

His plainness of manners and bluntness of speech were often against him, and not unfrequently made him enemies where he should have had friends. His honest practice of calling things by their right names differed widely from the wisdom of the world, and it was because of this that some people considered that he was at times uncouth, if not even rough and uncharitable. These manifestations of an apparent censoriousness, with him were never the dictations of a domineering spirit, or of any haughty disposition to give insult or injury They were the natural outgrowth of his bold and independent mind, which was ever ready to rebuke sin of any sort, and among any class of people. Always resolved on right himself, his aim and purpose was to enforce it on others in every honorable way in his power. In doing this, he sometimes showed an aggressiveness of spirit, which would startle the timid and lead them to infer that he wished to carry his points, if it was even at the expense of peace and love, and with physical power. It was this heroic energy of his Christian character which doubtless gave him the greatest success in his ministry; and it was to this trait, mainly, we may attribute his decided and prominent recognition among the people.

Wherever he went, and wherever he labored, he always dared to do right himself, and his purpose was to have all others follow his example. With him, the arm of the right was above all show and all pretense; and therefore he was never ready to compromise it with either friend or foe,

"In any of the tricks that are vain,
Or the ways that are dark."

The proud manliness of his nature scorned the littleness of all scheming and soulless policies, and wherever he detected such a spirit he detested it with his strongest impulses; and none the less when he saw it in the ministry than elsewhere.

The brave heart and the true man he always loved, no matter where he might find him; and through all his Christian life he was never known to slight the the weakness of unsophisticated honesty, or to turn away from the timely succor of any man of true or honorable purposes. What he was before God he aimed to appear before men; and it was this never failing integrity which gained for him so distinctively the high regards of the best and leading men of the State.

CHAPTER III.

DOMESTIC HABITS.

The question was once asked Rev. Allen Wiley:
"Do you know Mr. Thompson *well*, Brother Wiley?"
"I do not. I never lived with him"—was the response of the old itinerant.

How true it is, that the home circle alone, reveals our true characters. What we really are, is known only there. What we merely pretend to be, is what the outside world usually knows of us anywhere else.

The fact is patent that the true character of a man is not always known by his public life. No, not even when he is a minister of the Gospel—for he, who is usually bland and polite in society, may often, in his own home, be selfish and morose, and display anything else than the Christian graces. Domestic integrity is not always evinced in the home circle in the blandishments of social cheer, or even by the reciprocal tenderness of becoming recognitions. The sternness of stolid abstraction often assumes the place of affectionate geniality, and the home hearth is made desolate on the most suicidal principles. Home tells the true story, for it is there that real character is tested; there only the inner man speaks out, and the true animus of the soul *is* read without any glossary.

With his wife and children, he becomes familiar, and they know him in his *weakness as well as in his divinity.*

At home the curtain is lifted and the man is on the

stage in *his* true character, in all his measured proportions.

As was once remarked, by a lady of her husband: "you can never see him except in his slippers—he is then himself."

Most people put on a face to receive their friends, and a very different one to accommodate themselves to their enemies. Hence, we must know what a man is at home with his wife and children, in order that we may understand what we may think of him when he is abroad. Mothers, wives, and children, are all made to stand on their home virtues, and it is only justice that the same law should be applied to men. Indeed, it is quite likely, that many men, who have had most respectable public records, would have lost much of their personal prestige had their domestic idiosyncrasies been fully revealed. In such inspections we know it depends much upon the kind of wife a man has whether he will display many home virtues or not, for her power, as all know, is frequently the arbiter of his character as well as of his destiny. Yet it is often the case, even when the wife is all she should be, that the husband is cold in his affections, and consequently careless in his family associations. Therefore, we aver that the mere pulpit performances of a minister should not be the chief exponents of his real character, for he may have splendid talents to preach but not the virtues to practice. The theory of goodness may be well on his tongue while his nature may be as rugged as the cliffs.

Such suggestions as these have come legitimately before us, in the effort of our pen in the delineation of

Mr. Havens' domestic character. If we did not investigate his spirit and history in this connection, we would not, and could not know him in the inner greatness of his spirit, or be able to fully appreciate the simple tenacity of his Christian virtues. Then, in addressing ourselves to this somewhat delicate task, we but render justice to the unpretending and good woman who was the partner of his life, who had undoubtedly much to do in the distinguished usefulness of his itinerant history, as well as in the well regulated government he had over his own disposition, which was naturally impetuous and fiery.

The eulogy once pronounced upon a good and great man, on the occasion of his funeral services, was, in an eminently honest sense, applicable to Mr. Havens:

"He was a good man, ever kind to his neighbors, and loved his wife and children as he did himself."

The fortunes of his itinerant life led him to seek a home in our State, and directly after coming to Indiana, in 1824, he entered a quarter section of land about three miles west of Rushville. Here he and his boys put up a small cabin, into which he moved his family, where he determined, as far as possible, to make them independent of all church stipends, and where he could raise them to habits of industry and economy, and at the same time give his own services to the itinerant work of the ministry. This humble cabin home was surrounded by an almost unbroken wilderness; but humble and obscure as it was, he felt that it was his own—that there his family would be happy, because they would neither be dependent, nor suffer for the want of bread or meat.

His circuits of course were large, and his frequent and long absence from home threw much of the management of the clearing up and labor of the farm upon his wife, who, with the aid of her sons, ultimately brought the place into such a state of improvement and production as to give them as comfortable a home as the country afforded.

That little farm enabled him to give his life to the labors of the itinerant ministry, and that wife, the mother of his fifteen children, through all those years, taught him by the simplicity of her spirit, and by her uncomplaining sacrifices, to love and reverence her with an affection which grew stronger with his years and held him with more than silken cords even down to the very Jordan of death.

Men ordinarily love their homes as they love their wives, and though the professional calling of Mr. Havens demanded his frequent absence from home his presence there was never prevented save by his itinerant obligations. What the church required at his hands he always attempted to accomplish, and therefore he yielded the sceptre of domestic government to his wife and children to a much greater extent than is common among fathers. To their economy and plans he generally yielded with grace, because he felt and acknowledged that his calling was that of the ministry, and to its special duties he directed so much of his attention, that often his return to his home was received more like the visits of a stranger than that of the proprietor.

The religious deportment of the household however, was always readily yielded into his hands, on his return from his circuits or districts, and the family bible and well worn Methodist hymn book were laid before him night and morning, for each member of the household felt that he was the High Priest of the family, and both wife and children listened to his song and prayer with devout solemnity as to one whom they knew to be sincere, and for whose character and pretensions they ever exercised the highest reverence. He often sang from memory a few verses of hymns familiar to the family, for he never was tedious, and the quivering tremor of his voice, both in song and prayer, carried with it, even in his private devotions, the strong convictive power of an earnest sincerity.

Mr. Havens' personal dignity and unostentatious spirit, made him both at home and abroad, the humble gentleman and the decided Christian, whom to know was to respect and hence the voluntary reverence which was always extended to him by his children, his neighbors and even by strangers.

They had intuitive confidence in his sincerity, and were well satisfied with his Christian honesty, for they always found him favoring the right and opposing the wrong, on all subjects, without regard to either fear or favor.

It mattered not with him where he was, in whose house or home he happened to be, he seemed never to forget either his position or character as a minister. What he professed to be he was always ready to make manifest, and therefore even among strangers, he frequently spoke out bravely in defense of the principles and claims of Christianity, where others, even of his ministerial brethren, would not even make themselves known. It was never Mr. Havens' conviction that he was under obligations to compromise with wrong in any society. He believed that God was everywhere and that there was principle in everything, and while he was not unmindful of the rules of a respectful etiquette, he but seldom yielded to a passive silence in any company where he saw there was a want of respect for honest principles.

In the earlier days of his ministry it was quite common for some Methodist Preachers to be extra careful of what they ate or drank. Of course in some families such particular guardianship of the appetite was prudent, to say the least of it, for otherwise they might have masticated more than their usual "peck" of earthly matter. But this fastidious squeamishness was rather ignored by Mr. Havens, because he thought it savored too much of Priestly pedantry, which, in his view, reflected but poorly on the self-sacrificing character of the ministry, and therefore he usually ate without questions anything that was set before him. He drank coffee, tea, milk or water, just as it was provided for him, at any meal, and at all places. He endeavored to be pleased wherever hospitality was offered him, and he aimed to give as little trouble to families as possible.

On one occasion he was invited to dine at the house of one of his friends where the lady was very profuse as well as premature in her unnecessary apologies.

"She was very sorry she did not have more notice of his coming, for then, she would have had him a good dinner. To-day," she added, "we really have nothing fit to eat."

The table was before him and Mr. Havens saw there was an abundance, and what was good enough for anyone, and he drew back from his chair as if he would retire, saying, "Well, sister, if you really have nothing fit to eat on the table, I will go somewhere else for my dinner, for I am really very hungry."

The good lady could but blush, for she felt the eccentric rebuke of the good old minister; and yet she could but smile a tacit consent to his admonition when he added: "But I believe, sister, I will try and make out with your poor dinner to-day by making my dessert on the faith of the one you will get me when you know I am coming next time." Mr. Havens ate many a good meal in that house afterward, but the sister never again troubled him with apologies.

He once said to another lady: "Don't, sister, make any apologies; I never like them. They are neither fish nor flesh, and they always embarrass me." To him they were like empty compliments—something he did not like to deal in. He preferred the plain manners and frank expressions of the olden days. He thought, and perhaps correctly, too, that the habit of making apologies frequently lead to falsehoods, and he often used to say that he but seldom ever heard a preacher make an apology and afterward preach a successful sermon. Mr. Havens loved the old domestic habitudes, the primitive manners which accorded with the customs of his earlier years, because he believed they were less tinctured with pride and duplicity, and had in them much more of the genuine spirit of a heart-warm hospitality. As might have been expected of one reared amid the elementary developments of our western civilization, Mr. Havens never cared much for conventional rules or metropolitan manners. Having himself in early life enjoyed none of their advantages, it was not to be expected that he would readily swerve from the habits and customs in which he had been so long educated. He loved to stop and make his home, in his itinerant travels, with those families whose manners were plain, and whose hospitalities were never measured or given for display. It was on this consideration that he never had many stopping places on his circuits and districts. When he found a good home, however humble it might be, he would always drive right to it as if it were his own domicil. For forty years he had been in the habit of stopping in the town of Brookville, in Franklin county, with Mr. Samuel Goodwin, the father of Rev. T. A. Goodwin, who was a tanner by trade, and whose residence was by "the seaside" of the White Water, where he always felt that he was a welcome guest. Though he spent hundreds of nights in that place, and visited many of the families of the town, he always had his lodging room at the home of Mr. Goodwin. He had his bed there, and he would never sleep, when in Brookville, in any other.

Such, indeed, was his unassuming domestic disposition that he was never easy if he saw that the hospitality extended to him was either studied or troublesome.

He but seldom asked for any sort of extra attention, and when an effort was made to force it upon him he felt that "the cost would not quit the expenses," and he did not often yield to a second invitation to any such namby pamby hospitality.

He had learned to eat whatsoever was set before him, asking no questions, and wherever he stopped he never seemed concerned about what they would give him to eat or drink, and it was but very seldom that he ever passed a criticism on the culinary character of the table.

In these peculiar habitudes Mr. Havens evinced his unselfishness, and set an example to the younger ministers, which, to say the least of it, was creditable to the man. He did not think that his being a minister gave him any preferred rights at another man's table, and when he accepted of their proffered hospitality he did so with his own personal understanding that he had no right to bring in any "extra bill of expense." The plain and simple kindness of his friends was always remembered by him with a gratitude which was as ardent as it was both true and constant.

CHAPTER IV.

PERSONAL ECONOMY

EXTRAVAGANCE in personal expenditures is often an indication of selfishness, as it also is of a general moral recklessness; for what men spend, regardless of a prudent and sound economy, is always means wasted; no matter whether the gratification is limited to ones own self, or is lavished upon others. This order of moral philosophy, though it may not be readily acknowledged by the thoughtless and worldly, undoubtedly involves the welfare of nearly all classes. Some learn it well in early life, from the teachings of their parental examples, while others receive its instructions from the fortunes of necessity only.

The limited stipends of the Methodist itinerancy, particularly in the earlier days, taught its pioneers the most rigid economy; hence, it was not strange to find such a man as Mr. Havens, fully systematized in the most limited expenditures.

The fixed salary of the Discipline of the Church, was then only one hundred dollars for the preacher, and the same for his wife; and sixteen dollars for each child under seven, and twenty-four dollars for each child over seven and under fourteen, which age ended the frugal chapter in these appropriations, and which were certainly both full and ample, as, "in the course of human events," even these meager assessments were but seldom realized on any of the circuits. How those early pioneers managed to live and keep a horse besides, has been a puzzle to many, much more difficult of solution than many mathematical problems. True, their incomes were small and their liabilities numerous; but, as Bishop Janes once asked, "Who ever knew a Methodist preacher's family to starve to death?" The good Bishop's experience was doubtless on the other side; but if he had lived in Indiana, and had had the honor of traveling some of the circuits to which he has appointed preachers, even in his day, he would have, perhaps, learned a lesson, such as his Episcopal philosophy has never taught him. But the fields had to be supplied, and some one must go to the new and poor circuits, as well as to the old and richer ones, and where they were all poor, as was the case in the earlier days of Indiana Methodism, the lot of even the most fortunate was a hard one, and was only endured by the heroic, in the humble spirit of zeal and self-sacrifice.

The old records of Quarterly Conferences tell many quaint stories of "quarterage," which, in these days, would place the blush of shame on the cheek of even the most penurious. We have read them where the Presiding Elder was paid fifty cents for his quarter's services, while even the "circuit rider," himself, counted his *pro rata* share in a sum less than five dollars. How men could keep soul and body together while playing such a conspicuous part on such a small financial basis, as we have already intimated, to many, in these days, would, doubtless, be "the mystery of mysteries."

The nearest explanation which we may give of the

matter is, to say that the people of those days were not half so selfish, and money-loving, and preacher-charging, as we find them even at the present time. Money, in the West, in the early settlement of the country, was scarce, because there were no markets, and what the farmers raised brought but little. Wheat sold then for thirty-seven and one-half cents; corn, for ten cents; butter, for six and one-quarter cents, and flour as low as one dollar and fifty cents per hundred pounds. Wood, nine feet in length, brought thirty-seven and one-half cents a load, which is well-remembered by Mr. William McEwen, of Columbus, who hauled many a load to the preachers in that vicinity, at that price.

It is said of John Strange, whose memory is immortal in the history of Indiana Methodism, that on one occasion, when he was traveling the Charlestown Circuit, Mrs. Strange informed him, one morning, just as he had mounted his horse to go to an appointment, that she had not a handful of flour in the house.

"Is that so, my dear?" asked the good man. "It is;" Mrs. Strange responded. "Well, now," said the eccentric and eloquent preacher, "I'll tell the Lord all about that, and we'll see whether He will allow the people to treat us in this way" When off he rode toward his appointment seemingly as unconcerned as if he owned a dozen flouring mills. Meeting Hezekiah Robertson in the out edge of town, he addressed him as follows: "Brother Robertson, my wife told me this morning, just as I was leaving home, that she was out of flour. I have to preach twice to-day; and you know you can't preach at all, but you can take her a bag of flour. Now, you and the Lord for it, Brother Robertson." Then bidding him good morning, Strange rode on his way to preach to the people, as confident that Mrs. Strange would not be without flour for dinner as he was that he would not be without grace in preaching his sermons—for the day.

To take money from a "circuit rider" for almost anything, was thought by many of the people in those good old times to be very nearly akin to sacrilege. Indeed, but few did it among *white* men; and with *black* men with straight hair, who did charge them, they soon learned to have but few dealings. Of course, the families of the preachers were often sick, and required the services of a physician. To the honor of the medical fraternity, it may be truthfully said that but few of them ever thought of presenting a bill against a Methodist "circuit rider." Medical services were a free will offering, almost uniformly. We only remember of two exceptions. One where the doctor belonged to the Friends, and had to charge to keep the rules of his church; and the other made out a bill against the preacher, because he heard that he would not take his medicine through fear that it would kill him.

The high honor and professional pride of the medical fraternity would not allow them to take a fee from these poor self-sacrificing itinerants, whose incomes were so small, at best, that liberal minded men could only wonder how they managed to live or keep out of debt.

The disposition of Mr. Havens had been through life so trained that he cared but little for money for his own use, and such was his high strung spirit of personal independence that he would much rather stand up before the people with an untrammeled freedom without a cent in his pocket, than to have their gifts and feel that his freedom of speech or reproof was thereby restrained. His greatest pride was that of personal independence, and poor and dependant as he sometimes evidently was, he was the last man to either make his wants known or to ask to have them relieved.

He learned early in life to have but few wants, which gave him the habits of economy, which continued with him through all his after years. When he received his "quarterage," as the quarterly income of the "circuit riders" was called, he carried it home as if it was not his own. It was but seldom that he ever spent a dollar of it for himself, though frequently his garments were seedy and his boots were badly needing recuperation. In any new departure in this line he had to have the counsel of "Mother," as he called his wife; and often, even when she had counseled him to purchase a new garment, he postponed it with characteristic carelessness, until his careful and tender hearted companion urged him to the duty by her expostulations.

Display in dress was always an evidence, in his estimation, of both pride and weakness; and he but seldom formed a very high estimate of any one, male or female, whom he saw "arrayed in purple and fine linen." His conceptions of extravagance and pride were of course gleaned from the economical habits of earlier years; and if they were sometimes thrown out in private reproofs in rather a severe style, it was because he believed, as did most of the early Methodist preachers, that conformity to the world in dress and extravagance was a palpable as well as a sinful indulgence.

The regime of his economical instructions was of course rigid, and at that time constituted a prominent principle even in the discipline of his church. Therefore he felt obligated, both by example and precept, to vindicate his ideas of non-conformity with the world, and to lead the people under his charge to plainness and simplicity as consistent Christians.

The wants of families in the early settlement of the West were supplied chiefly from their own resources, and, consequently, they were as simple as they were often economical and meager. Extravagance was taught, with emphasis, to be a sin; and on this account, the children of that day grew up with very strict ideas of economy. Of course, the old styles prevailed, and new departures from them were naturally viewed with jealousy and suspicion. In all these regards, Mr. Havens had been raised after the strictest sect of economists, and, therefore, he had learned to supply his own personal wants with very small considerations. Always plain in dress and moderate in all his wishes, the limitation of his means was never a drawback to his enjoyments, or any hindrance to his efficiency or active usefulness.

We have heard a story of one of the straits to which Mr. Havens was once driven, which, if true—and we rather guess it was—must have made him feel that "quarterage" was getting scarce and was bringing him to his nakedness.

Tradition, at least, tells the story on him that his

wardrobe, which he always as a general thing carried in his saddle-bags, got so far reduced that he had but one shirt, and that, of course, was on his back. While it was there he felt no ways embarrassed, and could meet his appointments with a regularity and nonchalance which would have done honor to the highness of an archbishop. But when the time came for a change he found the predicament an awkward one, from which, however, he was happily relieved by going to bed and taking a nap while his better half washed and ironed the aforesaid linen, which, on awakening, he found at his bedside as white and clean as if it had been especially prepared for his approaching quarterly meeting.

The personal expenses of Mr. Havens were of course chiefly directed by himself, and the small amounts he deducted out of his always limited income, gave a true index to the liberality of his character, and showed what was real in his history—that he did not live for himself. Nature had made him a nobleman in his dignity and mien, and the graces of the Christian life had taught him the liberal self-sacrifices of his profession. What he did for others was, in his esteem, only the obligations of the higher law, and intent on these simple purposes, he seemed to think that worldly speculations were no part of his life services. He felt that he was a Methodist itinerant preacher, and that whatever honors or emoluments that official relation would give him constituted his legitimate and chief boon, and outside of this his thoughts seemed never to run in any other channel only as they were called out by his obligations as a citizen and neighbor.

Even in his habits and personal indulgences he was always gentlemanly, and particularly careful of the rights and privileges of others; and in the daily use of his pipe, though it seemed often to be essential to his proper equilibrium, he would never light it in a strange house without asking permission.

In 1852, Mr. Havens was a delegate to the General Conference of his church, which met in Boston, and as is the custom on such occasions, he was appointed to board with one of the families of the city. He was introduced to the gentleman and his wife and to the sons and daughters, and after early tea he was shown to his room on the second floor, the husband and wife both assisting him with his baggage.

"Well, now," said Mr. Havens, "I see that this room will just suit me. You know we, Western Methodist preachers, sometimes smoke, and I will ask the privilege of sitting out on that portico when I smoke."

"No, Mr. Havens," responded the kind-hearted Yankee merchant, "we will not allow any such thing about our house. If you want to smoke, sit right down in this large rocking chair, and light your pipe, and smoke as much as you please. We did not invite your General Conference to Boston to take away from you any of your rights or privileges. We just want you to pitch in and enjoy yourself just as you do at your own home out in Indiana."

"Thank you, thank you, sir," said Mr. Havens; "I perceive you are a gentleman of good sense, as well as of politeness; and I shall take it for granted that I am at home while I am under your roof."

Some exceedingly nice people, who are as intolerant and exclusive as they are radical and temperate, would no doubt have played a different part with the old western pioneer, by saying we would prefer to have no smokers as our guests. We have generally found all such superficial reformers as proscriptive as they were exacting.

It was certainly one of Mr. Haven's highest virtues that he asked but few indulgences for himself. The strictness of his personal economy gave him a marked advantage in the restriction of his expenditures, and made him less selfish and less covetous both as a man and a minister. Indeed, it is probable that if his annual expenditures for himself had been strictly kept, it would be seen that he did not lay out fifty dollars a year for all his purposes.

The personal sacrifices of such a minister may well be recorded, for they remain, and should, among his loudest and strongest sermons. Posterity can not but be benefitted by their recital, as his own high integrity is more richly indorsed by their remembrance. He made no extortionate demands upon his congregations to enrich his coffers, or to justify his personal extravagance, nor did he ever harp upon the starving order of his pay in the itinerancy, as some have done; for he appeared, from the beginning, to comprehend the situation, and therefore he placed his family on the land which he had entered in the woods, where, under the guidance and counsel of their excellent mother, they dug their living from the soil, while the father gave himself to the arduous labors of an itinerant minister.

Surely such a man is a hero, even in the moral world, as he tempers his ambition to the restraints of virtue, in order that he may build up the fortunes of others at the sacrifice of his own.

CHAPTER V.

CHARACTER OF HIS FRIENDSHIPS.

The measure of men's greatness is often made known in the character of their fraternal spirit. What they profess may give us their relative positions in society, and what they do may indicate their energy and ambition; but we have to look to the fraternal spirit of men to know their real animus, as well as their geniality and true character. In the investigation of this point we may learn more of the inside nature of men and of their real stamina than we can at a hundred public receptions. In business life many are social, but often only to their customers. They take no interest in men only as they have a personal interest in them. Indeed, they seem so absorbed in their own self-interests that they know nothing and no one outside of these selfish purlieus. They can smile upon a man of dollars if he is replenishing himself at their own crib; but if he is feeding at any other, to them he becomes both "a heathen and a publican."

Even in the ministry the same spirit is often manifested. Men who profess to be disciples of the Master, and whom we would suppose, from their high standing in the Church, were possessed with the same broad humanities, are exceedingly complacent when in the presence of patron saints—but when they have no ax to grind they appear to be wrapt only in their own selfish mantles. Evidently born to take care of themselves, they make their "calling and election sure" with a wonderful assiduity.

The fact may be contrary to the general conviction, but it is painfully true that the weaker imbecilities of our nature often crop out even in the history of the professedly pious gospel minister. It does not follow at all that because he is in holy orders he is therefore a saint, any more than it does that he is a gentleman or a scholar. The one we know is an attainment of grace, while the other is the result only of long and faithful study. But neither the one nor the other is ever forced upon a man just because he wears the sacred ermine.

Human nature is ever jealous of her rights, and her well known weaknesses cling to some with a remarkable tenacity all through their lives, notwithstanding they are sometimes found even in the front ranks of the holy ministry. The friendship of Judas Iscariot reflected but poorly upon human nature, while even that of Peter was of a very doubtful stability. If on such high *roles* of apostolic fame men were found whose fraternal integrity bore such poor evidences of any true and real friendships, it ought not to be thought sacriligious if we say in this chapter that the friendships of ministers of the gospel are, in many instances, to say the best of them, but little above par.

It is said that men of the same profession are frequently jealous of one another, and we presume there is a world of truth in the declaration, often when it is applied to the Christian ministry. This liability doubtless lies with a strong weight even on the Methodist ministry; indeed, much stronger now than it did in former days, for in an Annual Conference of Methodist itinerants where men necessarily must stand in each other's way, even for years, the temptation with many is almost irresistible to be somewhat jealous of the men who supplant them. True, the common ills and misfortunes of the grand system generally make warm friendships, and often life time brotherhoods, but as it is in other departments of life, so is it in this; there are often too many exceptions to the general rule where men who are deficient in education, as they also are in the larger ideas and the more liberal sentiments, hope to maintain their ascendency or their temporary positions of fortune, by throwing check lines over the equal or, perhaps, even over the superior abilities of their brethren. Things of this kind, no doubt, happen, as perhaps they always will, in all conventional assemblies of even gospel ministers. The admission may be considered a sad one for the honor of the ministry; and some may even deem its statement in this connection inappropriate, if not imprudent. But we aim to be frank in writing of one who was always known to be frank himself; and as we have nothing personal to accomplish in doing so, but aim only to give to our readers, as nearly as we can, our life sketches of Father Havens in the characteristic language of the man as he would say himself, if still living, "without regard to fear or favor." We aim to speak plainly, and to "set down naught in malice."

As we have attempted to demonstrate in another chapter, but few men in this day have read character with any greater or more definite readiness than Father

Havens, and on this account he was sometimes shy of some men whenever they came about him with their pretended friendships; for even, while he would admit their sincerity, he had but very limited confidence in their fraternal integrity. He had lived long enough to know that the friend of to-day might and often was the enemy of to-morrow, and therefore, toward many, he maintained a respectful reserve, which, however, was always accompanied, on his part, with an honest frankness, which was ever as fearless as it was sincere. Even among his brethren in the ministry, he sometimes created enemies, because he did not feel it to be his duty to play the patron or hypocrite, or to carry a Janused countenance. It was not, indeed, his weakness to implicitly place too high an estimate on human nature anywhere, for he well knew that it was all made of the same frail material, and he well understood that, now and then, in spite of all reforms, it would indicate such an admixture, as was even worse than "dust" itself.

Coming up, as he did, from the lowest rung of defective education, and having his entire growth in knowledge and experience, in connection with the ministry, his chances of the practical test, gave him, perhaps, as clear perceptions of friendships' numerous faces and changeful characters as perhaps fell to the lot of any minister of his age.

But always tenacious of the right, and jealous of the consistency and purity of the Church, he stood fearlessly in the breach whenever the one was in jeopardy, or the other was trampled upon, no matter who was the transgressor. In these vindications, he spared neither friend nor foe; yea, he spared not even himself, for he feared not to assume even the responsibilities of prosecutor, and thereby he sometimes brought upon himself the excited and keen displeasure of those who otherwise would have been his friends. But, then, while he asked no man's friendship at the expense of principle, he never turned his back upon a friend for the sake of personal policy.

What he did for a brother in his character as a Christian, or as a presiding elder, in his official capacity, he did because he believed it was right; and if a favor was conferred he never named it to the recipient, unless it was done as a mere matter of history, for he scorned to buy up friendships with the patronage of his official power, or to join in with "rings" to retain his ascendancy. His warmest manifestations of friendship were always toward the "outs" rather than the "ins," and such was his spirit of untrammeled independence that he never played the sycophant before his Conference, to win its applause, or to gain its popular favor. What he was in person and fact, he was always willing to be measured for. Indeed, he never turned weather-cock to catch any popular breeze.

That such a minister should have foes as well as friends might well have been expected; but that he had the capacity to vindicate his positions, as well as his fair fame, none ever doubted who knew him. Like the hero on the field of battle, he showed himself possessed of sufficient energy for the strife, and the bold friendships of his heart always gave him hosts to stand by his side. These and similar affinities made him a leader among the armies of Israel, and held him up through a long and distinguished ministry.

In the later years of his life Father Havens did not trust himself out very far in the line of friendships, for as the fire of his years died away, and the sun of his public labors began to set, he felt that his friends grew few, and that the boundaries of his fraternal confidence became more and still more limited. The facts, however, were not always as he felt them; for many thousands still reverenced him, and the memory of the good old man was as fresh and green in their hearts as when his trumpet tones rang out with his mightiest personal power.

The fact will readily be conceded that no Methodist preacher who ever labored in Indiana had more true and admiring friends, among the general public, than Father Havens. Men of all faiths, and creeds, and churches respected him, while those most distinguished, and who ranked among the first minds of the State, held for him the very highest regards. Such men as Hon. James Raridan, Hon. Oliver H. Smith, Hon. Samuel Parker, Hon. Caleb B. Smith, and Hon. P A. Hackleman, and all such celebrities over the State, looked upon the old heroic preacher as being one of God's special and most worthy messengers. They respected him for his talents, and reverenced him for his high moral integrity, and for his sacrificing and heroic efforts to build up and protect the citadel of the public morals. They had heard him often at his quarterly and camp meetings in the days of his strength, when thousands gathered to hear him, and when he stood up before the vast multitudes, with that dignified and commanding presence and eloquence, which, under the divine blessing, brought many hundreds to acknowledge the truths of religion, and led them to give their hearts to God.

When Father Havens was in the zenith of his ministerial strength and efficiency, he found a young and gifted Minister in his District by the name of Lucien W. Berry, to whom he became warmly attached. He saw that he had great powers of mind, and at times exhibited a pulpit ability almost equal to the eloquent friend of his early ministry, Rev. Henry B. Bascom. He kept him in his District on several different Circuits, and in a few years had him stationed in the Capital of the State, which was then the most important charge in the Conference—where Mr. Berry remained two years, when he succeeded Father Havens on the District as Presiding Elder. In this relation to the Church, Mr. Berry served several years on different dictricts, when he was elected President of the Indiana Asbury University. The friendship of Father Havens, doubtless, had much to do in the rapid elevation of this able and eloquent Divine, to so important a position, and undoubtedly, gave him something of the prestige which he carried with him to his high and distinguished responsibility. No man was more grateful than Dr. Berry. He felt that he owed much to the kind considerations of Father Havens, and down to the latest period of his life, he entertained for his venerable patron, the tenderest emotions of gratitude and reverence; and had he outlived him would have been with pride and gladness his willing and able biographer.

Some brethren, no doubt, have thought that in these freaks of friendly partiality, Father Havens showed a weakness; but we opine, if some of them had made the effort and played the part of "patron Saints" to somebody, they would have placed jewels in the crowns of their own distinctions which they have utterly failed to accomplish. Some Ministers, who are good and honorable men at that—have somehow never had any patronage to bestow upon any but themselves. They see young men of promise around them, but they keep their distance, lest by the light of their countenances the student might eclipse the master. We can not but honor the memory of Father Havens, because he was a stranger to jealousy, as he also was to selfishness. His fears of being eclipsed by a rising rival never drove even a beggar from his door. He had known what it was to be a stranger himself, and had frequently felt the darkness of his own surroundings, when there was scarcely a star light upon his path, and yet he often gave to the young candidate for future honors in the Church that grip of friendship which would help him up and on, unless he subsequently forfeited it by his own willful delinquency.

His fondness for debate, and the keenness of his sarcasm, sometimes led the venerable minister to the utterance of language much more biting and severe than he even thought it was at the time; but when the coolness of reflection, and the "sober second thought," convicted him of his wrong, but few men were more ready and prompt to ask pardon than Father Havens. He did not claim infallibility, and he was always confident of his own weaknesses. No matter whom he had offended, if he thought he was wrong, he considered it no dishonor for him to beg their forgiveness with the utmost respect and sincerity.

In his own neighborhood, in Rushville and vicinity, where his family so long resided, he was well known, and always respected by every class of society. He mingled with them, when he was at home, as if he was the moral guardian of the entire community. With even the wickedest men of the place he would frequently hold street conversations, and many of his most effective sermons were preached in this way to men who but seldom ever darkened a church door. They knew he was honest, and they believed him sincere, and hence they listened to him with respectful deference; and the probabilities are that many of these men remembered these street exhortations better and longer than any plain moral lessons they heard from any other source.

In the later years of his life, Father Havens adopted into the family of his friendships a young minister of a somewhat eccentric eloquence, by the name of John W T. McMullen. He had known him from his childhood, and when he found him in the ranks of the itinerancy, stirring up the churches and moving among the unconverted, with all the wild eloquence of "a son of thunder," he seemed himself to be strongly captivated with the trumpet music of his preaching, and he at once adopted him as one of his favorite sons in the ministry. The relationship was one of mutual acceptance, and for aught we know of mutual enjoyment and profit. No such union of hearts was known in the Conference. They were always together when it was possible, and though one was old and the other young, their ties of brotherhood were like those of David and Jonathan. The honest simplicity and lofty eloquence of young McMullen appeared to have a charm for the old hero, and held him like the enchanted wand of some spirit power.

This ardent and last friendly attachment of Father Havens continued until his death, and then, as had been agreed upon, Mr. McMullen preached the funeral oration of his venerable and departed friend, in the court-house yard of Rushville, in the presence of some two or three thousand people. It was our privilege to hear this oration. It had evidently been most elaborately prepared, and nearly three hours were consumed in its delivery. The effort was, indeed, a grand one. It was both beautiful and eloquent, and abounded in the rich figures and tropes for which the eloquent minister is so distinguished. Still, our thoughts were on the father who had gone from us, and we could not well do justice to the son.

CHAPTER VI.

HIS MORAL FIRMNESS.

As true character is known by its devotion to moral principle, and as truth is truth always and everywhere, he who gives his life to its support and upbuilding, carries with him along down the years the conscious elements of his own protection, as well as that of the public welfare. Even the most splendid talents can not impart character where simple truth is disregarded, or where moral principle is set at defiance. In all such cases, even genius itself is found to be but a flash of deception, and its brightest corruscations are nothing more than sad deceptions.

But the world is full of such failures, and men are found mourning their personal defeats, when they should only be blaming themselves for their own moral delinquencies. The dead dog lies at their doors, slain by their own hands, and if the stench of his demise has created sickening disgust, they should have the good sense, if not the honor, to place the mortuary credit to their own disregard of morals and principle.

What strength is to the physical man, moral firmness is to the Christian. The one gives energy and life to bone and muscle; while the other endows the moral hero with the mastery of himself, and the resources of a life of the highest and noblest activities. Even education itself fails to give character or stability where the honor of moral principle is disregarded.

At this very point thousands err. They think that intelligence is attainment, and that wealth is power; and so they may be, but the one without principle is but the dashing steed without his rider, while the other mocks its possessor with only the foulest distortions.

In the lives of many, policy assumes the guardianship of both truth and morals, and holds the reins of its empire with a grip of tenacity as determined and obstinate as though there was no reality in either. They seem not to believe there is wrong in any sort of duplicity, and as for sound and consistent principle, it appears to be totally unrecognized by them. Hanging only on the outskirts of moral goverment, such men are never ready to assume responsibility—no matter to what extent it may involve the right, or comprehend the public welfare. Personal interest is their motive power, and to this they cling, with tenacity, as if it was the only plank of their individual safety.

The lives of all such time-servers, are but miserable comments upon either worth or goodness, and we can not but hold them up as moral abortions.

The exemplification given us in the unflinching integrity of the martyr Stephen, stands in eternal contrast with all such moral instability; and though he lost his life by his steadfastness, he gained the glory of a personal renown which is second only to that of the great Master himself.

The display of any such virtue is more than heroic, because it gives to principle its noblest adherence, and sacrifices interest on the alter of integrity.

It was this sort of devotion to principle which gave

such honorable prominence to the Christian life and ministry of Father Havens. What he understood to be right and true he adhered to, no matter who opposed him, or what might be the circumstances of his opposition. He felt that his commission as a gospel minister, held him responsible for the cause of truth and right, and the honor and purity of the Church everywhere, that in the pulpit or out of it, he was God's embassador, and he always appeared to recognize an attack upon truth, or right, or virtue, as an insult to himself and his profession, and whether it raised a storm, or looked like casting pearl before swine, he instinctively entered the contest if he even had to fight the battle single handed and alone. Fearing no one but his Maker, particularly, when religion or virtue was in jeopardy—he often entered the arena of contest when other ministers, who he believed were as good if not better than himself, would beg for him to hold on, least the effort might make the matter even worse than it was.

An incident which occurred on one of his circuits will illustrate this moral firmness of Father Havens, as well as give to the reader some idea of the manner in which the old time pioneer preachers laid the foundations of the great Church of the west.

The wife of an infidel in the bounds of his circuit was reported to be in a dying condition with consumption and anxious for some minister of the gospel to visit and administer to her the consolations of religion.

A minister of another church had already made an effort to visit her, but he had been driven away from the house with violence by the wicked and infidel husband.

At one of his appointments some six miles distant, Father Havens learned of this lady's condition and health, and of the effort of his brother minister to serve her, and he determined at once to visit her let the consequences be what they might.

Persuading one of his congregation to accompany him, the fearless "Circuit Rider" started for the place, while his entire congregation felt that he was going into danger that might cost him his life.

Arriving at the house a little before sundown, they hitched their horses and entered the dwelling, where in a small room they found the almost dying woman. Her mild blue eyes, now deeply sunken beneath their pale arches, her high forehead and intelligent contour, indicated her to be much more than of the common mould. Her long tresses of auburn hair hanging loosely about her head, showed that the poor woman notwithstanding their wealth was cursed with physical, as well as moral neglect.

Aroused by the sudden entrance of the visitors, she cast her eyes on them with a wild glare which showed her surprise. But soon learning who they were and the object of their visit, her countenance brightened up with mingled emotions of joy and sorrow, and she said with a sweet voice:

"I am very glad to see you, Mr. Havens, but I fear my husband will abuse you, if he should come in and find you here."

Mr. Havens informed her that she need have no

fears in that regard, for he was well protected, and felt fully prepared for any emergency.

He then enterered into conversation with her and found that she was deeply interested in the subject of religion, and anxious for her soul's eternal interests. He sang, and talked, and prayed, with her, and as the husband did not appear, and it was getting late in the evening, he suggested to his friend, who had accompanied him, that they had better put up their horses and feed them, as they would probably remain through the night.

Mr. Havens, after the horses were put up and fed, returned to the sick chamber, and renewed his conversation with the dying woman. He was thus engaged, when the husband made his appearance, and the dying wife informed him who Mr. Havens was, and explained to him the object of his visit.

The vicious and infidel husband, regardless of the tender feelings of his poor wife, cast the look of a tiger, when it is about to spring upon its prey, on the minister and said:

"A Preacher, ha! Well, who sent for you, sir?"

"No one," responded Mr. Havens, firmly. "I heard of the low condition of your wife's health, sir, and I considered it my duty to visit her."

"Well, sir," retorted the unfeeling husband, with a scowl, "the sooner you get out of this house, and quit my premises, the better it will be for you."

"It is now dark," responded Mr. Havens, "and as there is no place within reach, where we can find lodgings, you will not surely turn us out of your house."

Calling to mind a pious brother of this inhospitable unbeliever, Mr. Havens said:

"I knew your brother, sir, and if he were still living, he would be most deeply mortified to know you refused to entertain a minister of the gospel, who has traveled six miles to visit your sick wife."

"Do not talk to me of my brother," said the enraged man. "He is dead. While he was living, we promised each other, that whoever died first, that he would come back and give some account of the other world. But he has either gone to hell, and can not come back, or else there is no hereafter."

"You are in doubt then," said Mr. Havens, enquiringly.

"No sir, I am not," he responded. "I do not believe the bible at all, although I have as good a one as anybody. I sometimes read it, but I do not believe a word it contains." Then gathering it from his book case he handed it to Mr. Havens, who opened it and began reading one of the Psalms, and when he had finished it, he said: "Let us pray once more with your poor dying wife."

He then knelt by the side of the dying woman, down whose cheeks the warm tears were coursing, and offered up a fervent and feeling prayer in her behalf. The cowed infidel stood like a statue, gazing upon the minister, and then upon his wife, and when the prayer was finished, he left the room without a word.

Mr. Havens and his companion soon after retired for the night, in a room to which the sick wife directed them, but they scarcely got to sleep when they heard the running of horses and the yelping of dogs, and it was not hard for them to devise what was up. Their horses had been turned out of the stable and the dogs were set on them.

Mr. Havens and his friend sprang out of bed and made for the barn yard, where they found the poor effete skeptic crouching in the shadow of the barn. Driving off the dogs and approaching their owner, Mr. Havens enquired of him what he meant by such conduct, and assured him if he did not desist in his meanness, he would set the dogs on him.

Avering that the horses had got out themselves, the fellow swore that if they got out again, he would "dog them to hell and back." "There is where you are going yourself sir," retorted Mr. Havens, "without any dogging, and if you don't do better you will get there before you are aware of it." The horses were put up again, when they once more retired to their bed, where they slept undisturbed until morning. They arose early with the intention of leaving before breakfast, and passing into the chamber of the sick wife, they were about bidding her good bye, when the husband accompanied by two large rough looking fellows entered the room, and requested them not to leave so suddenly.

"You would not go last night when I wanted you to," said he; "so now, before you leave us, we want one of the best specimens of your praying, that we may know what sort of religion you have." This he said in a leering and contemptuous manner; and as he finished, he handed Mr. Havens the Bible, "that the performance might begin."

This was just what the preacher desired, and opening the Bible he deliberately read several portions of scripture, and then knelt by the bedside of the afflicted wife, and with his eyes wide open he began his prayer. He thanked the Lord for his mercies for their preservation through the night, and asked, with great sincerity, that his richest blessings might rest upon the poor sick and dying woman. He then told the Lord what sort of a husband she had, putting in a few iron-clad utterances, which, under other circumstances, might have been called pointed and personal. The husband sat in his chair, as did also his two companions, all wincing under the withering rebukes given them. In the hands of the man and preacher, on his knees, they were seemingly held spell-bound, and the prayer was finished without the least interruption.

After breakfast they left, feeling that God had given them the victory, and that they had done their duty toward an amiable Christian woman, whose transient life here on earth was soon to terminate in that of the immortal.

It was thus some of the early ministerial pioneers were called upon "to beard the lion in his den," and unpleasant and even dangerous as the duty sometimes was, many of them met the emergency with a heroic faith and fearless spirit, which but seldom quailed under any circumstances.

It was difficult for the heroic soul of Father Havens to submit to anything like an officious dictation in regard to any duty he felt was due to himself, to his congregations, or to his Maker. In all such sacred matters, he felt that the responsibility was peculiarly his own, and on this account he chose, in most cases, to be his own arbiter.

A few years before his death, he paid a visit to Cincinnati, where he spent a Sabbath and preached one of the most vigorous and eloquent sermons of his life. The minister who invited him to preach took special pains to tell him that the people would not listen to a sermon over a half hour in length; and the venerable old Presiding Elder read his text and started out in his discussion of its doctrines in his usual style, without much reference to either time or circumstances. The congregation was deeply interested, and every eye was fixed upon the earnest and eloquent white-haired stranger. They knew that he was Father Havens, of Indiana, for he had been so introduced by the young pastor. Just as he came to the middle of his sermon, he pulled out his watch, and looking at it, said:

"I am sorry, my brethren, that my half hour is up. This good young brother, your honored pastor, told me this morning that you would not listen to a sermon over a half hour long. My time, I see, is up, and I must quit and take my seat."

"No, no," "go on, Father Havens," "we will hear you," "go on, go ahead," came from all parts of the house. The whole congregation seemed to have caught the inspiration of the sermon, and they were unwilling that the services should close with only half of it.

"I thank you, my brethren, for the compliment you

pay to the Gospel, and to its divine author," said the venerable preacher, and then, with an energy even beyond himself, for another half hour or more, he held the large assembly with that old time gospel grasp, which many remember he was wont to do in the best days of his strength and power. Many who heard him that day, said, "Indiana Methodism may well be proud of that 'old man eloquent.'"

CHAPTER VII.

HIS HEROIC SPIRIT.

Nobility of character is, perhaps, as definitely illustrated in the moral heroism of ones life, as it is, or can be, in any other specific trait. "Quit you like men," is an apostolic injunction which points to this distinctive excellency with inspired power. St. Paul was himself a moral hero of the highest caste, and in commending this noble trait to others, he understood the high and imperial force of its character. In the heroic manhood of life, which he so distinctively demonstrated throughout his entire apostolic history, he gave legitimate proof of that superior claim which he had, as "the chiefest among all the Apostles."

Heroism, indeed, is always essential to true greatness, and men are men, in any relation of life, only in proportion as they develop and sustain the heroic virtues. A coward in principle is never a hero in anything. He may shift his positions and make pretensions, where nothing but his own selfish interests are at stake, and when many better men than himself are guarding the posts of danger, but after all he sums up only a practical cypher; and living or dead, the world has but little to boast of in his history.

With Mr. Havens the New Testament contained the true theology of life, and hence he made it the basis of his thought—the ruling authority of all his devotions. He there saw concentrated purity, stability and all the benevolent charities of the heroic life, which he aimed to demonstrate in his own career, and in which he succeeded in an admirable degree, as all will admit who knew him well, as one among the many itinerant advocates and defenders of the Christian faith. Indeed, there was always something in the very spirit of the man, indicative of the hero, for he appeared ever to be master of the situation and ready for any and every emergency. The fulfilment of his duties as an itinerant Methodist Preacher gave him frequent opportunities of making his record before the public eye in such characters as led many to style him "The Old war horse of Indiana Methodism," while Hon. Oliver H. Smith, who knew him for forty years, gave him the *sobriquet* of "the General Jackson of Indiana Methodist Preachers."

In almost any of the relationships of life, Mr. Havens would have won heroic laurels, for he was a "character," *sui generis*—original, independent and fearless. In all the relations he sustained in his Church—though making no pretensions himself—he was always honored and recognized by his brethren, as a Chief worthy of double honors. These he often received, but seemingly, without any conviction of their flattering character, for he placed but a light estimate on the compliments of popular favor, because he well knew that the breeze which created them was often only incidental, and that the breath which could destroy them was as inconstant as the winds. In his own belief, his duties to God, and his obligations to man, constituted the ruling laws of his life, and he consequently bowed to them as to the only fulcrum which could raise him to power, or that could confer upon him any permanent honor. It was this knowledge of his responsibilities, which had grown to be a part of his nature, that gave to his whole action and life, the straight edge of a scrupulous conscientiousness, and often led him to deeds of daring in the performance of his duty, where others winced and faltered, least they might meet with defeat, or mar the noncombativeness of their character. It was consequently in agreement with his genius, to meet responsibilities with manly firmness and to endeavor under all circumstances, to execute his life mission, fearless of the whims of human caprice, and often apparently reckless of any ultimate worldly fame.

Many stories are told of him that he sometimes even used *physical* arguments in extreme cases. But it was very evident, in all these instances, that he considered this mode of argumentation the only one such men would listen to, and the only one which could give him the victory.

At one of the Conferences Mr. Havens attended, some member, who professed to have a complaint against him, objected to the passing of his character until he would have a private talk with him. Conscious of his own integrity in the case of the brother's involvement, and nervously sensitive of his own good name and standing in the Conference, the old fires of his younger years were stirred within him, and he demanded of the chair that the vote be taken at once, "as he was ready to waive all by laws on the subject."

He wished, if any one had aught to say of him, or of his acts or character, that he would speak out right there before the whole Conference. He was ready for any revelation that might be made, and prepared to meet friend or foe in any dissection that might be made of his character.

It was late in the evening, and the Conference was about to adjourn for the day, and the President proposed that his case should lie over until the next morning. This proposition, though coming from the Bishop did not savor well with the old veteran of a hundred battles, and he insisted that the vote be taken then. "He did not wish his character hung up all night." The Bishop said it would do no harm to lay it over. This, Mr. Havens thought was a partiality unbecoming the chair, and he turned to the Conference, and said, "I am sorry to see the Chair lending itself to a party" The Bishop who knew Father Havens as well as he knew any minister, and perhaps respected him as highly—but still intent on having everything done in accordance with the by-laws of the Conference, only remarked, "I think, brethren, that Brother Havens is insinuating."

"No, Bishop," responded Mr. Havens, "I am not; for I mean just what I say, and say just what I mean."

The Bishop well knew who was meeting him, and not wishing to have any collision with the oldest itinerant of the State, made no reply, but passed on to other business, and so it happened, to use his own phrase, that "his character hung up all night." But when the morning came, in company with two others, he had seen the troubled brother, and his character passed, as it always had for more than forty years, without the smell of fire on it.

Mr. Havens was not disposed to be disrespectful to official dignitaries, nor was he unmindful of the honors due to station or power. He was respectful to all, but still he feared no superior in office, when he thought he was in the wrong, however great might be his intellectual strength or his personal dignity

The self possession of Mr. Havens was usually sufficient for every emergency, and whenever vice was to be rebuked, or wrong was to be put down, his heroic spirit was manifest, and his language was never equivocal. Hence many opportunities were seized by him which others would perhaps pass by, to reform, if possible, even the most reckless. Thus many, who were found by the wayside, received the benefit of his labors as a minister, who otherwise, might have gone down to their death without a sigh of sympathy or an effort of redemption.

On one occasion, when on his way to Conference, which was about to convene at New Albany, he in company with a number of his ministerial brethren, took passage on a steamer where Mr. Foote, United States Senator from Mississippi, and Mr. Samuel Houston, Senator from Texas, were passengers, on their way from Washington to their distant southern homes.

Mr. Havens and his brethren—Wiley, Simpson and others—were introduced to these distinguished statesmen, and the company engaged at once in that sort of agreeable chit chat which is so often the life of traveling greetings. Of course the conversation was toned well if it was not altogether clerical. But they were surrounded by the mixed throng of a crowded steamer and it was not long until they were interrupted by the profanity and vociferous disputations of some young men, who were engaged in playing cards near by. Of their conduct and profanity Mr. Foote, who was distinguished for his polished and gentlemanly bearing, said, "I wonder if those young men have any moral feeling?" adding with evident indignation, "if they have, it is certainly shamefully obscured." One of the ministers thought they had none, which conclusion became general. The matter was referred to Mr. Havens, as he was known to be an expert in reading character, when the old apostle threw his eye on the gambling crowd, and pausing for a few moments, he remarked that one of the young men, whom he pointed out, was, in his belief, possessed of even high moral feelings.

"How do you learn that Mr. Havens?" asked Senator Houston.

"If I can't convince you of the fact" he replied, "I can satisfy myself whether I am right," and he arose from his seat, and approaching the group, he laid his hand kindly on the shoulder of the young man, and said, "Young man, as soon as you get done playing out your hand I desire to speak to you in private." Then folding his arms he stood over the young man a silent spectator of the game. The young gentleman was evidently taken by surprise and grew quite agitated and nervous. Several times he turned his head and looked up in the venerable face before him, but seemed unable to analyze the mysterious influence it was exerting over him. At the close of the game the young man arose hurriedly and informed Mr. Havens he was at his service. Conducting him to the rear of the cabin Mr. Havens said to him:

"Young man, you will probably regard this as a great liberty and intrusion, when I inform you that I never saw your face before to-night. But I hope you will pardon me if I have done wrong, as it is your present and future welfare alone which has prompted me thus to speak to you."

Here he paused, but still kept his eyes steadily fixed on the young man's.

"Go on," said the listener respectfully, "I will hear you."

"I am the father of eight boys," resumed Mr. Havens, "and I love them as a father loves his children. I have seen the company you have been in to-night, and I have witnessed the wicked practices into which they are leading you. You are a respectable looking young man, and doubtless have good and pious parents who pray for you every day of their lives. How do you think," he asked, "they would feel if they knew the company you have been with to-night?"

"I have parents who are living," the young man responded, "and I would not like for them to know one word of where I have been to-night. I know they love me as a son, and always remember me in all their prayers."

"I thought so," resumed Mr. Havens, "for I am a father myself, as I have already told you; and I know if any one should find one of my boys in such company as I have found you in to-night, and would endeavor to persuade him from the error of his ways, though he failed in his effort, I should feel that I never could repay him for his kindness. I saw you first," continued Mr. Havens, "to-night, and I may never see you again, but I feel a strange interest in your welfare. I hope, my son, you will forever quit all such associates, and I have no doubt if you do, you will always be thankful to God for it."

When Mr. Havens ceased, the young man was in tears. He felt the power of such an exhortation.

"I will play no more to-night," said the young man, "and I will try, sir, to remember your advice."

He asked for the name and residence of Mr. Havens, which were freely given to him, when they parted with pleasant adieus for the night. Two years after this, Mr. Havens received a letter from this young man, who was a citizen of Tennessee, giving him the gratifying intelligence of his conversion and reform.

In hundreds of instances of this character did the old itinerant hero display the personal excellencies of his ministry, for it was in this way he won many who became stars in the crown of his rejoicing. His Master's work was always his highest obligation, and if he performed a deed of daring in any of these plunges after a sinking soul, it was never in view of any personal aggrandizement, or with any purposes of egotistical accomplishment. The ardor of the hero was his, without one spark of his vanity. Flattery he hated, because he esteemed it as the language of deceit; and as he was a stranger to cowardice, he but seldom dreamed of danger in any act of duty. He never hesitated to speak against sin, no matter how great might be the sinner, and his attacks were often personal ones, like the one we have just related.

Hon. O. H. Smith, in his Early Reminiscences, says: "I knew James Havens well. He seemed to be made for the very work in which he was engaged. He had the eye of the eagle, and possessed both moral and personal courage that never quailed. He was the Napoleon of Methodist preachers of Eastern Indiana."

It was this heroic feature in the character of Mr. Havens, more than anything else, which gave him power among the people and made him prominent. They loved him for his decision and firmness, and for his personal sacrifices; and whenever they attended any of his meetings, they expected a square gospel meal of honest truth, without any of the sickly condiments of flattering eulogy, or the plastering compliments of a yielding sycopancy. He bore bravely, all through his ministry, the banner of a soldier who never feared to fight, and who dreaded no defeat, no matter who was the foe.

CHAPTER VIII.

KNOWLEDGE OF MEN.

To be a christian, one must know himself, but to be a practical and successful minister, he must have a knowledge of men. Human nature furnishes the objective points of his official action, and therefore he should master the philosophy of human idiosyncrasies, in order that he may know how and where to strike the chords of moral emotion. Hundreds who are scholars, both in thought and science, have almost utterly failed in their profession as ministers, because they have never understood human nature. Defective in what is termed "common sense," they have read books, but not men. Masters in technical theology, they are only stunted infants in their knowledge of men. They have been patient students of the divine truth and purposes, and yet they know but little of that human animus on which they are to operate.

The demonstration is of frequent occurrence, where the mere teaching of "the theology of the books," to a people who have never read them, or much of anything else, has resulted only in the production of a sort of mechanical Christianity—where the brains are polished but the heart is left as unregenerate, as if it had never even been aimed at.

The admission is often made even among the evangelical, that it is not the province of science or scholastic theology to regenerate. They tell us they may enlighten and elevate, but they can not initiate the soul, or convey it into the Kingdom. This work is done by the Divine power, alone, and yet we know man's nature and man's weaknesses must be studied and understood, in order that his moral predilections may be comprehended and his special depravities be fully known. Where this is done, the minister may move among his fellow men with the requisite knowledge of his holy office, and be able to direct them according to their several capacities.

It was in this department of ministerial accomplishment especially, that Father Havens excelled most of his brethren, for it was the great book indeed, of his elementary study; and early in life, he was led to its mastery by the law of necessity as well as from the natural dictates of his own common sense. To know men in their dispositions and in the inner workings of their thoughts and faith, and in their moral determinations, was much of his life ambition, and to accomplish this purpose, he often brought men of all classes, whom he would happen to meet, to a test point, by arguments and questions; and when he once learned where they stood, however much they might differ with him, he frequently complimented them for their bold thought and intellectual independence; and yet before leaving them he almost always cautioned them against living a life of moral carelessness.

In his life-long study of human character, he became convinced that "the stuff it is made of" was not all gold. He also well knew that the moral defect was universal, and that instability, both in purpose and character, was the common inheritance of all. Hence it was but seldom he ever misjudged any one, when he had once thoroughly scanned him. But if he ever did, and was afterward made sensible of it, no man was more free or frank to confess it, or more ready to acknowledge it. He has often been known to go to individuals, who were much inferior to him in everything that constitutes respectability or character, in order to apologize to them for the opinion or belief he had expressed in regard to them. The nobleness of his nature was such, in this regard, that he but seldom failed to express the same opinions of men in their presence that he would or had in their absence. He read men as scholars read books, and he turned over page after page of their characters, until he was satisfied; and when he was done, there were but few who had the power to deceive him.

The work of his ministry was chiefly all performed in the itinerancy, in which, in the earlier days especially, he was often brought in conflict with men of the baser sort—reckless and careless men, who were always ready for any sort of an onslaught on the church, her ministry and membership. But it did not matter how boastful these men were, or how daringly they threatened, Father Havens was always ready to stand his ground, and to maintain his rights and privileges. He was not disposed to fall back and yield, even for the sake of peace or quiet. His own ideas were, that if the devil was mad, he had no authority to order or command him. Then, he well knew that a defiant, boastful sinner was nearly always a coward, and that men of brass countenances could but seldom lay claim to superior brains. Hence, he had but little reverence for the one, or fear of the others. His command over such characters was generally as peculiar as it was heroic. Most of them feared him, and they not unfrequently manifested toward him a respect and reverence which they were not disposed to show toward any other minister. They knew that "old sorrel," as they often called him, "was game to the backbone," and when he was about, they understood they had to be on their good behavior.

In etiquette Father Havens was always as frank as he was sincere and independent. Still, he made but little pretensions to style or polish, and on this account he was somewhat more liable to personal collisions with uncouth characters than was common with many other Methodist ministers. But this peculiarity only served to give him the greater prominence, and to open up before him a wider door of personal influence and power among the people wherever he traveled, or was sent to labor.

Always profound in thought and cautious in forming his opinions of men, he but seldom uttered an expression of any one that he subsequently found himself mistaken in, and obligated to retract.

There were times and circumstances however, when some thought him severe—for he but seldom "sugar coated" his pills, particularly, where he knew that the parties charged, were playing the game of hypocracy, and were aiming to deceive "even the very elect."

If he ever stood like a wall of adamant against a

man, he believed in the wrong, it was because his own convictions of right would not permit him to do otherwise, without compromising, either the truth of facts, or the rights of principle, neither of which he could do, and still respect himself as a man, a Christian or a minister in the pulpit. Father Havens often displayed his thorough knowledge of human character. He understood that his public teachings were for the benefit of the multitude and therefore he often dealt with them with a knife of dissection, which at times was sharpened up to the keenest edge, and which he applied without regard to social pretensions or even religious professions. With that fervid and pungent eloquence so characteristic of his pulpit efforts, he would give to saint and sinner his due portion of truth with but little thought of what any of them might think of him when his discourse was finished.

Many who heard him often trembled for his popularity. They feared that his plainness of speech and withering rebukes, would bring down upon him the hot indignation of his audiences. But he understood when and where to strike, as he also knew that the impudent boldness of sin, required a bold hand to bring it down, and therefore he stood up before the people, as one who feared not the face of man.

The remarkable success of his ministry was undoubtedly largely attributable to his plain personal admonitions and reproofs, "in season and out of season," which he often administered without regard to persons, places, or circumstances. He knew men too well to consent to sinful compromises with them. However wealthy or distinguished for their social force, they could bring no power to bear against him, to make him afraid to meet them, or to tell them of their wrongs. Those who knew him well always knew where they might find him on every moral question, for he wore no disguises and never held back his opinions for fear they would be unacceptable or unpopular.

Even when he was in the wrong as it is admitted he sometimes was, he always gave evidence that it was an error of the head and not of the heart. But being a minister of the heroic stamp, and always subject to the power of impulse, it should certainly be set down to his credit, that it was but seldom he ever misjudged men, or their motives, or called in question their rights or privileges. What he accorded to others he however rigidly claimed for himself, and therefore it was always a dangerous experiment to come in conflict with any of his reserved rights or privileges.

The following authentic story is appropos on this point:

At one of his camp meetings in the State of Ohio he became very seriously annoyed by the rough and boisterous conduct of a large and robust man by the name of McDaniels, who was creating a disturbance of the religious services. Nearly every one was afraid of the huge monster and no one dared to approach him.

Father Havens being fully convinced in his own mind that McDaniels would not dare to strike him, he determined "to beard the lion in his den." He found him, a half hour later, some distance from the encampment, surrounded by his boon companions, and still planning mischief against the meeting. He approached him alone, and commenced conversation, and began to rebuke him for his mean and cowardly conduct. McDaniels tried to defend himself, but Father Havens going a little nearer to him, said:

"I know you, sir; I know your name and family; and I know, sir, that you have a respectable father and kind mother, who would blush with shame to learn of your conduct at this camp meeting. I think, sir, you had better resolve to come into the congregation, and take your seat like a decent white man should, and you will feel at least that you are a more respectable, if not a better man."

"Who's agoing to preach?" asked the reckless rowdy.

"Why, sir," responded Father Havens, "I am going to try to preach myself."

"Well, if I go in and hear you, will you agree to pray for me?" the rowdy asked.

"Yes, sir, I will," Father Havens responded.

"Well, then, I'll be on hand," said McDaniels; "go and get your trumpet ready, and we'll all come in and hear you."

Father Havens took the man at his word, turned away from him, and repaired to the stand where preaching was about to commence. The horn was sounded, and the people assembled, and among them was McDaniels and his crew.

Father Havens read his hymn, and the people sang with spirit and power. But before he asked the people to kneel in prayer, he informed the audience that he "had made a solemn promise out in the woods, a few minutes ago, to pray for one Mr. McDaniels, who, he was glad to see, was in the congregation, and he wished every christian in the assembly to join him in praying for him. I know the man," he remarked, "and I am glad to say to this congregation that this Mr. McDaniels is respectably connected, and would, no doubt, make a good man and a valuable member of the Church, if he was only once converted."

The congregation then kneeled in prayer, and Father Havens offered up a most devout petition in behalf of his "improvised subject." Strange as it may seem, before that camp meeting closed, McDaniels joined the Church, and in after years he became a pillar in it, and remained such through a long life of usefulness and piety.

Many years afterward, at one of his camp meetings in the White Water country, as was customary, he was called upon as Presiding Elder to take up the regular quarterly collection for the support of the circuit preachers. It was Sunday and the audience was large, and of course he made his appeal for a liberal collection. He told his audience that all could give something, and that many should give liberally. Then turning to his right, where he saw seated a popular candidate for Congress, he added: "Here is my friend, Hon. Oliver H. Smith, a candidate for Congress, he will give ten dollars, I have no doubt." Mr. Smith of course felt himself sold for the occasion, and it only remained for him to come down with the "dust."

Father Havens read the character of men at a glance, and if it had not been for his conservative caution, he could have given the outlines of their characters with as much precision, perhaps, as most of our phrenological philosophers. His study of men, however, for the most part, had reference more to their moral status than to their intellectual. His business was with men's goodness and badness, and he gave his thoughts this direction as a matter of professional duty, in order that he might the better fulfill the great purposes of his calling, and show himself a minister who need not be ashamed.

CHAPTER IX.

OPPOSITION TO INNOVATIONS.

THE opposition which age sometimes offers to the innovations of the times, is often attributed to the ignorance or old-fashioned bigotry of the objectors, when, in fact, it should sometimes at least be taken as good evidence of their intelligent discernment and virtues. Society, as is well known, is not always benefitted by what is termed the footsteps of progress, and therefore due credit should be given to the conservative who are disposed to hold it in check, as well as to those who are so anxious to grease the wheels of its advancement to what they term the higher civilization. Simplicity of character often makes men better, rather than the ostentation of superior pretensions, and on this account some of our old time ministers have been led to think but indifferently of many of our modern Church innovations. They thought, and no doubt with some reason too, that the advances of pride were often more to be feared than that unsophisticated simplicity which is satisfied with its own native manners, rather than with the tinsel and allurements of any mere worldly display.

Personal goodness has not usually found its wisest preceptors among the innovators of the age, or its most reliable guardians in what is called the higher walks of society. The spirit of the world is there, we admit; but then the affinity between it and the sterner virtues, though it is sometimes polite and formal, is but seldom either genuine or real. The arrogant pretensions of the one is wholly antagonistic to the simple humility of the other; and therefore those who find fault with the latter, because it appears to be awkward and unsophisticated, only find fault with forms and appearances, when they should see and know there is neither lack of principle nor want of virtue.

The education of such men as Mr. Havens in the cabins of the West, as might well be presumed, would be both natural and simple, and without much polish of any sort. Indeed, the very simplicity of those early times gave to them the baptism of a native honesty, which became a part of their personal natures, and which, in spite of their future surroundings, governed them in their subsequent years.

But it was in his Methodist education that Mr. Havens became the most scrupulous. It was his first love in the science of moral principle, and he clung to it with a life-time tenacity in its original forms, because his early prejudices had taught him it was the *ne plus ultra* of the purest Christian truth. What it had done for him he knew was real, and therefore as an honest man he wanted all others to partake of the same pure waters.

Methodism, then, was as pure as it was simple, and as sin-killing as it was spiritual. It was as innocent of all formal display as it was loud and dogmatic against the popular views of the day. It asked no favors of the world of fashion, and bore down upon the rich with as bold a hand as upon the poor and the insignificant. Its theology recognized no divinity in wealth, and wherever it was preached it was understood to be a crusade against "the world, the flesh, and the devil," without regard to persons or relationships. It was this fearless independence which gave it character as well as power among the people, and enabled it to win its way, and to establish its dominion in almost every neighborhood of the great broad West.

In the growth of the country and the developments of society, as it became more wealthy, there was a natural desire to leave behind many of the old land marks, and to fall in with more popular and new fangled notions. The old styles, many thought had had their day; and led on by some intelligent and enterprising Yankee, or seduced away by some half way but worldly minded Methodist, the people were ready to forget the simple economy of the good old western Church, and to fall in with almost any popular "progression" which might be made. It therefore became necessary for the Circuit rider to keep a sharp look-out among his people, and to warn them against all the delusions and seducements of the day.

Among the early preachers of the west the use of notes in the pulpit was considered almost as great a dereliction, as the reading of a sermon out-right. With most of them this conviction was a palpable one; as they were taught by even their ablest marksmen, that all such gospel services could only end in formality and in most instances would be exceedingly displeasing to the people.

Of course Mr. Havens with the rest adopted these prejudices, and they more or less governed him all his life. No matter how well written a sermon might be, the reading of it was not called preaching; and when one of these reading preachers, one Sabbath in the court house in Connersville called upon him to close the services, Mr. Havens prayed the Lord to bless the sermon which had just been *read* to them. Of course the young Presbyterian Brother felt the *cut;* but as his Church justified his course he made no effort at retort. Mr. Havens thought the practice an innovation, and whether right or wrong, we give him credit for his effort to rebuke the evil, although the young minister belonged to another denomination.

To Mr. Havens, the future of even his own Methodism was an unexplored territory, and at that early period he could not even guess what his plain Church would come to in this particular. But he acted from his own stand point, and we honor him for it, not because he was always right but because he was always bold, and always honest.

It should not be understood however that Mr. Havens was opposed to the writing of sermons for he was not. It was the reading of them before the people that met his disapproval, for in the earlier days most Methodist Preachers, as well as their people, measured sermons not by their rhetoric and good English; but by their power and spirit, and the bold and eloquent manner of their delivery. Even notes were looked upon as being a hinderance to any manly rebuke of sin, or to any effective exhortation to the attainment of spiritual life.

The fact however is patent to-day in every community, that read sermons, as a general thing, only interest the scholar, the thinker—men of limited, or partial education always prefer the off hand talk, and the ready declamation, whether it is all grammatical or not. In the past days of Methodism, if a circuit rider had read to the people even the sermons of John Wesley himself, they would have been ready to have "shipped" him at the first quarterly meeting.

It was not in the sense of a moral reform negation, however, that Mr. Havens opposed these innovations, for it was the common teaching and sentiment of most of his compeers. They went in for power—for present effectiveness, and if they did not make their congregations cry, or shout, or resolve to quit sinning by joining the church, or coming to the mourner's bench, they felt that the effort was comparatively a failure, and that they had done but little good. But the following little incident will show that grace never fetters itself to any forms:

Rev. Augustus Eddy, who was widely known through Ohio, as well as Indiana, for many years, as a distinguished and popular presiding elder, once went to one of his quarterly meetings on Saturday, where he found a meeting house full of people all waiting to hear him. In the pulpit, on his arrival, he found Rev. John Meek, an old-time pioneer itinerant who had fought a thousand battles, but always without a single note. Seeing Mr. Eddy take some notes out of his beaver, he said to him in a whisper:

"You must not use notes here, Brother Eddy. The people won't stand it."

But Mr. Eddy laid the notes in the Bible, and began

the service. He sang, prayed, and read his text, and commenced preaching without reference to a note. In this style he went on until the congregation was fired and lifted to more than fever heat. Some were almost moved to shouting, when Mr. Eddy, lifting his notes from the Bible, and turning and shaking them in the face of the preacher behind him, he said:

"Ah! Brother Meek, I thought you told me this congregation would n't stand notes!"

"Yes," retorted the old pioneer, "but your Holy Ghost fire has set your notes in a blaze!"

Just so, Mr. Havens thought, if the preacher has the Holy Ghost fire, he could say anything without much regard to either matter or manner.

Rev. John S. Bayless, who was once stationed in Indianapolis, when the "Second Charge" was first organized, in 1842, was preaching in the old "Western Charge" pulpit, one Sabbath afternoon, to a crowded house, and Mr. Havens and several other ministers were in the pulpit behind him.

Mr. Bayless often used notes, and was an eloquent and an able preacher, albeit he had a lisping delivery. On this occasion his sermon was being listened to with great interest, when, near the close of it, he attempted to make a poetic quotation, and said, in his peculiar lisp:

"As the poet says— As the poet says—" with his arm elevated, as if he was determined to give the beautiful poetic thought; but as he could not catch it readily, he instinctively turned toward Mr. Havens, as if for relief, as he exclaimed the third time, "As the poet says—"

"Am I a soldier of the Cross,
A follower of the Lamb?"

ejaculated the old presiding elder, with a sort of sarcastic sympathy. But as this old poetic interrogative was not what the preacher wanted, the congregation was generally and deeply convulsed, and amid the confusion Mr. Bayless took his seat.

Mere attempts at display in the pulpit never met the approbation of Mr. Havens, and however highly he respected the preacher who made them, he was very apt to tell him of it, at the proper time.

Aberrations in the pulpit were more especially under the eye of Mr. Havens' guardianship, as he felt he had a greater privilege to criticise in this direction than in any other.

Innovations were made by the people, but these he did not so particularly notice, as he believed they had the right to make changes and though he did not always approve of them, he ordinarily contented himself with the mere expression of his disapproval, when he would let the matter rest, as he considered that they alone were the responsible umpires.

It was not until he had measurably retired from the itinerant work, that many of our most modern church innovations were fully inaugurated.

Steepled Churches, promiscuous sittings, organized choirs, organ accompaniments, theological schools and a classical ministry, comprise the chief modifications of modern Methodism, some of which Mr. Haven's doubted, at least, so far as the sin killing conquests of the old time fire were concerned.

He feared the spirit of the world and the fashion of the times would root out the old genius, the divine fire of revival progress, which he so well knew had always been the greatest honor, as well as the brightest star, in the coronet of Methodism.

He admitted that there was grand worldly dignity in a high, tall Church steeple, and that amateur choirs with the aid of organs could make the multitude believe that there was good music in religion if nothing else, and on these accounts he gave them but little favor either as an experiment in religious diaramics, or as a pretentious display in theoretic devotion.

His day of itinerant efficiency, however, was well nigh past, when most of these modern improvements in Church devotion began to be adopted in his own denomination, and knowing this, he bowed, to what many termed the spirit of the age, with what grace he could, although up to his last hour he greatly preferred the simplicity and moral beauty of the old-fashioned worship.

The mission of Methodism as he understood it, was to save souls, and not merely to cater to religious formalism, and therefore he advocated the use of the old machinery, as that which he had seen effective in a thousand conflicts, and which he believed could be wielded by an honest, conscientious ministry, simply and successfully, until the world should be converted to Christ, and the moral power of his Church become universal.

It should be remembered by our readers that Mr. Havens had been educated in the early Church discipline to oppose falsehood and fiction, pride and fashion, and it should not be thought strange that his antagonistic spirit was wont to show itself against all sorts of innovations. What he was in his profession he aimed to evince in his principles, and he was ever willing that the verdict of public opinion toward him might be governed accordingly.

At an old settlers' meeting which he attended, near Knightstown, a few years before his death, he was called upon to address the people, who were greatly delighted with his scathing sarcasms, and acute criticisms, on what the world calls progress in the Church, and which is set down as modern piety. He spoke of the state of the country when he came to the county of Rush, in the fall of 1824. He said he had seen society in its primitive organizations in Ohio, Kentucky, and Indiana, when cabins were universal, and when all that the people wore was spun, wove, and made up at home. He described the habits, manners, and customs of the early backwoodsman of the West, and contrasted them with those of the present age, in that style of sarcastic argument for which he was always so greatly distinguished. He was especially severe on the young men of the present day, who, he said, with all their acknowledged advantages had, as he feared, less conscientious regard for truth and character than the awkward and uneducated youths, who never knew any other homes but their cabins, or any other instructors save their mothers. He said he had long noticed the fact that the young man who relied upon either his father's wealth or fame, was apt to carry down to posterity but little evidence of either. To the female side of the audience the old hero also gave many severe cuts, which in a younger man would have savored of an antecedent rejection or a broken troth, but coming from Father Havens they were relished as a bright dream of the past, the music of which was pleasant to their ears. He said that in the earlier days it was not difficult to guess at a lady's weight, or to tell how old she was by her natural teeth. Women, he said, used to be domestic, but now they were but seldom in their element save when on a millinery rampage. He thought nothing was more beautiful on earth than a good and modest and virtuous woman; but he had been frequently told that the finest dressed ladies of the present day were often the very poorest representatives of either innocency or virtue. "What the result will be," he remarked, "of all this nineteenth century progress, I know not; but I confess I have my fears that when such women become mothers, their children will fear neither God, man, nor the devil."

CHAPTER X.

HIS DEVOTION TO METHODISM.

WITH the heroes of Methodism, both the faith and economy of the Church, were looked upon as an inspiration, as a new and great commission, whose special object was "to spread scriptural holiness over all lands."

Ignoring the emptiness of forms, and what they believed to be the powerless dogma of the Apostolic succession, they relied chiefly and alone, upon the "Divine rights of the Holy Spirit," and believing, that God had called them to the work, they went out into the itinerant field, "not knowing what would befall them there, save that the Holy Ghost witnessed in every city, saying that bonds and afflictions awaited them."

But "none of these things moved them, neither counted they their lives dear unto themselves, so that they might finish their course with joy, and the ministry which they had received of the Lord Jesus, to testify the gospel of the grace of God."

It was this heroic faith in their call, in their system, and in their work, which gave them their inspiration, and led them to the display of that self-sacrificing moral heroism for which so many of them were distinguished.

At this high fountain-head of spiritual commission and personal obligation, these old heroic Methodist

Preachers began their ministry; and though deficient, as many of them were, in the substantial build or polish, of any systematic scholarship, they were nevertheless, such workmen in the building of the Temple as any Church, or age, might have been proud of. Personal piety, and a spiritual commission, coupled with a zeal which "the Day of Pentecost" would have honored, constituted their set-out, and without "purse or scrip," or even the sheep-skin parchment of a Bishop, they mounted their horses, or started on foot, as they have often been known to do, "to preach to the spirits" in the cabins of the wilderness.

Strangers, as most of them were to the motives of the world, and ignorant of its tricks and policies, many instances might be given, where, like the immortal Doctor Primrose, of Vicar of Wakefield memory, they were wheedled out of their horses with a note or a song, by some hypocritical jockey, or sharper, which left them on foot; which often, as a matter of self-protection and safety, forced them to become good judges of horses, if they were not of tricky and over-reaching men.

Their early style of worship, was as unostentatious, as it was simple and sincere, and as it was for the most part, conducted in humble cabins and at Camp Meetings—where the people flocked on week days, as well as on Sundays, to hear the gospel, "without money and without price"—the unpretending Circuit Rider was often the only public character the people ever saw in their neighborhoods, and therefore it was no marvel, that they looked upon him as one sent of

God "to reprove them of sin, of righteousness, and of a judgment to come."

In these visits to neighborhoods of obscurity, and among a thoroughly domesticated people, the itinerant was not only "the observed of all observers," but he very frequently was claimed by them as being "the best man in the world."

The grand success which everywhere attended the circuit preacher's efforts of these early itinerants gave them a confidence in the adaptability, as well as in the real divinity, of the system which made them feel that they were "God's vicegerents" in communicating gospel knowledge to men; and it was, therefore, but seldom they ever dreamed that their ministerial commission was behind that of even the "Archbishop of Canterbury" himself.

Why men became so attached to this life of hardships and privations, to many often appeared mysterious. They could not see anything in it but poverty and worldly sacrifice, and yet they were compelled to admit that the men engaged in it were gifted and eloquent, as they were evidently sincere and honest.

Neither the cold of winter nor the heat of summer stood in their way in reaching their appointments; nor did swollen rivers or frozen creeks present impediments that they did not overcome. They were engaged in their Master's work, and the importance of their mission neither admitted of delays or furnished an apology for any cowardly delinquency.

Receiving their appointments to their respective fields, from the mouths of the Bishops at their annual

Conferences, the order was obeyed with a promptness which would have reflected honor upon even a military edict. They had joined the conference with the full understanding that they were not to select their own fields of labor, or to object to going wherever the Bishop might appoint them. They of course still retained the reserved privilege of locating, whenever they wished to do so; but this step was thought to be wrong and full of moral danger.

These principles and motives led Mr. Havens, when but a youth, to enter upon the work of the ministry—and although at first it was only in the sense of a local preacher, he, from the very beginning, evinced a zeal and devotion in the cause which foreshadowed the distinctive energy and success of all the rest of his life.

That which troubled him most, and gave him the greatest uneasiness, was the conscious knowledge of his own incapacity for such a high and sacred calling. This indeed was "the man of the mountain" on his back through all his years. But what he lacked in the polish of scholastic accomplishments, as far as he could he endeavored to make up for by his earnest zeal, his heroic devotion, and his life-long constancy

Though liberal in his sentiments, he was emphatically, if not dogmatically, a Methodist. What Methodism was, was his first religious life-lesson, and it ever afterwards made the foundation basis of his religious profession. Though in after years a very independent thinker on many subjects, he never turned "radical" against the economy of his church. He knew his Bishops had power, and that presiding elders had great influence, both of which, as he believed, were sometimes wielded unwisely; but all this was no more than he expected, for he knew they were but men, and that however well disposed they might be, they could not always comprehend the full situation of affairs, and, therefore, as a matter of course must make some mistakes.

He well knew, too, that any change of government which might be made would only shift the responsibility of power without giving any assurances of greater safety or protection.

Through most of the years of his itinerant life, there were more or less agitations on the subject of "reforms" in the government of his Church, and at one period the storm became so great that the very foundations of the edifice were shaken. But through it all Mr. Havens stood to his post as a hero, never once flinching or faltering, or showing any disposition to throw the destinies of American Methodism into the hands of speculative adventurers. He had seen the workings of the machinery as it was, and he was well satisfied that no other Church economy of the land excelled it in efficiency, or surpassed it in the economical and practical workings of its agencies. It was not in the principles of the government so much as in the occasional weaknesses of the men who executed it, that he saw defectiveness, and this evil, he well knew, attached to all governments, both civil and ecclesiastical. His own chief aim was to build up a plain and substantial christian civilization, and he was well convinced that this could be done with the machinery of Methodism as it was, both wisely and safely, if Methodist preachers would be honest and faithful toward one another, and the people continued to care with any degree of conscientiousness for their moral and future welfare.

At one period, Mr. Havens had what was termed, in the common parlance of the day, a Radical Methodist preacher as one of his not very distant neighbors. Hearing that he was learned in all Church economy, as well as a talented preacher, Mr. Havens, for a long time, was quite anxious to fall in with him that he might learn what "new light" the gentleman had, which made him so great an enemy of the "old ship" in which he had made his first sailings.

Meeting him one day in a store of the village, he asked for and obtained an introduction to him. After some general conversation on the subject of Church affairs, the following dialogue ensued:

Mr. H. "I understand, Brother T, that you were once a minister in the Methodist Episcopal Church?"

Mr. T. "I was."

Mr. H. "And a traveling preacher?"

Mr. T. "Yes, sir, I was."

Mr. H. "Well, will you think me impertinent if I should ask you why you severed your connection with the Methodist Episcopal Church?"

Mr. T. "I left it, sir, because of its tyranny."

Mr. H. "Because of its tyranny! Why, in what respect did that tyranny affect you?"

Mr. T. "I was expelled from the Conference, sir, unjustly and without law."

Mr. H. "I am sorry for your misfortune, sir; but

let me ask, had you not been lecturing against the Bishops, the Presiding Elders, and the government of the Church generally?"

Mr. T. "Well, yes, I had been speaking out my honest sentiments, which I had a right to do, and it was none of their business, so long as I filled all my appointments."

Mr. H. "You certainly knew that we have a rule forbidding any preacher from inveighing against our doctrines or discipline. Did you not know that you were violating this wise and provident rule, when you were delivering your public lectures on your hobby of reform?"

Mr. T. "This is a free country, as I understand it, and I claim the right to advocate any reforms I please, either in Church or State."

Mr. H. "Well, sir, I admire your independence, but I can not say as much for your discretion. You are now I believe, Bro. T., a member of what you call the Methodist Protestant Church?"

Mr. T. "I am, and also a traveling preacher in that Church, and President of the Conference."

Mr. H. "I acknowledge your official dignity, sir. But let me ask you, what would the result be if you were now to deliver lectures over the country in favor of having Bishops in your Church, and Presiding Elders, and so on of all the rest? Would they not expel you from your Conference and Church?"

Mr. T. "It is very probable, sir, they would. But if they did, that would not make it right; for I hold it that this is a free country, and every man has a right to his own sentiments."

Mr. H. "So he has; I admit it. But whenever he makes use of those sentiments to tear down and destroy the moral power of his own Church, he certainly should not complain if the sane and sober members of his Church should take him by the hand and lead him out as one who was no longer fit to be a member of their body. Such an act would have no tyranny in it, for it would be demanded by every law of peace and safety"

Here the Protestant brother evidently began, if he had not before, to see his mistake, and he left Mr. Havens without much ceremony, but not until the *old landmark* Methodist had grasped his hand, and exhorted him never to forget that he was converted to God through the instrumentality of the Methodist Episcopal Church.

But few ministers we have known of any Church could lay claim to a higher integrity in his devotion to his own particular denomination than Mr. Havens; still this devotion never amounted to bigotry, for he was both liberal and tolerant, and never turned his back upon any man, merely because he differed with him in his religious sentiments.

Coming from the Terre Haute Conference in the fall of 1841, he, in company with some eight or ten of his brethren, stopped at a hotel, near Greencastle, where he found sitting at the fire side Rev. Jonathan Kidwell, a Universalist minister.

It was about dark when they entered the sitting

room of the tavern, and Mr. Kidwell was sitting alone, and as he had his hat on it was difficult, as he kept his head down, to tell who he was.

The venerable Universalist seemed to know he was surrounded by Methodist Preachers, and he evidently did not care much for the sudden intrusion, which had been made upon his company, as he sat with his hat slouched over his ears, as if he did not wish to be even recognized by them.

Mr. Havens recognized him as soon as he entered the room; but as Mr. Kidwell did not raise his head, or salute any one of them—so far as he was concerned he had the thing all his own way.

But this did not suit Mr. Havens, as he wanted to show the old apostle of Universalism, that though he was a Methodist himself, he wished to be impartial toward all in the house. Walking out on the porch a little while, Mr. Havens came in, and walking round to Mr. Kidwell's chair, he took hold of his hat as if he thought it belonged to one of his traveling companions, saying, as he did so, "Which one of the brethren is this, who is so sedate?" Turning up his head, Mr. Kidwell revealed his face, when Mr. Havens exclaimed, with apparent astonishment, "Why, if it ain't my old friend, Brother Kidwell! Why, how do you do, Brother Kidwell, I am glad to meet with you."

Mr. Kidwell arose and greeted Mr. Havens with apparent cordiality, when the two old theological antagonists took chairs together and entered into quite a social chat.

When supper was announced, we all walked out to

the table, and took our seats, of course it was supposed that Father Havens, as he was the oldest minister, would say grace. We waited, until Father Havens broke the silence by saying—" Brother Kidwell, will you please ask a blessing." Of course the blessing was asked, both devoutly and reverently, and during the supper, and throughout the evening these two old war veterans of antagonistic faiths, chatted as socially and with as much apparent pleasure, as if they had all their lifetimes fed from the same table.

All the next day the old Methodist itinerant, seemed to feel that he had gained a victory over both bigotry and himself, and he appeared to feel that he was more the man and the Christian, because he had treated Mr. Kidwell, who was so down on the doctrines of Methodist Preachers, both as a man and a brother.

CHAPTER XI.

PREPARATION FOR THE PULPIT.

ORIGINALITY of character is usually found in the thoughts of the man, rather than in his actions, for it is the inner man which gives the true type of life, and to it must we look to make any definite recognition of ones real animus. Even the very mode of thought has much to do with the character of the man, for it tells us whether he is impulsive, phlegmatic, acute, or suggestive, and to some extent it furnishes the personal as well as the intellectual measure, as fairly as any other view.

It does not often occur to an audience how, or where, or by what process of thought, or intellectual labor, the sermon they have just listened to, was made, though this or that had much to do in its production, as well as its character.

To those who have never known any other mode of preparation for the pulpit; but with the pen, it may seem preposterous to even speak of any other. With them composition must precede every public effort, and they are only able to appear before an audience, when they have their sermon written. Extempore effort is above and beyond their capacity. They are pen orators only, their manuscripts being their only stronghold—for any public display, or any preaching abilities.

The fact may not be admitted, but nevertheless it is true, that the practice of reading sermons can be sustained with a much lower grade of talent than that of extempore preaching. Writing may require the better education, but off-hand speaking demands the higher talents. To write is mechanical, and can be learned as one learns a trade, but extempore speaking, where it is effective, requires genius and oratory, as well as ready knowledge. The one is the work of the mechanical scholar, while the other is the evidence of the gifted and ready orator.

Among all who write, and even write well, we find but few who can read so as to give the touches of oratory, with any marked efficiency. Orators, like poets, are born, but "writists" are turned out from the schools, like hubs from the factory.

The practised writer may make men think, but the power and music of the orator, is requisite to move them to action. It is such facts as these, that throw light upon the wonderful success of Methodism. The preachers were extempore orators. They aimed at the hearts of men, rather than at their heads. The "Jerusalem philosophy" taught them that, "with the heart, man believeth unto righteousness," and they caught the refrain with pious avidity; and directed by Wesley, they poured upon the world for a hundred years the grandest, because the most effective, sermons it has heard since the Apostolic age.

It was not ignorance that led the Methodist ministry to ignore the reading of sermons. It was their theology—that theology which aimed to strike down the sinner at a single blow. They did not start out to reform the world by the slow process of systematic education, but to move it with the power of a moral avalanche. They aimed indeed "to shake one world with the thunders of another," and their very motto was to "cry aloud and to spare not." Their preachers "went everywhere preaching the word." "Many heard them gladly," and everywhere the exclamation was uttered, that "they who have turned the world upside down, have come hither also."

Laughed at, as many of them were, and even are still, they swept the Churches of the land of much of their formalisms, and kindled a spiritual activity and fire among the people of different and distant countries, which, it is to be hoped, they will never cease doing until the last trumpet "peals the dirge of time."

It was under such spiritual impetuousness that Mr. Havens was first led to an acquaintance with Methodism, and having full confidence in the sterling divinity of his own experience, he preached the facts as he had learned them—told the story as he knew it in the moral protection of his own life, and as he had seen it in ten thousand cases around him. With him Christianity was no mere theory, but an order of law and precepts, of spirit and power, such as the world could find in no system of its own philosophy, and to these he directed both his thought and soul afresh, whenever he was called to preach a sermon. Never having given himself, to any great extent, to the use of the pen, thought and reflection, and prayer to Almighty God for his assistance, became the fixed preparatory habits of his life.

To this habit may we attribute that rich vein of living, original thought, which made him so prominent as a preacher, and drew around him wherever he labored the best thinkers, and even many of the best educated minds of the country. Mr. Havens was no "English Sketch Preacher," nor did he entertain his audiences with revamped sermons. With him every sermon was a new one, and he sank or rose with the circumstances of the occasion, and yet he but seldom ever made a failure.

Believing, as he did, that he was accountable to God for the spirit and manner, as well as for the matter of his sermons, his preparatory agitations were often very great before going into the pulpit, and sometimes for many hours before he delivered his sermon, his mind would seem in a perfect storm of agony and excitement. In pleasant weather he would go to the woods with no companion but his Bible; and in winter he has often been known to walk the floor of his room during a large part of the night before preaching one of his bold, spirit-stirring sermons on the Sabbath.

The mystery with many who knew him, and who were fully aware of his scholastic deficiency, was to account for his original and profound thought, for his logical force and argumentative impressiveness. They saw that he moved out on the line of his investigations with a master's power, and that it was but seldom he ever failed to give to both "saint and sinner his portion in due season."

In theological schools it is the custom to read all other books in order to get a clear understanding of the Bible, but with Mr. Havens this order was almost wholly reversed. He read the Bible to know what was, or should be, in all other books. What it taught was his theology; and drinking, as he did, daily at the fountain head of all truth, all doctrine, and all hope of life—temporal, spiritual, and eternal—he came before the people at each pulpit greeting with a fresh and divine commission which gave him authority to speak the truth, no matter whom it might hit, reprove, or please, totally irrespective of the pride of wealth or the display of dignity

On nearly all occasions his sermons were prepared and intended to rebuke all manner of sins among the people, and to warn them against the moral presumption of "rushing on the thick bosses of Jehovah's buckler." If his personal ambition led him to make an extraordinary effort it was not with the selfish idea of building up himself in the esteem of his hearers—but it was with the higher and nobler conviction of showing himself a minister that needed not to be ashamed, rightly dividing the word of truth.

The mechanical stilts of mere human knowledge were never his support in his pulpit reliances. Hence, he never fed his congregations on the husks of human science, when they came before him for spiritual food, or to have the doctrine of the atonement explained to them, or when they wished to be led up in thought and devotion, to the higher walks of immortality and life.

Though wholly an extempore preacher, Mr. Havens was not always ready to preach. He wanted time, ordinarily, to prepare his sermon, or, at least, to get his mind in frame, and when this was done he was always ready—though it was not uncommon for him to change his text even after he had begun the services.

On one occasion a brother minister of another church came to him and informed him that he had been very busy during the week making some improvements on his property, and he had only one sermon prepared for the Sabbath, and wanted to know if he would not preach for him on Sabbath night? Mr. Havens gave his consent to do so, and at the proper time he reported himself at the brother's Church and was politely escorted into the pulpit.

Presenting Mr. Havens with the bible and taking the hymn book himself, the Pastor asked, in view of selecting suitable hymns for the sermon of the evening:

"Mr. Havens, what will be the subject of your discourse to-night?"

"Well, sir, I don't know yet," was the response of the old Methodist itinerant, "I have not exactly fixed on that yet," he added.

The confession took the brother by surprise, for he had been educated in the regular line of sermon preparation, and he thought it strange that a preacher of such long standing as Mr. Havens should agree to preach for him, and then come into his pulpit without knowing what he was going to preach about.

"I want to select suitable hymns," said the minister.

"In that matter just suit yourself," responded Mr. Havens.

The hymns were sung, and the prayers were offered, when Mr. Havens read his text:

"God forbid that I should glory, save in the cross of our Lord Jesus Christ."

For a full hour that assembly listened to a sermon as full of bold thought on the moral heroism, and self sacrifice of the Christian life, as perhaps they had ever heard in their lives. The brother said he never listened to a sermon with greater interest, or with more astonishment. "It was," said he, "full of the purest thought and richest divinity, and was delivered with a readiness and pathos, which perfectly astonished me." "I thought," he added, "if Mr. Havens preaches that way without preparation how must he preach when he does prepare his sermon."

This good brother did not understand it. That sermon, doubtless had cost Mr. Havens more study, more pure mental agitation, than a dozen written sermons usually cost a mere sermon writer. Though he may have preached it even hundreds of times in his life, he had no outline of it, and every effort he made to preach it was a new one. The subject, to his mind, was ever like a grand temple, which he would occasionally visit, to inspect its beauty, and to learn the divinity of its architecture. When the spirit of his thought led him in this direction, and he felt the subject appropriate to the hour, he would enter the spacious gates of such a temple of truth, and walk down its inspiring corridors, and with his soul wrapt in the etherial atmosphere of the higher life, he would closely scan each chamber of the divine edifice, and thus impressed, and thus inspired, he would come before his congregation feeling that every truth he preached was an inspiration, which on the pains and penalties of an immutable law, they should both hear and obey. Though in no mechanical sense a scholar, Mr. Havens was most undoubtedly a profound thinker on all the great leading subjects of Christian theology. His mind was thoroughly disciplined to the practices of thought, and he understood the order of successful argument, as if he had been an expert logician. Of course his pulpit efforts lacked the finish of the scholar, as well as the profundity of the thorough reader, for he was not the one, nor did he ever lay claims to be the other. But feeling, as he always did, the educational misfortune of his early years, he was the more studious and particular in the thorough investigation of all such subjects, as he from time to time adopted as the themes of his ministerial efficiency.

Mr. Havens was once invited to an evenings entertainment among a large number of Presbyterian ministers, where as was natural the subject of pulpit preparation was extensively discussed. The conversation was general, and various opinions were expressed in regard to the best time for study, as well as the proper mode of preparing sermons.

Though the oldest minister present, Mr. Havens, with his usual modesty on such occassions, sat and listened, and while the younger divines were all giving their respective experiences in regard to the matter, he was running back on the wings of his memory, over the vast fields of his life-toil, where in cabins and school houses, court houses and log churches, he had met and addressed so many thousands of the old and pioneer citizens of the West. But still he listened with respectful reverence to what he termed "the more learned theories of these theological scholars." The most of them he found placed great reliance on a good supply of well written sermons. Noticing this fact, when one of the company turned to him for his views, and asked what he thought of the matter, he facetiously remarked:

"I was just thinking, Brethren, what the result would be if one of you was going to assist one of your brethren at a Communion Meeting, and was to lose your written sermon by the way." "What would you do in such a dilemma?" he asked. "That is a contingency, Mr. Havens," replied one of them, "which I presume but seldom ever happens." "Well, but it does happen," responded another, with a laugh, as I can testify from my own experience. "About a year ago," said he, "I rode twenty miles over to an adjoining Presbytery to get one of its members to come and spend a Sabbath with me. I succeeded in my mission, and obtained a good brother who is said to be a fine scholar to ride over with me. But on our arrival we found the little satchel of my companion, in which he had his sermons was *non est*, and the result was the next day I had to preach twice myself."

Of course the laugh was against an implicit reliance on written sermons, and more particularly so when one is going from home.

CHAPTER XII.

STYLE OF HIS PREACHING.

The fact that Mr. Havens ranked among the ablest and foremost preachers in the West, to many may seem anomalous, particularly when it is admitted that he was neither a scholar nor even a general reader. But of him, more especially than of any other minister of Indiana, it may be said that he was a man of one thought, of one purpose, of one book. The "holy Bible" was his *vade mecum*, his life-long companion, which not only commanded his devotion and absorbed his thoughts, but it furnished the basis of his religion, the circumference of his philosophy, and the obligations of his lifelong labors. To "this book of books" he made all his appeals. It was his souvenir in all the sacred memories of the past, and whether in doubt or trial, through all of life's vicissitudes, this inspired volume, "the book of the ages," was his only supreme and infallible reliance.

Though possessing a mind which was largely and naturally skeptical, Mr. Havens never suffered his thoughts for a moment to doubt either the authenticity or credibility of this great book. With the immortal Bard of Avon, Sir William Shakspeare, Mr. Havens made his best and strongest quotations from its words of wonder, and gathered also the theory of his moral ethics from its holy teachings.

Thus drinking from the fountain head, it was not

necessary that he should taste of any other waters, for with his inner soul filled with the blessings of this higher inspiration, he scarcely had need of any of the lighter sprinklings, to either give zest to his knowledge or zeal to his mission.

Like most of the early Methodist preachers, Mr. Havens aimed chiefly at the conversion of sinners, and to this end he drove his forces, often with a speed and power, which not unfrequently moved his whole congregation. His texts themselves were often startling, and he generally selected them in view of striking the truth home upon the hearts of his audiences, for he had but little faith in "catching men with straws," and therefore he charged upon them often with an impetuous storm of fiery eloquence, which made his hearers tremble as if their impending fate was just before them.

It was never the purpose of his sermons to merely entertain an audience. This policy he thought might suit a tragedian, but not a gospel minister. He preached as he believed, because he was sent, and relying for his effectiveness wholly upon the gift and power of the Holy Ghost, he entered the pulpit somewhat like a general goes into battle, and always with the resolve, if within his power, to have the victory.

His best efforts were usually made under the pressure of excitement, when the people were gathered by thousands to hear him, and when the circumstances of the occasion seemed to demand it. On such occasions his nervous organism was strung up to its highest tension, and he became "a hero on the battle-field," no matter how fierce was the strife. Earnestness and zeal, sincerity and high resolve, marked and distinguished his spirit; while in language and utterance, look and gesture, he so far became the orator, that it was but seldom his congregations ever grew weary of his effort.

Many pulpit orators are either pompous or ornate, but Mr. Havens was never the one or the other, for it was not in the dignity of his personnel, or in the flowery elements of his language, that he ever aimed to excel. Indeed, he disdained to even look in these directions, for his high sense of ministerial obligations, utterly forbid any display of vanity in the pulpit, and his evident sincerity and sterling Christian honesty always kept him in another sphere.

Ever aiming at execution in his holy office, and chiefly anxious to convert men, and to reform the malignant spirit of the age, he mostly forgot himself in his preaching, and seemed not even to care, whether his efforts would lead on to his personal fortunes or not. Indeed, but few ministers we have ever known excelled him in this regard. It was this fearless moral independence, doubtless, that gave him such prominence, as well as such great success.

Earnest in thought, as he was fervent and determined in spirit, he gave utterance to both, in language that was expressive, and in such a style, as always impressed his audiences and held them with the chain of his power.

It is a well known fact in all oratorical efforts, that every speaker has his own particular forte, which constitutes his chief strength, and opens his way to the minds and hearts of his audiences, as with the power of a mysterious divinity. This forte Mr. Havens possessed in a peculiar manner, though he never appeared to be conscious of it, only in the aims and purposes of his holy calling.

But few ministers ever talked to his congregations in plainer language than he did. This in fact, was his style of address, and whether in the pulpit or out of it he always scorned to be Janus-faced. He loved the direct style, the frank expression, the honest and determined word. Such manner of utterances belonged peculiarly to the genius of his own character, and if he ever prided himself in anything connected with his pulpit performances, it was the fact that he was never afraid to preach the truth to any congregation, or even to tell any man of his sins and meanness even to his teeth.

Though thus fearless of men, but few ministers we have known were more fearful of God. He believed most sincerely in the great Omnipotence, and as it was by such authority and commission, he had entered the ministry, he never lost sight of his high responsibility. Nothing could lead him to forget that he was one of God's moral almoners, and through all the years of his official life, we never heard of any one accusing him of daubing with untempored mortar.

What he preached, he gleaned from the word of God, and as he knew the source of his doctrines, he never hesitated to make them known in their eternal richness, as well as in the terrible fearfulness of their present and eternal penalties. What the bible says of both Heaven and hell, Mr. Havens believed most implicitly, and therefore he often gave the allurements of the one, and depicted the horrid agonies of the other, with all the nervous and eloquent language of his soul, while listening thousands shook before him under the fearful power of the word.

In conversation with Hon. Charles H. Test a few days since, he spoke of Mr. Havens as follows: "The first time I ever heard Rev. James Havens preach, was at a camp meeting a short distance below Connersville." "I was," said he, "over at Connersville attending court, and remaining over Sabbath I was induced to attend the camp meeting. The congregation was large, numbering several thousand, and Mr. Havens, I found, was the preacher for the popular hour. I took my seat as near the stand as I could get it, and after singing and prayer, the preacher read his text in a distinct but husky voice, and began to preach. I soon became impressed that he was no ordinary speaker or orator; for soon he had the people interested in his subject, and for an hour or more he held the vast assembly as if they were enchanted. I thought I never heard a finer sermon from the lips of any man than Mr. Havens gave us that day. It was clear and terse, eloquent and able, and under its delivery the people sat during the long hour with an extatic pleasure such as I have but seldom ever witnessed."

It was the earnestness of Mr. Havens' preaching, perhaps, more than any other distinct feature, which gave it its resistless and eloquent force. He never trifled with eternal interests, when he was in the pulpit, for there he felt he was an officer standing between

God and man, and he well knew that if he proved recreant to the truth—

"The traitor's doom would be his only future trust."

Some of our readers may be ready to ask whether Mr. Havens' style of preaching was of the instructive cast? The question, we admit, is a natural one, for we are well aware that many have the impression that the impulsive extempore preacher does not teach—that he only excites, and therefore is limited in his influence to only a single class.

That some off-hand and excitable preachers may be thus limited is probable, but Mr. Havens was not of any such class. His preaching comprehended the divinity of truth, the genuine power of religion, the genius of eloquence, as well as the earnestness of soul of a warm-hearted and zealous gospel minister.

True, he dealt but sparingly in speculative theology, or in metaphysical phylosophy. Gospel facts and Christian morals, in connection with the evangelical experience and hopes of a religious life, made up the chief sum of his pulpit themes, and these he laid before his congregations with such plain and earnest force that they could not well fail to feel and acknowledge their true character and power.

Preaching through many of his years to very large assemblies of people of all religious faiths, and of every shade of morals, many of his sermons were especially designed for the outside world, instead of the Church. On this account they were often of that bold character which some would term rough. But the true secret of the matter was they were only plain.

10

They contained the truth, and doubtless in most instances went in the right direction. It is possible for some congregations to listen to what is called preaching—and preaching which is well paid for too—that never touches the worst sinners among them—the rich, the fashionable, and the licentious.

It may be said of Mr. Havens, however, that no man ever had a dollar big enough to buy him, or any assumed human dignity that could awe him into silence. He had seen bears and panthers, and even the native and fiery red man, in his youth, and there was no pale face that could make him wince or fall back from his high responsibilities. It was this decision of character, this positive make up of his ministerial pretensions, which constituted him the giant among men, and the hero among gospel ministers. He was not afraid to say what he ought to, and as he was not given to flattery even among his friends, he never held back the truth even for their accommodation. In plain words, Mr. Havens was an honest man. But that all his sermons were clear and graphic, orthodox and prudent, it might not be safe to affirm. Of course he meant them all well, yet there were times and circumstances through which he was called to pass, that transcended his education and abilities, and if he showed confusion of thought or trepidation of mind at any time, it was because the sudden pressure of circumstances had not given him time for proper reflection. On such occasions he was exceedingly distrustful even of himself, and apparently as unwilling to confide in his own judgment as in that of any other man.

In almost every profession of life there are vicissitudes of history where men are not themselves, where some foreign genius seems to possess them, and under such confused and monopolizing control the real animus of the man is for a brief period obscured, if it is not wholly perverted. With Mr. Havens, however, such freaks of character but seldom occurred, and when they did, he seemed to recognize their presence in himself as readily as he did or would in any other person. It was this knowledge of his own weakness that led him to the exercise of such leniency toward others, and often in his public services, while he would be most scathingly severe on the derelictions of transgressors, he would earnestly plead that charity should be extended toward them, and that as far as possible every one should lend a hand to help them up again.

Hon. James Rariden, for many years a Representative in Congress from the "old Burnt District" of Indiana, whose residence was at Centreville, in Wayne County, was a great admirer and strong friend of Mr. Havens. They had met first when both of them were young in their respective professions, one a lawyer and the other a preacher, but both of them, in the common language of the day, styled "circuit riders." The lawyer carried Blackstone and the preacher John Wesley in his saddle-bags, and as they were very much alike in many things, their congenial associations were often as free and unrestrained as if they had grown up on the same fire-stones. Raridan was not a professor of religion, however, and indeed among many it was thought he had but little faith in anything of the sort.

But Mrs. Raridan being a Methodist, Mr. Havens was often their guest, where he met her husband, the Congressman, who always greeted him in the most familiar manner.

At one of Mr. Havens' Quarterly meetings in Centreville, he preached on Sunday morning, one of the severest and most scathing sermons against infidelity he was ever known to utter. Quite a number of the skeptical citizens of the place were present, and prominent among them was Mr. Raridan. They all sat and listened with the utmost reverence, as they knew "Old Sorrel," as thousands called Mr. Havens, had the floor. Many furtive glances were made by the congregation at these supposed infidel gentlemen, as Mr. Havens poured the thunders of Sinai around their heads, and held up to them the milder splendors of the New Testament philosphy. What, and all he said, on that occasion, of course is lost, both in its matter and manner, but like the terrific storm which has swept in its wildness through the giant oaks of the forest, the track of its footsteps were everywhere visible. When the meeting was over, Mr. Havens was invited to dine with his old friend Mr. Raridan. While at the table there was not an allusion to the sermon. All was pleasant and marked with the kindest hospitality, and the old Presiding Elder almost began to think he had made a clear convert of the eccentric and talented Congressman.

The company rose from the table, and took seats in the parlor, when Mr. Raridan came in with his pipes and tobacco for himself and distinguished guest, to have their favorite *recherche* Indian desert.

The pipes filled with the best old Virginia fine "stub and twist" and lit, the two old "Ex-Circuit Riders," sat puffing out their graceful curls of rolling smoke, as if there was not a single string of discord between them. Mr. Raridan felt that "Old Sorrel" was "one" ahead of him in the matter of the sermon he had just preached, and he was itching to get even with him.

"Do you pretend to believe, Brother Havens," Mr. Raridan solemnly asked, "that Jonah swallowed the whale?"

Mr. Havens not noticing the catch, very promptly responded:

"Yes, I certainly do."

"Well, well," said Raridan, laughing at the good success of his humor. "I don't know which was the biggest fool Jonah or the whale. You tell me that Jonah swallowed the whale"—

"No, Raridan I didn't," said the Presiding Elder.

"Yes, yes, you said you believed he did, which is the same thing," responded the facetious Congressman.

Mr. Havens, seeing that his humorous friend had taken advantage of his absent-mindedness, cast a leering glance at him and remarked: "Raridan, I'm afraid the Devil will get you yet."

The little joke evidently gave Mr. Raridan the victory, for he used to tell it with fresh gusto, on all possible occasions.

CHAPTER XIII.

CHARACTER AS A REVIVALIST.

The distinctive mission of Christianity is fully exemplified only where men are led to acknowledge the majesty of moral laws and where their lives are made to strictly conform to it.

That such an order of society can be accomplished by the mere process of "catachetical teaching" has been doubted by many, whose faith and experience have taught them, that spiritual life is only enjoyed by such as are "born again."

Having discarded the old doctrine of "a legitimately descended Priesthood," and of "baptismal regeneration" in the impartation of spiritual life, they became ardent zealots of revival reforms. On this faith, they moved out on the works of the enemy, and among the masses of the people, with a power which has often demonstrated that "the day of Pentecost" might be repeated as long as time might last.

It was this spiritual theory, in connection with the great doctrine of Martin Luther, of "Salvation by faith," which formed the outline and revival mission of Methodism, and which for more than a century has been known in England and America, as the Wesleyan reformation.

The spiritual results of this wonderful mission have largely silenced the dogmatic criticisms of the older churches, and in many instances have, indirectly at least, wrought a reform among those who even denied their divine legitimacy.

It was not what Methodism was that made it popular, *but what it did*, and what it was still doing. The world did not care so much for its theory as they did for its practical reforms and its self-sacrificing, executive enterprises. They saw there was life in it—that it "stopped not on the order of its going, but went at once," to any country, to any people, " without money and without price." No order was able to resist its force, and the grand result has been that its working boundaries have been universally unlimited.

Here in the West particularly this wonderful religious enterprise seemed to find its natural element, and its growth became commensurate with the advance of society. Its popular tide often ran so high that even ministers were not so much esteemed for their intelligence and scholarship as they were for their zeal and the revival power of their ministry. The burning fires of revival energy, transcended all other accomplishments; and even men of letters, whose ability was only to teach, often felt, in these great religious awakenings, that they were only mere children of the Kingdom.

It has often been reported that this work was fanatical and temporary; that its subjects were made up only of the ignorant and lower classes. If this had been true, it would certainly have been the higher compliment; for, that the " poor have the Gospel preached unto them," is one of the very best evidences both of its divinity and legitimacy.

The fact that genuine revivals are essential to the

life of the church, is ultimately the experience of every people. Methodism learned this in the beginning, yet in some of her localities, of late years, the long absence of revivals, and the chilling monotony of icy formations, have so far enfeebled her pretensions and dwarfed her evangelism, that her lights have become dim, and her simple forms of worship have grown to be but the shadow of their shade.

It is not the purity of theology, as has been fully tested, that keeps up the Church, any more than the wealth and social status of its members. Christian life can not fatten upon empty theories, or on any sort of mere pompous displays. Its vitality is of the higher growth, and flourishes only when it faithfully carries the spirit of the Master. What he was, in the mild tenderness of his ministry, the Church itself must be in its spirit, if it will live. Therefore, it becomes necessary that revivals shall be constant in their working economy, as simplicity and fellowship always are in their genuine demonstrations.

These, and similar sentiments, were well vindicated in the life and ministry of Mr. Havens. Indeed, he began his experience with them, as they belonged to the very genius of that Methodist element in which he was converted.

Fully satisfied, as he always was, that God was the author of his commission, he inferred that what had been done for him, would be done for others. Consequently, when he entered upon the ministry it was not with the view of becoming a great man himself, but the hope of making great and good men of others.

This, in fact, was the old primitive idea among Methodists everywhere, and, as we have already intimated, the people were ready to doubt the sterling piety of any preacher, no matter how able he might be, if he had no revivals under his ministry. This distinguishing feature in the work became the mark of goodness, as well as the measure of ministerial greatness. So common, therefore, did revivals become throughout the boundaries of Methodism, that the increase of hundreds in a single circuit was only looked upon as an ordinary circumstance. Such, indeed, was the mighty growth of the work, that circuits were multiplied annually, and ministerial additions to the annual Conferences called out young men from shops, and farms, and schools, and colleges by scores and hundreds.

These facts and circumstances may furnish some idea of the times in which Mr. Havens served in the public ministry, and may also give some conceptions of the zeal and fire which made him so prominent a leader among such a host of evangelical revivalists.

Being naturally independent and fearless as a man, he only needed the graces of Christianity to constitute him a hero in any such excitements, and the storm of revivals soon became his most favorable element; and when he was in the midst of them neither the confusion of the crowd, nor the roar of the troubled waters, ever, for a moment, disconcerted him. On such occasions he was "himself again," and the fervent eloquence of his exhortations fell upon the listening crowds before him, like the thunders of an Apostle upon the gathered multitudes of the ancient Israel. At these times but few men excelled him, for he was as bold and fearless as he was sublime and effective.

Standing in the pulpit, or looking from the altar upon his congregations, his deeply exercised spirit caught the inspiration of every passing breeze; and watching the work with a guardianship as vigilant as it was sensitive and protective, he always aimed to rule it in its order, and to guide it in its extension and continuance, as if the fortunes of e'en his own destiny depended upon the grand results.

On such occasions he usually had but little patience with objectors and critics, and if any interloper attempted to create a disturbance, he was driven from his position with as little respect and ceremony as the case would honorably admit of.

In a revival of very great power, which occurred in the bounds of one of his old circuits, Mr. Havens learned that a brother minister of another church had made some disparaging remarks of the work, and was further using his influence to keep some away from the meeting, and he became at once exceedingly indignant. To be wounded in the house of his friends, was to him always a sore trial, and this act in one from whom he had expected better things, aroused him as the lion is stirred when the hand of the stranger touches her young. Without giving any names, he mentioned the matter publicly, and remarked that he would give fair notice that all such parties might have a clear understanding of the conflict which was going on, and he then added: "If they want peace they can have it on peaceable terms; but if they want war, they can have it to the knife!" The bold and positive declaration, as all fully understood, was not intended to be literally construed, yet it was a proclamation of war, after all, if they wanted it.

Mr. Havens understood the points of church etiquette as well as the responsibility of a minister of the Gospel, and nothing excited his indignation sooner, or to a greater extent, than the opposition of ministers of other churches when he had a revival on hand.

It was then, more than at any other time, that he showed himself a hero, fearless of the face or frowns of any foe. Nothing could make him cower or yield, on such occasions, to either the spirit or power of wrong. He felt that he was about his Master's work, and such was his impetuous spirit, that he would have maintained his ground, like Peter of old, even to the smiting off an ear of his foe.

In one of these revivals, where the ecstatic enjoyment ran high, and where a great many of the members were rejoicing on the largest Methodist scale, there was a female of doubtful brains, as well as virtue, who gave great umbrage to the congregation by her continual shouting. But few had any faith in her, and yet, none, even of her own sex, dared to warn her to desist in her excessive genuflexions. Mr. Havens was spoken to on the subject, and he watched her for some time, until he became convinced that the woman was not sincere, when he approached her and said, in rather a low whisper:

"I think, my sister, you are wasting your ammunition here in this meeting. I learn there is not a woman in the house who has any confidence in you, and I think you will make a better reputation by taking your seat and behaving yourself."

This advice, though seemingly rude and severe, had the desired effect, for the woman immediately took her seat and gave no more trouble during the meeting.

In the same revival meeting one of the wickedest men in the county came forward to ask an interest in the prayers of the church, and after being some time on his knees he requested that Mr. Havens should come and pray for him, especially. Of course he went, and kneeling down beside the wife-whipper, drunkard and bully, whom he had known for years as one of the most high-handed sinners of the country, he began to pray with great earnestness for his conversion. But he first told the Lord who the professed penitent was. "This man, O Lord, has been one of the wickedest of men. He has been a drunkard, a swearer, a Sabbath-breaker, and a terror to the neighborhood in which he lives. He has whipped his wife, and often driven her and her children from their home. We know, O Lord, that he has brought upon himself and his household misery and wretchedness, and almost the horrors of hell itself. If thou canst pardon him, Lord, grant him this boon to-night." While Mr. Havens was praying, many of his friends trembled, for fear his seeming penitent might become angry and make one of his accustomed "splurges" at him. But the devout and honest old Presiding Elder had no such fears, for he well knew that the guilty are always cowards, and, under the circumstances, he was prepared for any emergency.

It is sad to relate, that although this old penitent made a profession of religion and joined the church, at that revival, and clung to his temperate integrity for some eight or nine months, he at last fell, and in a drunken attack which he subsequently made upon his poor wife, one of his daughters struck him with an axe, which ended his life.

To clear up the moral forests of the great West demanded much of that sort of heroic faith for which Mr. Havens was so especially distinguished, and which he so often displayed to the sudden terror of even the wickedest of men. A milder spirit would have totally failed in carrying, as he frequently did, the war into the camp of the enemy. As an ambassador of the Gospel of peace, he felt that he should establish peace everywhere, even if he sometimes had to conquer it; which, indeed, he not unfrequently had to do at the expense of a seeming contradiction of the doctrine of non-resistance. Well versed, as he was, in the knowledge of human nature, he became aware of the fact that often desperate remedies had to be adopted with desperate men, and in view of their salvation he sometimes struck out on a line of action to accomplish his purpose which often made others around him turn pale with fear. He did not hesitate at any time to tell wicked men what he thought of them; and when it came in his way, either publicly or privately, he made known to them the consequences of their immoral course of life, with a plainness of speech that frequently completely cowed them, and led them to confess their wickedness.

But few men in any profession had more nerve than Mr. Havens, and this courage appeared to be natural with him. Though simple as a child in the tenderness of his affection, he was, when aroused by the spirit-stirring power of a revival, or the fiercer storm of opposition to his church or religion, much more the lion than he was the lamb. He appeared, indeed, to be set for the defence of the Gospel with an ardor as firm as it was decisive, and, therefore, he would stand his ground unflinchingly until he felt that he had the victory.

His energetic, and often eloquent exhortative talents, gave him prominence in revival scenes, as they also made him well known to the multitude. It was remarkable, too, that as severe as he sometimes was upon them, the few only uttered their maledictions upon his head, while the great majority looked upon him as being a moral hero, as well as a true minister and an honest man. They saw that he was no panderer to the prejudices of wicked men, and that he was at no time willing to compromise either his own character or position in order to preserve his worldly popularity with any class, however high or low.

The grand results of this heroic spirit can never be written by mortal pen, for what he was, and what he did, as a divinely commissioned instrument in the great revivals of the nineteenth century, while it has given to his fame the *eclat* of a high moral heroism, can neither be counted nor measured.

Thousands who have preceded him to the spirit-land were warned by his timely exhortations, and stirred to duty by his thundering appeals; and if they did not in this life, they will in the next, honor him as their Spiritual Father. With thousands still living he prayed when they were drinking the wormwood and gall of repentance; and when their faith laid hold of the promise, no heart rejoiced more than his. With him such scenes constituted his highest triumphs, as they were the grand objective points at which he aimed through all his ministry.

Down to the latest period of his active labors the war cry of revival power always moved his soul as with electric inspiration, and though feeling that he was growing feeble with his accumulating years, he yet, like a hero, as he was, still panted for the active fields of battle.

CHAPTER XIV

MINISTERIAL SUCCESS.

To teach truth and to advocate virtue, to officiate as a circuit preacher and unfold the moral economy of the Methodist Discipline, a half century ago in the West, did not require the knowledge of letters or the educational polish of the present times. Then, the people had no grand churches for pious worship, or even fine clothes for any personal display. Both in manners and spirit they were plain, simple, and honest, and in their intellectual capacities were not so apt to demur against blunders in grammar, or defects in rhetoric, as in these days, with their spiritual advisers.

Wherever they made any profession of religion, no matter what might be the character of their theology, that profession was understood as having direct reference to right and wrong; and therefore, in their investigations they looked more to the goodness of the man who preached to them, and to the spirit and revival zeal he exhibited, than they did to any literary qualifications he might possess.

This simplicity of manners, and want of education among the early settlers of the West, made them practical rather than speculative, and though usually easy of access they were not readily moved by either the wit of learning or the arguments of philosophy, and therefore they commonly failed to see the point of the one or to appreciate the conclusions of the other. Their Gospel food was the spirit and pith of religion, which they understood to be that spiritual life and power which not only reformed men but made them happy. They had learned that religion was an ecstacy, as well as a moralizing agency, through which the humble and obedient were prepared for the trials of the present life and for the rewards of the eternal future, and they were not disposed to listen to the dry details of scholastic lectures, or to the monotony of any philosophic discussions. Their mental positions were somewhat normal on most all theological subjects, and therefore the preacher who gained their confidence and fed them with Gospel food, had to be careful of his dress as well as of his address. They cared but little for dead languages, and even but little for living ones. Good grammar might be violated without let or hindrance, but in no event would they show much favor where the preacher either read his sermons or minced and mouthed them with any seeming pretensions. They felt that they had been too well raised to feed on husks, or to be directed in the way to heaven by any sort of a pedantic coxcomb.

Under such circumstances of society, what is called an educated ministry would have failed, not only of success, but they would not have commanded even the commonest attention of the multitude.

In saying these things we do not wish to be understood as admitting that the ministry of those early times was an ignorant one, for this was not the fact as was well demonstrated in the success of their work, and in the bold and successful expositions of all sorts of heretical ideas. The fact that Mr. Havens was not a scholar did not imply that he was an uneducated minister. Not at all; for he was thoroughly educated in all the practical workings of the ministry of his day He had studied, and understood well the moral wants of the people; and, as he had made himself master of the scriptural theory of religion, he knew well what his congregations needed. This he could give them in plain English, and in such order and argument as they could and did understand. He felt that he was in the ministry to preach Christ, not himself, and therefore to do good was the great specific purpose, as he always viewed it, of his holy calling.

Though exceedingly fearful, as he ever was, of his own poor abilities to do justice to the great themes and doctrinal precepts of the Gospel, he nevertheless flinched not before the majesty of his duties, but heroically took them up according to the best of his abilities. Defective, as he felt that he was, in the knowledge of the sciences and in any eminent scholarship, he well knew that the simple Gospel was his special field of thought, and though he read it not in its original tongue, he had gathered its spirit and moral doctrines from the idiom of his own vernacular; and, with the vim and zeal of an implicit decision, he bore them to the people in such figures of speech, and with such spiritual power, as always proved successful

Indeed, but few public speakers ever knew better than the old heroic itinerant heroes of the early times, how to touch the audiences who came to hear them. They well understood the native genius of the people, and when assembled for worship they knew that their devotions had to be led by their own spirit and voice, as well as by the appropriateness of their subject and the style of their argument, and therefore their custom always was to look well to their own spiritual conditions, if they wished to move the people.

Of course, many in those days were not general readers; but then they were often good thinkers as well as cute critics, and if a preacher did not steer straight in his arguments and doctrines, they could play the dogmatic on him with as much severity and with as great decision as if they were masters.

Congregations frequently found fault then, as they do now, with their preachers, but the style of objections was altogether different from the present day. Fashions, among many, were considered terrible evils, and they would often condemn their preacher for roaching his hair, wearing whiskers, sporting gloves, or even for strutting in a double-breasted coat, as one and all of these indulgencies were considered to be following the vain pomp of the world; and many a good and talented preacher, who had been brought up somewhere in more advanced society, found when he went on to a circuit that he had to " lay aside every weight and the sin which so easily beset him" in any of these directions, or else he would more than likely be driven from his circuit.

As Mr. Havens was one of the people, himself, and as he had all his life been used to the plainest garbs, as well as the plainest manners, temptation to dress, and the variety of personal display, never troubled him. He was satisfied with his woolsey-linsey suit, and as he always made a clean shave of it, in the whisker line, he was ever in conformity with the usages of the day.

One of his colleagues, however, Rev. Henry B. Bascom, was his antipodes in dress in every respect. Though as poor as Mr. Havens, Bascom was naturally a prince in his manners, and, as his clothes were generally given to him, he always dressed in the most fashionable style of the day.

Many used to come to Mr. Havens and ask him if he did not think Bascom proud? But as he greatly admired and loved the young and gifted orator, he was not disposed to condemn him, or to hear him condemned, merely for the clothes he had on; and time and again he sent fault-finders of this character away from his presence " with a flea in their ears;" because he well knew that while Bascom was independent in spirit, he was one of the most humble and honorable among his brethren.

In those primitive times the tide of success in Gospel labors depended greatly on the popularity of the preacher; and yet, while Mr. Havens understood this fact, he always scorned to either pander to the ignorant prejudices of the people, or to bow in sycophancy to any of their arbitrary whims. He, too, had the independence of Bascom, and they both, alike, found that the attribute was one that could only be maintained at the expense of many a conflict. From the field of strife, Bascom was disposed to retire; but Mr. Havens was generally ready to fight it out, if he was attacked, on any line the enemy might choose. His independence of spirit, he well knew, only had reference to men like himself, and he was not disposed to be ruled anywhere, or at any time, by either the captious or the impertinent.

Having once taken his positions, he maintained them, especially when he was confident that his aims were pure, and that his cause was right. When such circumstances ruled him, few men surpassed him in heroic virtues or firmness, and a still less number ever mortified him with defeat. Devotion to principle appeared to always give him the courage of inspiration, and he would enter the area of conflict certain of the victory.

Though out of the usual line of his ministerial duties, he once attempted to play the part of a lawyer in the prosecution of one of the "baser sort" of men, who had been disturbing his Camp-meeting. The fellow had employed a lawyer to defend him, and on this account Mr. Havens assumed, for the time being, the duties of prosecutor in the case. The culprit being guilty, his counsel was driven to the extremes of legal defence in maintaining his case. The lawyer gave several points of law, to which Mr. Havens demurred, and he even denied the authority altogether. The struggle was somewhat protracted, but was finally closed with a pretty heavy fine on the violator of the laws of the State.

The next day the lawyer approached Mr. Havens, and wanted to know where he had studied law?

"Why, sir," he responded, "I do not know that I ever studied law a whole day in my life."

"How then, Mr. Havens," asked the astonished lawyer, " could you stand up and contradict me so positively in my legal positions on yesterday, in that case?"

"Why," said Mr. Havens in reply, "I knew that all true laws were founded on common sense, and this your law points contradicted; and therefore I felt free to contradict you."

The lawyer could but laugh at this new conception of the basis of law principles, and he turned away from his clerical opponent, fully convinced that he had better steer wide of these old preachers, particularly when he had a guilty client to defend.

In the associations of the ministry Mr. Havens, as a matter of course, was often thrown with learned men, some of whom differed with him very greatly on many points of his Methodist theology, as well as in the principles of his church discipline; and, as he was not very strongly disposed to yield any of his principles to the laws of either courtesy or compromise, he was frequently led into fireside debates, where often his powers of defence and success were as severely tested as they ever were anywhere else.

Methodism in Indiana was in the enjoyment of its chivalric days, during a large portion of his ministry, and its numerous sweeping revivals, and its high toned sacrificing itineracy had given it a prestige of majesty which perhaps no other church in those days could claim.

The clarion voice of Rhoderic Dhu, among the clans of Scotland, was not more soul stirring than the trumpet tones of many of these backwoods ministers; for most of them had drawn the old Jerusalem blade of

Gospel power when they were in the full fire of their youthful blood, and having thrown away the scabbard, they were always ready for the battle on any field, and at any hour.

Like the minute-men of an army of well drilled warriors, they were ready to say to their commanders, "Here am I; send me." The very spirit of their sacrifice gave them a moral pre-eminence, and a personal power, which awed into respect, in most cases, even the obdurate, and not unfrequently opened their way among the first and foremost families of the conntry.

When such a man as Mr. Havens was going to preach, the best educated and most prominent citizens of the community were to be seen in the congregation. They went out to hear him, not because they were Methodists, for frequently they were not. Governors, Senators, Congressmen, Judges, Lawyers, Physicians, and Ministers of other churches were there, to listen to the Gospel of the Son of God, and to take notes of the eloquent originality of a native orator.

On such occasions these old Gospel heroes well knew that it would not do to make a failure, and, moved by the wild but evangelical inspiration of the hour, they often preached away above themselves; and the whole audience would feel when the sermon was over, as if they had been listening to the deep-toned melodies of Calvary itself. Such, indeed, was the effect of many of the sermons preached by Mr. Havens and his associate hero brethren of the Indiana itinerancy; and it was not strange, therefore, that thousands applied to them the ancient attestation, " of a truth these men are

Christians, for their preaching is with the demonstration of the Spirit, and in power."

In one of Mr. Havens' Quarterly-meeting visits to Indianapolis, he was stopped on the street by His Excellency Governor Noah Noble, and invited to be his guest during the occasion. Of course, Mr Havens felt it to be his duty to accept the kind invitation, as he knew the Governor had been raised a Methodist; and though not yet a member himself, he was satisfied that the best hospitalities of the Gubernatorial mansion would be granted him, and he wheeled around his old roan and followed the distinguished statesman to his home.

Conducted to the parlor, after he had disrobed himself of his overcoat and leggins, Mr. Havens was kindly and politely seated in the best chair in the room, when the Governor informed him that he had been thinking about him for several days, and he had been ardently wishing for just such a visit.

"Well, Governor," responded the old itinerant, "if I can do you any good I shall prize my visit as providential, for I had intended stopping at another place; but, as I am now here, I will ask the privilege of saying one thing to you before I leave, which, I have no doubt, if you will act upon, it will be classed among the best acts of your life."

"Well, Brother Havens, what is it? Let me hear it, just here and now," asked the venerable Governor.

"You know, Governor," said Mr. Havens, "that I have always been your friend, both politically and personally, and I have felt often, that after all, I had not been true to you."

"Why, yes, Brother Havens," the Governor responded, "you have, as far as I know, in every particular."

"Yes, but I know that I have not," said the old and conscientious itinerant. "I have never told you," he then added, with his eye fixed on that of the Governor, "that you owe it to yourself and your family, and to the education your mother gave you, to join the church."

This sort of an appeal was certainly more than the Governor was looking for—for, in a moment, the great tear of contrition was in his eye, and, turning to his venerable friend and giving him his hand, as if guided by some unseen power, he said:

"Brother Havens, I have always intended to be a Methodist; but a thousand influences have prevented me from carrying out my resolution, and I will say to you now, that I will carry it out yet, and that, too, before very long."

Mr. Havens was highly gratified to hear the Governor thus express himself, and of course, reminded him that "procrastination was the thief of time."

In less than a year from the date of this visit, the amiable and popular Governor of Indiana was on his dying pillow, and, Mr. Havens being forty miles away, the Governor sent for the stationed minister of the old Methodist church, Rev. Lucien W Berry, to come and see him, which he did ; and, at the Governor's request, he received him into the Methodist Episcopal Church, and administered to him the Lord's Supper; and a few days after he preached his funeral sermon, to an immense congregation of deeply stricken and sorrowing relatives and friends.

CHAPTER XV.

PERSONAL POPULARITY.

The capriciousness of popular fame has always rendered it dangerous to the ministry, for in this profession, more than in any other, it is apt to be attended with such a profusion of compliments, such a flood of flattery, as has often spoiled, for all future time, many a young man who, but for such manifestations, might have done some substantial good in the world, and made a reputation which would have gone down through the ages.

The multitude run after the star of the hour, and worship it only for its glittering brilliancy. They care not for either its history or destiny, and they applaud it only for its present accomplishments. The circuit fame of many Methodist preachers has only had a short lived continuance, because of this very capriciousness. Operating, as they chiefly did, upon the multitude, a single sermon often sent them to the pinnacle of fame, while another just as often gave their names and efforts some other direction.

In the matter of ministerial supplies, the people have always been captious, and have demanded, as a *quid pro quo* for their stipends and confidence, that the man who taught them in holy things should possess nearly as many attributes as an angel, and especially, if not above all, that he should show himself able to "make full proof of his ministry" at the smallest possible expenditure.

In the early days of our Western civilization, when Mr. Havens was in his prime, the dogmatic captiousness of the people, was often as capricious and proscriptive as it was selfish and scrutinizing, as they often refused to accord either confidence or fame to such as carried high heads or wore fashionable clothes, or who put on the airs of either the fop or the pedant. The original settlers all had a partial eye for plainness in dress and for unostentatious piety, and they but seldom yielded the compliments of respect, or the ceremonies of politeness, to any minister who walked out of the ordinary track of the plainest simplicity. Hence, it was not an uncommon occurrence for a young preacher to be condemned, all around his circuit, because he had the gait of a dandy, or, which was but little less to be censured, was suspicioned for having "a touch of the big head."

The latter defection was thought, even in the olden days, to be fearfully prevalent; and, as some may not fully comprehend what is meant by it, we will attempt its explanation by the following little incident, which occurred in an Annual Conference of the African Methodist Episcopal Church, held some years ago in Indianapolis:

The usual examination of the preachers' characters was on hand, and the Presiding Elders in representing the young men, stated that several of them were somewhat afflicted with "the big head." Bishop Quinn who was presiding over their deliberations, finally said:

"Brethren, I have heard a great deal this morning about 'the big head.' I wish some of you would explain what you mean by it."

One of the brethren jumped to his feet and offered the following, which is perhaps the best explanation which can be made upon the subject:

"Bishop," said he, "I kin 'splain de matter to you all, in a very few words."

"I will thank you, brother, then, to do it," said the Bishop.

"Well sir!" responded the grateful expositor, "When any one preacher knows too much for one man, and yet not quite enough for two, we say he's got de big head, and it's not more dan one time out of ten, dat we ever finds ourselves mistaken."

It has often, no doubt, been the case even among white preachers, that conceit and brass have been substituted for brains and piety; but all such samples of the Ministry have been of but little real benefit to either themselves or the Church, until they were well cured of the malady.

With such scions of gospel itinerants, Mr. Havens was often as severe as he was plain and sarcastic, and he has frequently been known to administer such heavy doses of his caustic medicine when he thought the occasion demanded it, that the patient was either killed outright in his ministerial pretensions, or was so far cured as to never show any further symptoms of the disease.

In one of these instances he told the young preacher that he did not believe he had ever had a call to the ministry.

The young preacher averred that he had.

"Well," said Mr. Havens "it may be possible that

I am mistaken—but I am very much afraid" he added, "if you have ever had a call it was only a mere whisper."

To many it was always a matter of wonder that Mr. Havens should be so very popular as a minister— when it was so evident that it was an element of character that he never sought and which his independent spirit, as it seemed, would always hold back from him. But somehow, in spite of his personal indifference on the subject, he attained even in his earlier years the reputation of popularity both as a man and a minister, and he continued to hold it, up to the latest hour of his life.

Among those who knew him best, it was always well understood, that he would not turn on his heel from the line of duty, or from any of his rightful positions, to curry the favor, or to pander to the prejudices of any one, either high or low. The fact was always apparent, that he was neither a trimmer, nor a time-server. His was the spirit of the hero—which was always ready to fight for the right, and to battle against any foe, no matter how fearful might be the odds. Respectful, as he ever was toward all dignitaries, both of Church and State, he was nevertheless unwilling to yield to them the fawning knee of the sycophant, or the unmanliness of a subordinate truculency.

What he was, and where he stood, as well as what he thought, could always be known among friends and foes. He scorned concealments and detested hypocrisy of every character, and if, at any time, he suspected the one or saw the other in any of his brethren, he discounted them at once in his esteem, and mourned their weakness of spirit, as he would the aberrations and defects of his own kindred.

To wear laurels of popular favor in his day, cost many a struggle, for there were always around him, and sometimes even among his brethren, those who would have held him back, if it had been in their power. They felt that they were his superiors in educational knowledge, and therefore, expected of him those compliments of deference, which he was but seldom willing to yield to any one. What they were, in their personal claims he well understood, for his thorough knowledge of human nature, and his penetrating eye of scrutiny, gave him the insight of their characters, and when they made pretentious demands on his credulity, he looked the insult in the face, and brooked it only as he would the egotistical ebullitions of children. Among this class, Mr. Havens held not so much the popularity of ardent respect, as that of servile fear, for he forced them to a respectful deference by the truthful dignity of his positions, even when they had none, of any account, for the man.

It will therefore be perceived that his reputation and personal popularity were more the result of his heroism than of his truculent obedience to either the caprices of men around him, or to the time-serving spirit of popular compromise. Indeed, through all his life, his chief aim was to stand in the right, to maintain, as far as he could, that which was true and just, and if in doing so, he sometimes saw the laurels dropping from his brow, it neither awed him to a halt or deterred him from his purpose. To compromise with wrong, or to give way to the torrent of any sort of a corrupt public opinion, in his esteem, was yielding to moral cowardice the highest and best manliness of our natures, and on this noble conviction, which he always heroically adhered to, may we base the personal popularity of his entire life.

Men of all classes honored him because they knew he was honest, and they reverenced him because of his brave and fearless adherence to the truth and the right.

That these traits in his character sometimes made him enemies even among his brethren we are free to admit—but even this did not quench the ardor of his spirit, or in the least cower him into submission. Even when he was openly assailed, as he occasionally was for his brave efforts to vindicate the purity of the Church, and the laws of truth and justice, he stood his ground with the moral firmness of a hero, and seemed never for a moment to stop to ask whether his position would give him standing in his Conference, or make him more acceptable among his people. Any such consideration, would have degraded him in his own estimation, which he always felt to be a greater calamity, than the dogmatic censures of a thousand delinquents.

The fact that the attributes of the Christian Ministry, even in its ordinary grades, are necessarily more multiform than attach to the other professions, may be readily recognized in almost every community, and it is on this account that a continued personal popularity in the higher office is the more remarkable.

Skill alone will secure professional fame to the physician, even where there is but little else to commend him, and the lawyer may become a counsellor of renown, merely because he is well read in the law and possesses the powers of an eloquent advocate, but at the hands of the minister, who is looked upon as the expounder of the higher law, even the commonest people demand the sublimity of the highest example.

It is because of this rigid requisition that so many who fill the sacred desk, never rise to a higher standard than that of mere mediocres. The timidity of the man-pleaser holds them in tame subordination to the popular will, and yet, however faithfully they serve it, they never attain to any real popularity themselves.

To win and wear the chaplets of popular fame through a long ministerial life, requires the honesty of an unwavering integrity, as well as the thorough heroism of an unflinching moral aggression. If these are bartered off, in any way, to secure temporary personal preferment, the misguided wight will ultimately find himself as poor in fame and in the higher confidence of his holy office, as if he had made a public sale of all his sacred effects.

The simple duties of his station, which he always endeavored to perform for the honor of the Church and the good of the people, ever presented to Mr. Havens his highest obligations. To their honest and faithful performance he gave all of the best energies of his years, never turning to the right or the left to gratify any worldly ambition, or to serve the purposes of any mere personal and selfish policy. And so far as he became distinguished, it was the result of his heroic genius and indomitable will, in connection with his steady and stern devotion to the law of equal justice to all, and of his unwillingness, on all occasions, to daub with untempered mortar.

In the annual gatherings of his brethren in their Conference capacity, he was always deeply concerned in every question of vitality, and he always took his positions upon them regardless of what might be the majority on either side. Though not given to wrangling debate, or even disposed to contend in matters that did not concern his department of the work, he often felt it his duty to speak out when any policy was before them which he thought would have any bearing on the purity of the Church or the stability of the public piety. His influence on such occasions, though not always successful, was, nevertheless, both felt and acknowledged, and but few of his brethren, for many years, excelled him either in general influences or in conservative power.

Associated as he was with such Conference giants as Armstrong, Strange, Wiley, Ruter, Oglesby, Thompson and many others, Mr. Havens held the honor of being a peer among his equals, and in every respect maintained the credit and character of a leading member in these annual convocations. Never assuming and never aspiring to any sort of Conference favoritism, he yet was often honored with the suffrages of his brethren to the highest positions in their gift. In his case, these honors were the more reputable, because, as was frequently remarked, he never sought them by tricks of management, or with any special efforts to gain the popular favor.

Independent and decided, uncompromising and devoted, he always stood in his place, like a sentinel of honor, who occupied his position by divine appointment, and it appeared as if he would rather die than shrink from any responsibility or prove recreant to duty.

Among the people, particularly, Mr. Havens was very generally a favorite. They admired him for his heroic virtues, as well as for his personal integrity, and when they sat under his ministry, they felt they were listening to one who would dare to preach the truth, and who would not hesitate to rebuke sin, of any and every character, regardless of the civil or social standing of the transgressor, even though he was found in the ministry itself.

In the circles of private life he maintained the independence of his integrity with the same firmness of spirit which distinguished his public labors, and it may be safely said, that but few ministers who have ever been known in the State, were more frank or fearless in administering private reproofs, even where the subject, as was often the case, belonged to the highest social circles.

The great personal popularity of such a man was rather an anomaly in the workings of popular favor, for it was directly antagonistic to the common modes of securing such an end. For even his complacency had in it more of the dignity and independence of the reserved minister, than of the seeker of popular favor.

This, indeed, was natural with him, and he never troubled himself much in learning any other accomplishment. In this regard he did not at any time or anywhere even seem to think of popularity. He was too proud spirited to seek it, and he always had too much respect for himself to lay any plans to obtain it. And yet but few ministers who have ever labored in the State had a greater share of it or enjoyed, both living and dying, more of its honors.

We once heard one of his parishioners, Mrs. Julia Carr, of Rushville, a lady of intelligence and sterling integrity, say of Father Havens:

"I do not know what we shall all do when Father Havens dies, for we have looked up to him so long as our apostle, minister and friend, that I am often led to fear, when I think of it, that when he dies we will never again have a man to take his place."

Another lady of that vicinity, who has also long been a pillar in the Church, Mrs. Elizabeth Wooster, whose words of praise would do honor to any minister, once said of him:

"I have known John Strange and Russel Bigelow, and I have heard them and many others of equal distinction preach, but I must confess that my partiality for Father Havens makes me prefer to hear him above any preacher I have ever known."

These confirmations of the popular fame of Mr. Havens as one of the heroes of Indiana Methodism, though coming from women, are to be placed to his credit as being golden. They knew him well as a minister, and as a man, as a neighbor and as a citizen, through most of the years of his long and laborious itinerancy, and their testimony in his popular favor is worthy of record as being as intelligent and frank as it is truthful and appropriate.

Living witnesses by the hundreds would willingly take the stand to give evidence to the same import; and the fact that thousands, both old and young, have asked that a life of him be written evinces the deep hold the heroic apostle had upon the public mind.

The old had heard him in the days of his vigor, and the young had listened to his voice when it was husky with age, and now that he has gone they desire that some memento may be given them that they may remember him forever.

CHAPTER XVI.

HIS GENERALSHIP.

Every calling of life has its distinctive leaderships, as well as its subordinate relations, the one developing the higher talent of command and authority, and the other giving us, in the multitude, the more common order of implicit obedience. The one presents us with the hero "born to command," and the other congregates before us the million, who prefer to be led by a gallant captain rather than be at the trouble and expense of fighting for personal power, or of running the danger of having no protector.

More particularly than in any other church relation we have ever had any knowledge of, the Methodist itinerancy in its earlier days, furnished a field where moral generalship was not only in great demand, but where its authority was complete, while its victories were often of the most thrilling character.

The preacher in charge of a circuit held the command over hundreds who gave him their confidence, and who would follow wherever he led the way—while the yet higher dignitary, the Presiding Elder, ruled in a much larger field, and besides his preachers on the circuits, he had the commanding influence to direct in the moral and church movements of thousands over his District, who would keep step to his orders and sound the tocsin of revival effort, wherever he directed the onset.

With large Circuits and Districts, which covered, perhaps, one-eighth of the territory of the State, the *esprit de corps* carried with it generally, a revival power, which attracted the attention of all classes, and not unfrequently gave them audiences, numbering from five, to ten, and fifteen thousand people.

On these Quarterly and Camp meeting occasions, the Presiding Elder by general consent as well as from deference to his high office, was *ex-officio*, commander-in-chief of all the forces present, and what he said or determined upon, usually became the law and order of the meeting. Of course his responsibility was great, for he not only had to manage the pulpit and altar, but to a great extent he was held responsible for the general conduct of the congregation as well as for the entire order of the meeting.

To attend to all these important interests promptly, and in their Methodistic order, was certainly no ordinary obligation, and the talents and experience of a Major General were requisite for the victory. The crowds in attendance upon these meetings, were usually honest farmers, and good citizens from the towns and villages, who, with their families, came to hear the preaching of the Word, and to help on in the great crusade against the moral evils of the age. With the government of these there was usually no difficulty—for they were as honest as they were reverent; and if they did not make a profession of religion, they had for the cause and its ministers a decent respect, as they also had for the place of worship. But there were others who were not so orderly, for every class attended these meetings, and it was not uncommon for some of them, to so far forget themselves, as to disturb the worship and solemnities of the occasion.

At these meetings the preaching was designed to awaken every listener to an intelligent sense of his moral condition, and to lead him at once—then and there—to seek his soul's salvation. Frequently the storm raged high, and "the blasts of the horns of the people" shook the walls of Jericho to their very foundations.

The fact may appear as a strange phenomenon, but it was often realized on these occasions, that "the Devil got mad" before they were fairly in sailing order. Among such old war Generals as Mr. Havens, these ireful demonstrations were always considered ominous of great revival success; for it seemed that their greatest dread was "a dead calm," and when they saw the wicked angry at their simple and peaceable efforts to save souls, they were confident of a crisis, which, in their view, would result in a great revival.

The vast numbers who were converted under the labors of these heroes of Methodism, gave to the order its richest prestige, and added to the general Church many of the chaplets of its most distinguished renown.

These crusades were not for personal glory, but were always made in view of the reform of the people. No pains were spared or labor denied to secure this end, without regard to grades or classes, and totally irrespective of what the world, or even other denominations, might say against them. They defied criticism, and "pushed the battle to the gate," while the very music of the revival storm often attracted to their meetings hundreds who never left them until they went away wiser and better men.

On the 25th of August, 1836, Mr. Havens held a camp meeting on what has since been called the "Military Ground," immediately west of the State House. The attendance was large, and on Sunday was estimated to number some six or seven thousand people.

Quite a number of preachers were there to assist in the labors, and the zeal and devotion of the membership of the Church were honored with a success which was, at that time, counted extraordinary.

An incident occurred at this meeting which evinced the heroic generalship of Mr. Havens, and demonstrated the fact that a man may be brave before his equals, but when he is taken in hand by a moral hero, the ardor of his soul gives way to a power which he feels, but can not see.

One of the most notorious leaders of what was then called and known as the "Chain Gang," at the Capital, appeared at this camp meeting, and by his presence and threats, created quite an excitement. The fellow was strong and athletic, and prided himself on his physical power, and had often boasted that the man did not walk the earth who could handle him or put him *hors du combat*. Of course, even the officers of the law feared such a customer; and if he was regulated and made to keep in the bounds of order, it was thought that the Presiding Elder himself would have to accomplish the work by some sort of strategy.

On Saturday night word was sent in to the preachers' tent, to Mr. Havens, that this old Captain was on the ground, and great fears were entertained from his threats, that he would do some serious mischief.

Mr. Havens arose from his bed and dressed himself, and with a few chosen friends, sallied forth in quest of the depredator. The night was dark, and the dim camp-fires gave the only light by which any one could be recognized.

To take such a man prisoner was well understood to be a dangerous effort, and, as a matter of caution, the *posse* moved in a body, for a fight was expected, as they all knew that the rowdy Captain was afraid of nothing, and would not be disposed to yield to any mere ceremony.

When they came up to where he was, Mr. Havens spoke to him and gave him his hand, which he held on to, while a friend seized the other hand, and before he knew it the Captain was a prisoner. Of course, when he learned the condition he was in, he made some effort to rescue himself, but he soon found it was all in vain, and quietly yielding, he was led before a magistrate, who committed him to prison. The following Monday, however, Mr. Havens visited him at the jail, and after a good long talk, went to the magistrate and had him released. The old Chain Gang Captain never troubled Mr. Havens again.

At a camp meeting held in the Haw Patch, in Bartholomew county, in the summer of 1844, Mr. Havens was greatly annoyed by a number of "fellows of the baser sort," who were disposed to disregard the rules of the meeting, and who, to show their contempt for the authority of the officers and preachers, seated themselves on the benches which had been specifically designated for the ladies. To get them to move, the rules of the meeting were read; but still they kept their seats, regardless of their own self-respect and of the request of the Presiding Elder.

The young men had evidently reckoned without their host, for the spirit of order in Mr. Havens was stirred to its highest point, and he took his position in the stand and again politely requested them to move to the male side of the congregation, where he pointed to seats that were vacant. To this request all yielded save two, who concluded they would stand, or rather sit, on their reserved rights until they got ready to move.

Mr. Havens eyed them closely and gave them time to change their seats, and when he found they were determined to defy him he addressed them as follows:

"Gentlemen, you *must* vacate those seats. These people have placed them there exclusively for the ladies, and we can not allow such fellows as you are to occupy them.

"Gentlemen, I know something of your characters, which you, perhaps, are not aware of, and if I am forced to do it, I shall have to expose you before this intelligent and large congregation.

"The name of one of you, I see, is written plainly in your face, and it is *Hangman*. The other, I observe, has his name written in significant letters upon his hat, and I shall read it, *Scape Gallows*.

"And now Mr. Hangman, and Mr. Scape Gallows,

you have but five minutes to comply with my request.
I know there is a sufficient number of young gentlemen on this ground who will volunteer instantly to compel you to respect our rules, if you remain obstinate." Then turning to the audience, he said:

"Young men, are you willing that your mothers and sisters shall be insulted by a Hangman and a Scape Gallows?"

A hundred voices thundered, "No, never." Mr. Havens announced that four minutes had expired, and he immediately began to descend from the stand, when the two cowardly bullies feeling that "discretion was the better part of valor," arose from their seats and made for the woods, as if chased by the ghost of their own imbecile meanness.

To deal with the rougher classes of men in the early history of the country, required something more than mere wisdom. Many of them were of the more dangerous classes, and to hold them in decent check, even at religious meetings, it was sometimes necessary to use both language and means which were not common to the ministry.

Mr. Havens being instinctively, as well as, by common consent, a leader, he was always looked up to in cases of emergency, and at his own meetings, as well as when he was only a visitor, if anything turned up out of the ordinary line, he was always appealed to as the general of the hour. The people, as well as his brethren, knew that he was brave, and equal to any sort of a conflict, and when interlopers stumbled in upon his meetings, he was always prepared to take notice of them.

At a camp meeting held near Laurel, of which he had charge, some half dozen young men, who came on the ground carrying long spice-wood canes, took especial pains to make themselves conspicuous, and in moving about over the grounds created quite a disturbance in the congregation.

Mr. Havens noticed them, and as he wished to see as little of them as possible, he determined to teach them some gospel politeness and reverence, if it was even at the expense of their imagined respectability.

Taking his position in the stand at the close of public service, he said:

"I observe some very strange looking young men here to-day. They are not so very strange in their looks, however, as they are in their actions. I see they carry with them large sticks or spikes, and when they travel they march in single file. Some might take them for Indians, but they are not. If I were to guess, I would say they probably belong to that singular class of men known as Virginia Sand Diggers." At the mention of Sand Diggers, the young gentlemen all took their seats, and quietly hid away their canes under them, and the congregation saw no more of the the *impromtu* display of either their canes or faces.

The descision and promptness, which Mr. Havens at times displayed in carrying forward the great purposes of his ministry, may have savored somewhat of intolerancy; but this was never either his meaning or intention, for, full of the kindliest spirit, and always open to the impulses of a generous nobility—but few men carried a heart of purer motives, or aimed to deal fairer than he did, with his fellow men of all classes and conditions.

True, he was sometimes sarcastic, and dealt in the language of inquisition; but this was only the natural outgrowth of his desire to " do good of every possible sort, and as far as possible to all men." Even in his attempts to govern, he only aimed to draw men from the wrong, and to direct them in the right, and if in this, he happened to overstep himself, but few were more ready to acknowledge it, or to make a proper apology, for the utterance of any wrong expression or the manifestation of an uncharitable spirit.

With his life running through more than six decades of the present century, many of his dealings were with that race of giants and heroes, who have given such *eclat* to the early settlements of the West, and the spirit of firmness and self reliance, which was so perceptible in his character was the legitimate graduating result of his early associations.

What he was in action, he was also in thought, and neither in the one or the other, did he ever wish to overreach a friend, or even do any injustice to an enemy. For it was ever the pride of his honor, to demonstrate the true attributes of the gentleman in his life, and to show by his spirit that he was above the arts of any accomplished duplicity. His life struggle was with himself, as well as with others, and as he often acknowledged, he found no easy task in either direction. The war within—though unknown to any but himself—was often fiercely contested, but in the results he evidently came out the victor. But that which was without had been before the eye of the world, and as thousands believed, it has given him a *fee simple* claim to the honor of being a hero.

Others excelled him in learning, and many in the purity of their eloquence, but in all that constitutes the Christian gentleman, or the brave old pioneer, Oliver H. Smith's sobriquet may be justly given him, viz.: "The Napoleon of Indiana Methodism."

The race to which he belonged—of western pioneer itinerants—has become extinct, and the mere shadow of their fame, is now all that is left us. The light of their general examples may still linger around us, like the rays of the sunlight, when the substance has gone from our sight; we would not forget them or turn away from their teachings, for no future age of our race, we opine, will ever point to a higher moral in history or give to memory a brighter dream.

CHAPTER XVII.

LIBERALITY OF SENTIMENT.

THE sentiment is both conservative and true, that Christianity has but seldom been benefited by any mere dogmatic teachings, for dim in their reflections, as well as feeble in their moral beauty, all such instructions have fallen short of the tone and spirit of its true character, and, therefore, they have operated everywhere as palpable misrepresentations of both its genius and divinity.

Truth is known as being always simple, as well as conservative, and any dogmatic efforts to advance it must destroy in its manner, what it would aim to accomplish even by the profoundest sincerity.

Intelligent and liberal, forbearing and charitable, both in precept and doctrine, the entire system of its philosophy is as delicate in its love as it is tender and pure in its promises.

All that is good in life, or felicitous in associations, has found its counterpart in the beauty of its morals, and, therefore, it can not tolerate a dogmatic spirit without contradicting both the simplicity and dignity of its own genius.

If even history itself contradicts us in any of these affirmations, it but blots the pages of its own records, and mocks the practical operations of the purest philosophy the world has ever known. That it does so we are fully aware, for it is abundantly evinced in the history of the Church. But going back to the dictations of the "higher law," the authority is ours to write the declaration that intolerancy, under the surveillance of Christianity, has ever been recognized as only a degrading crime, for which it has never proffered a single apology.

The fact is a strange one, but it is nevertheless true, that illiberality of sentiment has always been the offspring of Church pride, instead of Christianity itself. The doctrine of one Church and one people may claim Divine paternity, but what particular organization holds the keys of legitimacy, either apostolic or exclusive, may not so easily be asserted. Organic divinity is not so palpable and definite as that which is spiritual, for the one is of human ministration, while the other is wholly divine. The latter, like the sun, is essential to life, but the former may exist as a mere ecclesiastical and presumptious automaton, as destitute of the true animus of Christianity, as it is of any royal claims to a divine exclusiveness.

Vegetative power gives evidence of the life of the world, as procreation does of animal vitality, and yet, neither the one nor the other is subjected to any exclusive jurisdiction. Even life itself has vitality only where it is blest with the light of the sun, and the moral life of the world is subject to a similar jurisdiction of the Sun of Righteousness. Therefore, where the spirit of Christ is there is liberty, is the safest creed of humanity, and has long been the special faith of intelligent millions.

The Popish claims of the Roman Church, and the

Episcopal pretensions of the English and Greek organizations, though standing on the highest hills of a venerated antiquity, are only sustained in their divine supremacy by the musty pages of traditionary history. What they are in their organic power may all be well enough and legitimate; but that this legitimacy gives any one or all of them the exclusive spiritual rule of the world of mankind is neither proved from the Holy Scriptures nor to be demonstrably maintained from the lights of history.

The doctrine of one Holy Apostolic Church is not vindicated by them, for they constitute three separate and distinct organizations, as independent of each other as those of the Presbyterian and Methodist churches, and it is this confusion, doubtless, which has led to the institution of so many sects and denominations.

Whether these multiplications of religious households will the sooner bring about the reformation of the world, remains to be seen. One thing, at least, is evident, even now, as is everywhere becoming more and more manifest, that is—the spirit of intolerancy is fast losing its hold on the christianized portions of the globe, and the divine right to an independant personal faith is rapidly assuming universal supremacy. The right to worship God in one's own way is being clearly set up in all lands, and the divine jurisdiction of the Church, in any of its organizations or pretensions, is being disputed by millions of the best minds of the age. The advance in these regards may, by some, be considered sceptical and infidel; but when the intelligent moral result is considered, it will be seen that the evidences of Christian civilization are higher and more permanent in the lands of freedom than in any country where church intolerancy rules the consciences of men.

As a part of the fruits of this spiritual independence, Mr. John Wesley, a priest of the Church of England, was led, nearly a century and a half ago, to organize his societies among the poor of that country, in view of establishing a higher order of spiritual life, and of bringing the multitudes of the poor and the ignorant of his countrymen to a better state of society.

The reform was evidently needed all over England, where they had long as grand a State Church as the world, perhaps. could boast of. This field was a large one, and he entered it with a zeal and success which everywhere astonished his countrymen, and though he did not expect it, God made him the spiritual head of a people whose sacrifices and missionary zeal have since placed them in the van among all the Churches of Christendom. Receiving the baptismal appellation of Methodism, and adopting the efficient economy of a universal itinerancy, its dominion in a hundred years has been made respectable and influential even in the four quarters of the globe.

In doctrine and formulary order, the body, both in Europe and America, has largely copied from the Church of England, and though they make no pretensions to any organic Apostolic succession, they hold with the Lutherans and Presbyterians that the spirit of the office of the ministry is alone essential, and that the order of ordination amounts to nothing more than a mere Prelatical pretension.

Taking no further notice of the Royal claims of the Church of England, the preachers of Methodism took for their motto, "The spread of Scriptural holiness over all lands," and driving to this point with a zeal which has known no defeat, they have kindled the fires of a free gospel and of a present salvation among almost every people of the polyglotic earth, and their ministry to-day will perhaps compare, in talents and accomplishments, with that of any other Church in the world. Mr. Wesley laid down the axiom that "he was the greatest preacher who saved the most souls," and on this basis it may, perhaps, be still said they yet make their ministerial estimates.

Among them a preacher like Mr. Havens has always ranked well, because he possessed the essential elements of character to vindicate his claims to the true ministry, and gave evidence of a life of piety, sacrifice, and honor.

The simple pretensions of Methodism opened up his way to the ministry when he knew that he had but few qualifications for the office, and in the subsequent years of his long and useful life he always remembered "the hole of the pit from which he was digged," which many ministers are prone to forget. But with him the lessons of the past were golden remembrances, and their power over him made him as liberal toward others as he felt the Church had been toward him.

It was this generous liberality of sentiment which gave him much of his ministerial nobility, and which added to his weight of character so extensively, not only in his own church, but among all others.

Though a positive Methodist, he was in no respects

a bigot, and though he often differed with his brethren, he never showed obstinacy, unless it was against an open and palpable sin—and even then, if he was convinced that the guilty party had repented, he would forgive him as a brother and stand by him like a man.

Towards all reputable ministers of other denominations, Mr. Havens always conducted himself both courteously and respectfully, and but few Methodist ministers of Indiana, perhaps, ever met with greater reciprocal kindness at the hands of ministers of other churches. He knew them only as ministers, and as such, no matter how much they differed with him in doctrines and discipline, he recognized their ministerial equality, and whenever he met them, he treated them accordingly.

In learning he knew that many of them were greatly his superior, and in this respect he thought it no reflection upon his own character to defer to their higher attainments.

We have only learned of one instance where there was any deviation from this accustomed principle of his life, and this was forced upon him by the egotism of the man and the circumstances of the occasion.

He had been called out by a young divine to defend the common ideas of his church on the subject of baptism, and as the contestant was professedly a great linguist, he made very free use of the original Greek. This mode of argument, of course, was above Mr Havens' pretensions, as well as of every other one in the large congregation; and to show the utter folly and hopeless pedantry of the young man's mode of argumentation before such an audience, Mr Havens gave some of his ideas in the dialect of the Pottawatomies, an Indian tribe with which he had had some acquaintance, and the result of the sarcastic exposure drove the young divine to the wall, and left Mr. Havens the hero of the hour.

In such conflicts many of the ministers of nearly all the churches frequently indulged. Indeed, such debates constituted to a large extent the animus of the times, and, in many localities, gave quite a polemic stamp to the religion of the people.

But to a mind like hat of Mr. Havens all such religious displays augured but poorly of any particular piety or Christian devotion, and he usually sparred all such attacks aside, as being beneath the dignity of his notice and unworthy of his steel.

In the mere matter of religious theories he never invested very extensively, for he was, in every sense of the word, a minister of practical life, and to this end he made his war on sin and its concomitant adjuncts, as he always felt that this, especially, was the great object of his mission.

In one of his quarterly meeting visitations in the northeast part of the State, a number of years ago, Mr. Havens put up at the only public house in the place, where he found that the Circuit Court was in session, and consequently the tavern was well crowded with members of the bar. The large room in which these lawyers slept contained three beds, and as there were only five of them, the landlord arranged, with their consent, that the Presiding Elder should sleep with one of the lawyers.

Taking Mr. Havens into the room, the landlord politely introduced him to each one of the lawyers, who were all seated around a table amusing themselves at a game of cards.

Mr. Havens took his seat by the fire without saying a word, and they went on with the card-playing as if there had been no interruption. Unknown to him, they played to decide which one should sleep with the preacher, and after that game was over, the lawyer who had been thus destined to be his bed-fellow, supposing Mr. Havens would wish to retire, pointed out the bed he would occupy, when they went on with another game.

Being a stranger, although he had but little faith in their card-playing, he did not say a word, but when he got ready, he took his chair to the designated bed, and began to undress; but before getting into the bed, he knelt, as he had long been accustomed to, to offer up his evening thanks to the Lord of all grace and for the mercies of the day.

Looking around and seeing the quiet and dignified minister upon his knees, the hands of each lawyer were laid upon the table as if struck with paralysis, and not a card was thrown until the minister had finished his prayer and laid his head upon his pillow and was hidden away by the covers from their eyes. This unexpected and silent rebuke, which was as liberal as it was intelligent and appropriate, so awed them into reverence that they all, a few minutes after, rose from the table, and the cards were seen no more.

The next morning they looked at him as if he had been a special Grand Jury, and each man seemed to fear that some specific indictment would be found against him for his past night's offence. Several apologies were attempted, but Mr. Havens assured them that he was not hurt, or even disappointed in their conduct. He gave them, however, to understand that, as far as he knew, it was the general sentiment that but few lawyers went to heaven anyhow, and if this was the case, he thought it would hardly be justifiable to rob them of any of their privileges here. Two or three of these lawyers were in his congregation the next Sunday, and listened to his sermon with the deepest apparent interest.

Mr. Havens, for many years, was extensively acquainted with the bar of Eastern and Central Indiana, and he had the pleasure often of seeing them in his congregations. A number of them became members of the Church, and in many respects did honor to their profession.

The fact that Mr. Havens, in his forcible and energetic manner, mainly aimed to reach the hearts of the people, and to reform society from the common evils of the day, and that he made no attacks upon sister churches or their ministers, gave him the high respect of all classes and the particular good will of the largest minded men of the country.

He had no love for bigots or bigotry, and just as little for upstarts and sycophants of any profession. If he met with any such, even in the ministry, he showed them no favor: but, on the other hand, he not unfrequently administered a withering rebuke, the remembrance of which they could but carry with them to their graves. But ever kind and tender to the weak and unfortunate, he always gave them his sympathy with the profoundest sincerity.

CHAPTER XVIII.

PATRIOTISM.

Among the virtues of men, patriotism is one of the highest and noblest, for it gives to the citizen the credit of fraternal devotion, as well as the piety of the honest man. Without it no one can merit the public confidence, or vindicate the character of Christian consistency—for the laws of God demand its obligations at the hands of all men. The ancients inferred that governments were permanent in proportion to the piety of the people, and it was not until the tyranny of kings had trodden the rights of the masses into the dust, that the heroes of liberty began to teach the more daring theory, that "resistance to tyrants is obedience to God."

The growth of this virtue, in its higher and grander developments, has been found to be a product of the ages. It is never an exotic; for though men have sometimes volunteered their services in behalf of countries to which they were strangers, the devotion has been only the impulse of temporary sympathy, instead of the inspiration of a long lived patriotism.

Even here in our own land this virtue may often be doubted, for devotion to private interests is no evidence of this public attachment; and where men from foreign countries have made this "the land of their adoption," the act has doubtless been impelled by their own personal welfare, and this principle alone has given us the greater portion of this class of our population.

The land of our birth, and the land of our fathers, the home of our schoolboy days, and the country of our personal fortunes, furnishes the only soil on which true patriotism can flourish. It is under such regime alone that we find its best developments—its noblest virtues. Nowhere else have its cions grown to any high or manly perfection, and no where else has history pointed us to its loftiest examples.

Leonidas gave to Greece the brightest coronet of her renown, and the glory of William Tell made Switzerland immortal. What Cæsar did for Rome, though called ambition by his mistaken enemies, was only the higher strides of an imperial patriotism. Even the great Napoleon loved France second only to himself, and with all his ambition, he never sought dominions to his own empire without wanting his beloved France to have the glory of his achievments. The greatest crime of his illustrious life was the sacrifice of the noble Josephine to satisfy the morbid greed of France to secure a legitimate(?) successor to wear his imperial crown.

In monarchial governments patriotism is not so much a virtue as what has been styled "loyalty," which has usually signified devotion to the ruling dynasty The support of the king, in all such countries, has ordinarily been considered the highest virtue of the government. But here in our own Republic, where every citizen is a sovereign, the responsibility of a patriotic life has, from the beginning, been held as the sacred obligation of all classes, and even of the most humble. Our constitutions exonerate none from the burdens of taxation, and demand that every constituent should be true to the ballot-box.

Even the ministers of religion are not exempted from the obligations of the one or the duties of the other. The laws of the land know them only as citizens, and as such, except in a few States, they are entitled to all the rights and immunities of their countrymen.

Having no established religion, and giving no preference to any ecclesiastical organization, our Government extends to all churches, and to all ministers, protection in their worship and a delicate guardianship of their faiths and creeds of every class and character.

What men believe in religion is not the concern of the Government, and their modes of worship are all left to themselves. But reverence for our constitutions and respect for our laws are made the tests of our patriotism, and wherever they are disregarded, the insubordination is esteemed as a breach of the public faith which no leniency can justify without penalty.

To the honor of our American clergy, the record may be justly made that the great body of them have always been found true to what they have understood to be the patriotic interests of the Republic. If there have been any errors, even in extreme instances, the dereliction has not been for the want of any patriotic devotion, but must be traced to that zeal which, though radical as it may have been, led them on in their mission of redemption, dark and fearful as was the storm.

That some, even in the ministry of the churches,

have been, at times, too much given to the partizan cares of political life, may be frankly and readily admitted; but their zeal in this respect should, doubtless, find some apology in the fact that it is possible for even a good man to be more excessive in his patriotism than in his piety. This, indeed, is apt to be the case in times of great commotion, and more particularly so when the questions at issue have the hue of a seeming morality. Under such circumstances, men will sometimes do wrong even when they intend only to do right. They see the moral beauty of their grand objective point, and often rush toward it with an impetuous fearlessness that snaps the cords of tenderness and breaks up the delicate affinities which bind societies together; but even when their victory is gained, they not unfrequently find themselves greatly exhausted, both in their personal power and in their relative influences.

We are aware of the fact that some have the conviction that a portion of the ministry of the country have greatly demoralized their power, as well as diminished the numbers in their congregations, by the part they took in the revolutionary commotions which have so recently shaken our Government to her foundations. In this conviction they no doubt are at least partially sustained by the general moral appearances of the country. But then all such persons should remember that we have, in these years, passed through the darkest national cloud, and endured the cruelest baptism of blood any nation ever realized. It was a death storm of fire whose kindled flames scorched the very life of our nation, and swept to the grave, prematurely, millions of our countrymen.

In such a crisis of war and death, we may well wonder that the evils were not even greater than they were. But, thank God, the storm is past, and we stand a nation still. The bitter cup has been tasted to its dregs, and the dead of the storm have all been hid away in the grave.

It was a war, a wild war, of kindred affinities, where passion and ambition, pride and chivalry, met in their deadliest conflicts; and though it more than half exhausted the Republic, it is to be hoped that the patriotism of our people, and the piety of our churches, may again vindicate our national destiny to a higher power and purity than we have ever yet attained.

Such thoughts and sentiments as these were often, during the war, and before it, uttered by the venerable Havens, as his proud and patriotic heart was moved by the stirring agitations around him. The native fervor of his spirit would not permit him to look on such a conflict unconcerned; and though he was an old man, and retired from the active field of the ministry, he often declared that the confederated Union of the States, unbroken and indissoluble, was his living sentiment, and that it should be incorporated in his dying prayer.

No man loved his country with a stronger devotion than Father Havens. He had learned in his youth the stories of patriotism exhibited by the heroes of '76, and the same fire had been kindled in his own bosom, when mingling with the Indian hunters who had passed through the fiery ordeals of our western borders, and as he moved up to manhood this patriotic fire burned the brighter when he saw what his country was in the purity of its Republican elements and in the grand extent of its territory.

In his political faith, Mr. Havens, like most of his brethren in the Conference, was a Whig; and though firm and decided in his party principles, as far as he had studied them, he was, nevertheless, often the supporter at the ballot-box of those who widely differed with him. The counsel of Shakspeare was fully developed in his political integrity:

"Let all the ends thou aimest at
Be thy Country's, thy God's, and Truth's."

These were the governing elements of his character, and to these great ends he willingly offered his devotions at any shrine. The virtue of mere names, he was well aware, was often doubtful, and on this account he felt it, at times, to be his duty to "scratch" or "split" his ticket, particularly when some one he knew was on the opposite side.

On one occasion he met Judge Logan on the streets of Rushville, and after the usual salutations of the day, he said:

"I hear, Judge, that you are a candidate again."

"Well, yes, Father Havens," responded the Judge, "I am."

"Well, who is going to run against you?" he asked.

The Judge gave the name of his probable opponent, when Father Havens ejaculated:

"Humph! I don't like either of you; but, Judge,"

he added, "if you can't get a better man to run against you, I suppose I will have to vote for you, and you know that will be a bitter pill."

The venerable itinerant voted for the Judge, and he was elected, and when he next saw Judge Logan, he said to him:

"Judge, I voted for you, the other day; but I did it on the principle of 'where there are two evils, choose the least;' and now I hope I have not done wrong, and if I find out that I have, it is the last vote you will ever get at my hands."

When Governor Samuel Bigger was a candidate for re-election to that office, in 1843, Mr. Havens met him on one of the streets of Indianapolis, and, as they had long been neighbors, the greeting was, of course, as frank as it was cordial. But as Father Havens wanted to touch up the Governor, he said to him: "Governor Bigger, I always liked you as a Judge, and I do not know that I have anything against you as a Governor, but I confess I do not feel much like voting for you again on account of your Presbyterian bigotry. I know you never had any love for the Methodists, and if I vote for you this time, which I now expect to do, I want you, Governor, to understand that I shall do so purely because I believe that you are honest in spite of your bigotry."

Governor Bigger laughed heartily at the frankness of Father Havens, and asked him if he didn't remember of his often coming to hear him preach in preference to the Presbyterian ministers.

"Well, Governor," responded the sarcastic and candid old itinerant, "I believe you have frequently been in my congregations, but I know you are not a Methodist, and I am a little afraid," he added, with a pierce of his eye, "that you are not even as good a Presbyterian as you might be."

"That's so, that's so, Father Havens," was the honest response of the Governor; and, bidding each other good by, they parted from that half-jocular greeting never to see each other's faces in the flesh again.

Governor Bigger's sudden demise, a few brief weeks after this interview, and which was so deeply lamented over the State, was most sincerely lamented by Father Havens also, for he had long known him and his excellent lady as among his best Presbyterian friends.

The very positive Methodism of Father Havens sometimes allowed him to suspicion others in the liberality of their sentiments, but then, he was in his religion, like he was in his patriotism, somewhat jealous of any man's consistency when he heard of any illiberal dereliction.

He believed that the true lover of his country, like the true lover of his God, was derelict, if he suffered his selfishness to over-top his moral sentiments, or in any way to interfere with the free progress of religious or public institutions.

His country's welfare, in association with the high interests of the public morals, had always called out his honest and frank devotions; and while his guardian eye was chiefly fixed on the moral status of the country, he was ever deeply concerned in regard to any and everything that involved either its stability or national purity.

Though opposed to slavery as a civil institution of the land, he was never, in a political sense, what was termed "an abolitionist;" for he was not in favor of either rash legislation, or of ultra measures. So far as this, or any other evil, existed, he believed that the thing would cure itself; that right would ultimately triumph, and that whatever of darkness or cloud might gather over the government, that God would remove it in his own good time, if the people would repent and humble themselves before him.

His faith in the Divine government was as strong as it was direct; for he had taken his cue from the Old Testament chiefly, and his ideal of moral nationality was based upon Jewish history, as set forth in the sacred Scriptures.

The theory of our own government always had his most sincere confidence, because he believed that its basis of equalization and moral justice were founded on the divine records, and his faith was, that as long as the Holy Bible is regarded in its moral precepts and penal sanctions, the Republic will bid defiance to its proudest foes.

Meeting him shortly after the terrible fight of Bull Run, in the summer of 1861, we found him seemingly more sad and desponding than we had ever seen him before. The wild terror of that fearful defeat of our Union forces had partially passed from our mind, and we were not prepared to appreciate the cause of his evident depression. Upon our interrogation of the reasons for his despondency, he spoke about as follows:

"For the last few days, I have been regretting, more deeply than I ever have in my life, the condition of the country. It seems to me," he continued, "that our sky is growing darker and darker every day. Lincoln doesn't seem to know what he ought to do, and the prospect now is that our government will be destroyed, and if it is, it will throw back the wheels of civil liberty and of free governments a hundred years.

"I can not see," said he, "any way that we can consent to the independence of the South, with either honor or consistency; and, yet, I do not know but we will have to do it to save us from annihilation. The men of the South are as brave as the men of the North, and God only knows how this thing is going to end."

The patriotic heart of the brave old moral veteran felt deeply touched at the delicate and threatening condition of our national affairs; and though he was too far advanced in years himself to participate personally in the fearful struggle, he could but look upon the conflict with the saddest emotions.

If the sun of his country's honor and glory had to set in blood amidst the raging storm of an internecine war, more terrible, on this account, than the devouring desolations of the Furies themselves, he felt that liberty would be swept from the earth, and that even the foundation pillars of Christianity itself would have nowhere to stand. To the old men of the country that lamentable contest of brothers of the same kith and kin was, no doubt, more mournful and sad than it was to any others. Such, at least, appeared to be the sentiment and feeling, both living and dying, of the venerable man of God of whom we hear speak.

CHAPTER XIX.

HIS ORTHODOXY.

Soundness of faith is said to be the only reliable foundation of substantial character. This at least has been the teachings of our churches, and as a general thing, they have all held to it with an uncompromising devotion, such as time could not change, or death destroy.

The phases of theology have been so numerous in human writings, that Bible truth has often been obscured, and many have so far fallen into error, as to be designated skeptics instead of Christians.

On these points, most churches have been especially particular, as well as suspicious. They have watched with an eagle eye the slightest aberrations in this direction, and even men of talent and genius and popular eloquence have at different periods been placed upon the rack, as being of doubtful, if not of dangerous orthodoxy.

Nothing has ruined ministerial standing more effectually, or with a swifter certainty, than heterodox proclivities, for such inclinations have been deemed to be not only sinful, but destructive of the peace and unity of the Church.

For brethren to differ was to divide. They could not live in the same house or drink of the same holy cup unless they saw eye to eye. Differences in faiths have made divisions in churches, until these institutions stand, in many instances, more as monuments of theological confusion than as land marks of the old primitive Christian doctrine.

Most of these differences, however, which have wrought these unhappy divisions, were not cardinal in the Christian faith, and it really would not have mattered much which side the contestants fell upon.

Church history shows us that most of these divisions were the results of differences in church government, rather than of theological notions. Assumptive ecclesiastical laws, in connection with their injurious execution by inconsiderate dignitaries, have made "come-outers" in almost every church organization in existence—while in general orthodoxy the most of them have remained conservatively respectable.

The doctrines of the Bible, as held by the Fathers, and as handed along down the ages, have been termed by pre-eminence our orthodox theology. What they have taught has furnished the churches with their systems of faith and order of moral economy, and if they had continued steadfast in their Bible reliances, the world would never have been thrown into ecclesiastical confusion, or the Christian Church been torn into a thousand fragments.

Whether the world is made better by these numerous divisions has been doubted by the best divines of Christendom, as they have been compelled to acknowledge, that the glory of Christian unity has been sacrificed at the shrine of ecclesiastical ambition. The standard of orthodoxy has consequently lost much of its genuine practical power, and the religious world has largely swung off on the hinges of an eclectic theology which reflects but indifferently upon the true and old time theories.

These aberrations have not been, as some would suppose, the instituted systems of an uneducated ministry—for in most instances such men are apt to follow rather than lead. The new departures have generally found their first impulse in educated brains, if not in regenerated hearts. Men of thought and education have broken away from the leading strings of their church authority, and rather than submit to the trial of fraternal conflict, they have set up for themselves on a new *role*.

It is not what Christian doctrines are, that has made these divisions and church alienations, but what men have tried to make them. New theories of religious doctrines have been of almost annual birth, and the old land marks have been pulled up and driven down again so frequently, that the ancient boundaries have grown so dim that but few can now discover them.

The 39 Articles of the Church of England which form the basis, with only two exceptions, of the Methodist Episcopal Church, have held the body together in doctrines with a cohesive power that may well be looked upon as being wonderful. In all the contentions and divisions of the Methodist family both in Europe and America, there has never been a single separation because of doctrinal conflict. All have been agreed on its doctrines. Government has been the difficulty—in connection with the administration of it, and to these causes may all her depletions be attributed. In moral principle and doctrinal teachings the families of Methodism are a unit to-day throughout the world.

It was this universal doctrinal unity which gave Father Havens his highest Methodist confidence. He had often heard of ministers of other denominations differing with one another, and preaching a strange theology; but, among Methodist preachers, he knew that such a thing was a rare and strange occurence.

Taken in connection with the fact that a large number of the Methodist ministry have been what is styled uneducated men, it is somewhat remarkable that they have been so universally true to the faith and doctrines of the Church.

With most of them the Bible was their daily book of lessons. It was "the charter of their faith and the record of their redemption;" and from it they gathered their religious convictions. The writings of Wesley and Fletcher, of Clarke and Watson, furnished their doctrinal comments with such clearness and power as no other books have, ever excelled.

The Theological Institutes of Richard Watson contain the most thorough and exhaustive expositions of the doctrines, morals and institutions of the Christian faith, perhaps, ever written by any theologian the Church has yet produced. Nearly every Methodist preacher of Europe and America has read the work, while thousands have made it the chief study of their years.

With such doctrinal guides as these, Methodist preachers could not well float off into error. The arguments and exemplifications of Bible theology are so clearly and satisfactorily sustained by them that but few who have ever read them have fallen from the faith.

With such a mind as Father Havens possessed, an unorthodox aberration was barely possible; for though he was unlearned in the schools, and even far from being a general reader, his brave and practical common sense made him cautious and conservative in assuming his positions in theology, as well as in action. What he preached he believed; and he examined his points of doctrine always with a prayerful and careful thought, which admitted of no deception, and consequently never permitted him to drop down into any theological error.

Aiming in his ministry to reform men chiefly, his subjects referred to the duties of life, rather than to their religious speculations. It was not his purpose at any time to merely convert the brains of men. Such work as this he left to others. He understood the doctrines of Christianity to refer to the morals of mankind, and not to their mere intellectual developments. Hence, the most of his sermons struck at men's hearts instead of their admiration, and he bore down upon them, like a brave man of war, with the high resolve and determined purpose of bearing off the flag of the enemy in every conflict.

Convictive truths were the chief weapons of his pulpit power, and when he stood before the people, he poured upon them the "hot shot" of the gospel as one who believed his commission was from heaven. Simple truth—vital and effective—he well knew was the chief instrument of gospel power among any people, and it was this knowledge to which he always so tenaciously adhered, that made him so distinguished as a sound divine as well as a safe moral guide.

With the speculative, the sensational, and egotistical gospel philosophies, he had but little acquaintance, as he never made them his study, or placed any confidence in their grace or efficiency. Whether in his own church, or any other, he gave them no encouragement. They did not meet his style, or open to him a single avenue of gospel usefulness, and he, therefore, counted them as but dust in the balance.

What was termed heresy, he always opposed with a zeal which at times was thought to be even severe, because the exposures he made of them were both sarcastic and annihilating. Indeed, he winced at nothing, as he felt that it was not meet that he should do so, particularly when the true faith was endangered. On such occasions his nervous excitement gave spirit to his efforts, and made him the hero of the hour.

He knew he held the commission of a gospel sentinel, and he allowed no man to cross the line of orthodoxy in his presence with impunity. If he was even a very Goliah in his pretensions, he would attack him in defense of the truth; and, when he did so, his antagonist had but one alternative, and that was to make good his retreat.

At one of his camp meetings, in the White Water country, he learned that a brother minister of another faith and order, had been making strenuous and protracted efforts to teach the people that without baptism by immersion there could be no hope of salvation. This theory had its advocates, who were teaching the system with a zeal and boldness which but few men of any persuasion could excel.

In his sermon on Sabbath morning, Father Havens made a tilt at this rather ultra-fluidic theology, and in his peculiar style, showed his audience that the theory was not sufficient for every emergency.

Seeing the Hon. Oliver H. Smith in the congregation, he made him a special case, to show the utter impracticability of the watery salvation. After giving his general arguments to expose the position, he said to the assembly:

"Here is a man you all know, who is sick, Hon. Oliver H. Smith. He is not religious—but on his sick bed he becomes anxious about his soul's salvation. He wishes to be saved, and he asks his friends around him, What shall I do to be saved? They tell him he must be baptized for the remission of his sins, and with the same breath they tell him also, that immersion alone is baptism. But he is sick—very dangerously sick, and too weak to be taken from his bed, and the question comes up, what shall be done? A runner is started after the preacher, but he has gone away, and is no where to be found. The case becomes a critical one, and Mrs. Smith and her family and neighbors are around the bed of the dying man—weeping in the bitterness of their sorrow and deeply lamenting the sad fate of the husband and father, who will die and be lost forever, not because Christ did not die for him—not because the Lord is not willing to save him—but because there is no human administrator to administer the saving ordinance of baptism.

"Riders are sent in every direction to hunt up the preacher. Mr. Smith is dying, and his soul will be lost forever, if some proper administrator is not soon found. Wild with grief and bowed to the dust in bitter and hopeless lamentations the friends stand around the bed of the distinguished dying statesman, without a ray of glimmering light to cheer them in their hopes of his salvation. Sincere as he is, and anxious to be saved as he may be, the poor penitent man dies and is lost, lost, lost forever, just because there is no human arm to save him."

The vast assembly were deeply excited, and showed their indignancy of the doctrine of salvation by water, instead of by faith, and as Mr. Smith, the imaginary sick man, was in the congregation, highly enjoying the demonstrative argument of the stern old hero preacher, every eye was fixed upon him. The stroke was considered a masterly one, and as Mr. Smith remarked, after the services were over, "No man in Indiana but Father Havens could have carried his point with such skill and shrewdness."

Some years after this the Whitewater country was greatly agitated with the doctrine of Millerism, that the end of the world was to take place sometime in the spring or summer of 1843. Many seemed to be falling in with the sensational theory, and the public mind was wonderfully stirred in regard to the doctrine. Quite a number of local preachers of very respectable abilities were carried away with the grand apocalyptic discovery, and as it is apt to be in all cases of "wisdom above that which is written," these men became impatient of rebuke and with great effrontery were willing to face the world in defense of their judgment theory

Some of them broke off their church connection, as the orders came from headquarters for all who wished to ascend with Christ to "come out of Babylon," which term was applied by them to all the churches of the land, without regard to history, character, or antecedents.

To meet these deluded people, Father Havens found it no easy task. They were full of self-conceit, and so much determined on being deceived that no argument could reach them. The thing was sensational, and they fastened upon it with the most obstinate tenacity. "The year 1843 was to close the history of time." This was their belief, and in its advocacy they spent their days and nights in trying to make converts with as much apparent sincerity and zeal, as if they had had an especial commission, to wind up old Nature's history.

It was soon discovered, however, by the more intelligent opponents of their wild theory that time alone would cure them of their malady, and on this account, as Father Havens once informed us, "he did not feel like wasting powder to kill it. It would die of itself from the statute of limitation." So, indeed, it did; but, yet, many of its miserable advocates were so disappointed by the failure, that they were of no more use to their churches during the rest of their years.

The next delusion following that of Millerism, was the theory of "The Soul Sleepers," as they were termed, who taught "that the soul sleeps with the body in the grave, and that at the second coming of Christ, the righteous shall awake to the resurrection of life, and that the souls of the wicked will be annihilated forever and ever." Many of the Millerites run into this latter theory, and still linger there yet. They are, it seems, infatuated with the marvelous, and carried away with any sort of doctrine that will throw contempt upon the old orthodoxy of the churches. These heterodox departures they endure with a resignation and submission well worthy of even the purest orthodoxy. They seem, indeed, not to suspect themselves of any heretical bearings, or to dream that they are not in the line of the richest vein of Bible philosophy.

Meeting one of them one day, Father Havens asked him "how he would like to live in the world of annihilation?" "Live!" exclaimed the astonished Soul Sleeper; "those who shall meet with that sentence will not live at all. They will be as dead as if they had never been born." "Is that so?" Father Havens inquired. "Why, certainly That is what the Bible teaches," was the responsive assurance. "Well, then," said Father Havens, with an audible sigh, "I pity you, for I have known you a good many years, and I can not remember of any good you have ever done, and I don't see, for the life of me, how you can escape the destiny of annihilation." Then, looking sideways at the somewhat startled victim before him, he added, in a little stronger tone of sarcasm, "If the Lord can save such a do-nothing fellow as you from annihilation, there will certainly be very few others that he need pass by." This, of course, was an argument *ad hominum*, but it was, doubtless, in this case, more effectual than a day's debate would have been with such a character. The strict adherence of Father Havens to the old land marks of the orthodox theology of the ages, gave him the just claims of being a theologian, and placed him among his peers in his conference as one of the pillars of the temple. Nature had endowed him with clear powers of perception, and experience and observation, had given him the advantages of stability. Thought had made him familiar with truth, and the devotions of his life constituted him a consistent worshiper.

CHAPTER XX.

HIS PECULIAR ORATORY

THE cant of the pulpit, and the sing-song monotony of many in the gospel ministry, have often been the subject of sport and ridicule even among the religious. The deep sepulchral tone, or the equally pious whine of quaint gospel teachers have given to the profession in many instances a comedian character, and furnished irreligious jokers with some of their best themes of ridicule. The old idea of "speaking only as the Lord gave them utterance," totally regardless of all rules of rhetoric or oratory, and without a single touch of any sort of natural elocution, has in frequent instances, brought the services of the pulpit into contempt, and opened the way for all classes of irreverence and infidelity.

Manner, jesture, and tone, are all important in the sacred desk, as they, indeed, are, in all public efforts of speech; but more particularly, as we think, are they imperiously demanded in the pulpit efforts of the ministry.

The expositions of gospel teaching appeal to the faith of men rather than to their senses, and the manner of making them, becomes essential, as listeners to the ministry—in their frequent attendance upon the same man, are naturally led to a closer and severer criticism of his efforts.

Oratory, like music, may be criticised by many who

have no capacity for it themselves, and who know little or nothing either of its rules or order. They look at the speaker himself, to see what he says in his appearances, manners and jestures; and they listen to his voice as they would hearken to music, to catch, as far as possible, the spirit of its power and to drink in the divinity of its inspiration.

In the early days in the west, it was common for all classes to go out to hear preaching, and more particularly, when any minister of repute was going to preach. The man drew them out, even when they cared but little for the solemnities of religious worship, and it was not uncommon for the preacher to have his whole congregation in tears, while he held them with the power of his voice, and the spirit of his almost inspired eloquence, as if they had no capacity for resistance.

The old war veterans of our early pioneer Missionary work in the west, had no college cants, and they were, seemingly, as ignorant of the mechanical tropes and figures of the schools, as if such inventions had never been known. Their style was that of nature rather, than of art. Indeed it had about it too much of the old natural divinity for any sort of artificial imputations; and its daring independence would have set at defiance and held in contempt the weak and *namby pamby* styles, so common in the pulpits of the present day. It was the boldness of their style, in fact, that gave it its greatest majesty—for they made no consultations with flesh and blood to obtain their oratorial key, or to learn how far they might go in reproving sin, or in warring against evils of any cast or character. They went before the people as God's ambassadors, and not as mere ecclesiastical hirelings. What they said was uttered fearlessly, without regard to popular fame, or the weakness of clap trap applause. No threats could intimidate them, and no flatteries could purchase them. They were a race of pioneer Apostles as heroic as the primitives, and perhaps but little behind them either in the ardor of their spirit, or in the wonders of their accomplishments. Occupying the different fields of district and circuit labor, they appeared not to care where the Conference sent them, just so they might have some place, where they could make full proof of their ministry

The very moral position of these men was eloquent, and their mission was considered divine, by nearly every one; consequently, wherever they went the people by hundreds gave them audience, and on this account they felt their responsibility was such as could not be measured.

It was indeed wonderful to witness the great oratorical powers of some of these men, when they stood up before the people on popular occasions. Their straightened forms assumed the loftiest dignity, while their countenances would become radiant with the inspiration of their chosen themes, and their voices, growing musical with their eloquent utterances, would ring out upon the vast congregations assembled to hear them, like the bugle blasts of some champion gladiator.

The camp meeting scenes often witnessed under the preaching of such men as Bascom and Waterman, Bigelow and Finley, Stamper and Christie and hundreds of others whose honored names have been made immortal in the annals of western Methodism, gave to the itinerancy its highest prestige, and added to the membership and ministry of the Church many thousands of its brightest characters.

It was among such men as these that Mr. Havens spent the earlier years of his ministry, and it could not well be expected that such examples of pulpit brilliancy would fail to give their impress to such a mind as he possessed, particularly, as it was in the open field of observation, that he obtained most of that eminent education, which gave him such distinction, and made his name a household word in so many thousands of families throughout the State.

Indeed, nearly all Mr. Havens knew had been gleaned along through the travel of life; and as he had no master in science, neither had he any in oratory. The school of nature had always been his seminary of instruction, and the lessons he learned there had given him his highest accomplishments. Therefore, as an orator, he was both simple and natural. No effort at display was ever visible in his performances, and the chief features of his oratory were sincerity, earnestness, determined boldness and exceedingly frank utterances. He had a taste for the poetic and the beautiful; but he was charey in treading the sublimated pathways of any such regions. None knew better than he did the strength of his sail in strange waters. With him the themes of the gospel were the only burden of his ministry, and to these he gave the thoughts of his life, as to their fearless vindication, he gave the labors of his years.

The natural earnestness of his style gave to his sermons the character of an honest and candid sincerity which, with his heroic boldness and eminent commanding abilities, made him an acknowledged champion among his brethren in the ministry, as well as a recognized leader among all the people.

As a man of eloquence, Mr. Havens made no pretensions, although he often was eloquent, and sometimes even sublime. His chief aim was to make his sermons plain and practical. He appeared not to think of himself in the pulpit, but only of the people, and his deepest struggles were how to get at them with the strong arm of convicting power. In making his appeals to his congregations, he used no clap-trap or "high-sounding words." His was the style of a plain, commanding argument, of an earnest and fervent zeal, which came from his heart as much as from his head, and it was this frank and honest sincerity, doubtless, which gave him such success in his ministry.

The Bible, being recognized by him as the only reliable charter of his faith, he gathered from it alone the theology of his sermons, as well as the style of his language. Not that he made up his sermons from scriptural quotations, for this he never did. His style of language was his own; but as it was modeled after that which was divine, it was, of course, simple and terse, and often both comprehensive and beautiful.

But few ministers excelled him in the fervency of his oratory; for he was always in earnest, and drove his forces for conquest instead of display. Indeed, he had a peculiar love for bold, energetic and earnest preaching—that sort of pulpit oratory which takes the kingdom of darkness by storm, and drives the powers of evil before it like the destroying hurricane which defies opposition, as it sweeps on to its destiny.

It was this high regard for an earnest ministry which made him so earnest and fervent—so energetic and successful. Aiming always to be honest, as well as sincere, he had but little faith in a ministry of any kind that operated for mere show, or that existed on the emoluments or the imagined dignity of the office. Empty ministerial display, however richly it might be associated with personal pretensions, or with professed scholarship, never attracted much attention, or held any high place in his esteem. His love was for the real in life, and it was because of this he preferred the plain and earnest to the pompous and pretentious ministry.

In the ranks of oratory he was more "a son of thunder" than he was of consolation, and to this class in the ministry it was natural for him to give his preferences. Still, he had for ministers of other styles of oratory than his own, even the very highest regards, for he well knew that all these different classes were needed in carrying on the work, and in building up the Church, and he was always ready to receive them with all due respect, and to recognize them as an honored portion of the Church of God.

We once heard him say to a brother minister, "I am always pleased to hear you preach. You give me something to think about—something that sets my head to working. You are," he continued, "a thinker, and I like to hear such men, for they often show up the moral beauties of religion in a light which the common people would perhaps never see if it were not for such sermons."

Mr. Havens was mistaken in himself in regard to his education, for he was always impressed with the belief that his educational deficiencies had so hampered his powers of thought that he could not claim to be "a thinker." In this inference he was undoubtedly in error, for but few ministers we have ever known, were better, or even deeper thinkers, than he was himself. His thoughts, to be sure, were chiefly of the practical caste—but they were nevertheless worthy of distinction even in the line of scholarship, for they were always sound and true, and not unfrequently partook of the deepest profundity. This he evinced in his sermons frequently and often in his conversation; and to this cause, more than to his fiery oratory, may we ascribe the fact that he was but seldom ever known to preach a dull or prosy sermon.

It was never sensational or speculative theology which gave him power over his congregations—but the plain practical philosophy of Bible precepts—such as he gathered from the infinite mine of truth, and which he always gave out to the people with such force and earnestness. In this grand source of preceptive thought Mr. Havens had, doubtless, earned as honorable a diploma of Doctor of Divinity, as nine tenths of the distinguished clergy who wear this honor.

Nature makes some men giants in thought as well as in oratory, in defiance of the schools—and in this class may we justly place such a minister as he was, for though he never studied elocution in his life, he was nevertheless an orator of no mean grade, and if he lacked in scholarship, he was not deficient in educated thought, or sublime sentiment. His soul had drunk largely of the crystal founts of Sinai and Calvery, and from these pure fountains of philosophic infinity, he had imbibed as rich intellectual treasures, as philosopher or scholar ever drank from the doubtful waters of the "Pierian Spring." A similar conviction must have pervaded the mind of the Bard of Scotland, or he would never have written—

"What's a' your jargon o' your schools?
Your Latin names for horns an' stools;
If honest Nature made you fools,
  What sairs your grammars?
Ye'd better ta'en up spades and shools,
  Or knappin-hammers.

A set o' dull, conceited hashes,
Confuse their brains in college classes!
They gang in stirks, and come out asses,
  Plain truth to speak;
An' syne they think to climb Parnassus
  By dint o' Greek!

Gi'e me a spark o' Natures fire,
That's a' the learning I desire;
Then though I drudge through dub an' mire,
  At pleugh or cart,
My Muse, though hamely in attire,
  May touch the heart."

It was this "spark o' nature's fire," which gave to

FATHER HAVENS' HOOSIER HOME, 1825.

Mr. Havens, in connection with the higher and purer celestial fire, which he had received through grace, and which made him the equal of scholars, the compeer of orators, and in many respects a model among even the masters in the ministry.

To become a disciple of thought without the process of education, and to rise to the highest oratorical distinction, independent of all instructions in the arts of elocution, constitute an advancement in intellectual life such as is not often made, and even where it is attained the evidence is *prima facie* that the elementary character itself must have been of nature's highest and purest mould.

That Mr. Havens was an orator, was readily admitted by the thousands who heard him preach, but how he attained to this accomplishment was only known to those who were familiar with his history, and who knew him well as a man. Among all such it was always understood that his style of oratory was peculiarly his own; that he neither obtained it from books, nor from men. For, starting out in the ministry with all the impulsive ardor of a soul fired by the grace of God, he stopped not to confer with flesh and blood, but feeling, as he honestly did, that he was a called embassador to preach the unsearchable wisdom of Jesus Christ to a lost and ruined world, he entered upon the work with that heroic zeal, which marked the spirit of his age, and distinguished so many of the preachers of his day.

What he was in these respects did not constitute him *sui generis*, for there were many others like him— men who had volunteered in the great field of the itinerancy, to cultivate it faithfully and fearlessly, without regard to what they would get for their support, or where would be the field of their labors. The very enlistment of these men was heroic, and gave to their mission the moral romance of a spiritual crusade, which pales in the ashes of an expiring insignificance all the bloody crusades ever made against Jew or Infidel, Mohammedan or Atheist.

Sounding the key notes of the gospel from the ramparts of truth and a gracious spirituality, they lifted their voices with a burning zeal, whose fires, like those of Pentecost, were as visible as they were consuming. They knew no surrender of their positions, and bowed to no infallibility, but that of God himself.

It was not language that made these men eloquent; nor was it the rhetoric of the schools. It was Sinai's thunder and Calvary's love. It was the grand result of the inspiration of the hour—the direct display of that higher baptism which comes down upon the souls of men out of heaven, and which kills sin and breaks the hearts of the obdurate. It was this divine power which moved the people like the sweepings of the storm-king upon the face of the great deep. The effect was everywhere the evident movement of the power eternal; and when the people beheld it, as it appeared to be wielded by these missionary embassadors, they knew not what to say. They heard it, and felt it, and could not stay away; and, though often for a time full of anger, their wildest passions soon melted before it to the humblest submission, and the march of the conqueror was like the shouts of the people when they tread the path of triumph as an army with banners.

CHAPTER XXI.

HIS OHIO CONFRERES.

LIFE'S earliest ties are often its strongest and most sacred. It is then that confidence is the strongest and the more implicit, for the heart is then young and has not yet learned the calculating schemes of sinister interests.

It is not usually the best to know too much of the world's friendships—for it is too often the case that distance alone lends enchantment to the view.

Like the man who had the ax to grind, many are exceedingly complacent as long as we turn the grindstone for them. But their ax sharpened, they at once assume the attitude of self reliance, as if our friendship would never again be needed.

The uncalled for treachery of human friendships, doubtless, has done much to destroy our confidence in the integrity of our kind, and therefore it is natural for men, as they grow older in years to have less confidence in professions and in the proffered affections of the world around them. What they have experienced in the history of the past, has chilled their affections, and the blandishments of policy henceforth become the only measure of their civility. The coolness of etiquette regulates their associations instead of affection, and doubt and distrust displace the simplicity of confidence, while the heart is made to grow solitary, amid the desolations of its own loneliness. Even the society of the ministry has not been exempt from such delinquencies—for it has often been evident even in the holier affinities, that we have "these treasures in earthen vessels." It is even here we see history repeating itself in imitation of Peter's denial, and not unfrequently in the more glaring example of Judas himself.

Nature's moral debility displays itself in spite of the sacred office and regardless of the higher integrities.

"The older I get, the fewer seems to be the number of my friends," was once remarked to us by Father Havens himself, and we did not doubt but he felt all he said. The sun of his life was no longer in its zenith, and the voice of the multitude no longer followed him. Though yet living, he felt that he belonged to a past age. The shadows of life's evening were fast gathering around him, and he could not fail to recognize their obscuring mantle.

To the men who drank so deeply of the genial waters and warm, cordial friendships everywhere found in the pioneer homes of the West, these transitions of life's apparent neglect, were doubtless severe and trying, because they had not been calculated upon, and consequently were not prepared for.

But few ministers had a higher appreciation of a true friend than Mr. Havens. He had learned in early life their extreme value, and where ever he found one, whom he could confidently trust, he would frequently place himself in his hands and power, as a child trusts its own mother. He knew but little of duplicity in himself, and he scorned it in others. Nothing, indeed, made him more indignant than the designing sycophancy of a scheming aspirant. When such a case came before him, he gave the subject no quarters, but on the other hand, he frequently administered to him such a rebuke as either cured him of his folly, or taught him to try some other court for the success of his plea.

The old style of friendships, which were honest and frank, simple and confiding, he had learned in the cabins of Kentucky and Ohio, among the people with whom he began his labors, and the imprint of their kindnesses was on his heart to the day of his death.

Among the ministers of the Ohio Conference he was associated, in the first years of his itinerancy, with a number who subsequently attained to eminent distinction in the Church, and with others who made such a record of usefulness as can never be forgotten.

Of those who were admitted on trial in the Conference with him in 1820, we may particularly mention Alfred Brunson, Charles Thorn, James Jones, Daniel Limerick, William Simmons, and Zara H. Costin. With these good names his own was associated in the very beginning of his Conference connection, and with some of these good men he formed, in after years, warm and abiding friendships, which were only severed by death itself. Of these ministers, William Simmons and Alfred Brunson, alone, are still living. With James Jones, Mr. Havens was associated for many years in the Indiana Conference; but from all the others he was separated from the time he left the Ohio Conference.

His first appointment being to Salt Creek Circuit alone, his Presiding Elder, Samuel West, was that year his only ministerial associate; and when the good old man came round to his quarterly meetings, his visits were like those of the angels, for they were both cheering and encouraging, as the venerable old apostle always spake words of kindness, and bid him not to fear any obstacle which might come in his way.

The Ohio Conference at that period was the great Methodist field of the West, and it had among its members a number who were thought to be the equals of any preachers in the United States. Dr. Martin Ruter, John P Durbin, Russell Bigelow, James Quinn, Allen Wiley, James B. Finley, and John Strange, may be named as among the ablest of the Conference, and with these Mr. Havens mingled with an unassuming sobriety, taking notes, as best he could, and closely observing the spirit and character of every member of the Conference.

The genius of the itinerancy, in those early days, partook largely of the heroic, for the men who chiefly directed the work were Brush College graduates, and they expected every recruit to their ranks should be ready to do valiant battle in any field which might be assigned him.

Mr. Havens' second year found him on the Straight Creek Circuit, with Greenbury R. Jones as his Presiding Elder, who was a man of great power in the pulpit, and who, for many years, was distinguished as one of the ablest members of the Conference. Each year added to his acquaintance the names of men who were rapidly rising to moral power, many of whom, in after years, in different conferences, became heralds of renown, and made for themselves a name in Methodist history which will now never be obscured.

The third year of Mr. Havens' itinerancy may be set down, as one of the most significant of his life. His appointment was to Brush Creek Circuit, with Henry B. Bascom in charge—Greenbury R. Jones still remaining on the district.

The colleague of Mr. Havens this year was one of the most eloquent pulpit orators of his age, and even at that period could have filled with inspiring command any pulpit of the country. The year before Bascom had labored on the Hinkstone Circuit, in the Kentucky Conference—but as his father's family lived in the bounds of the Brush Creek Circuit, he had asked for and received this appointment, as a special favor. Here on this large four weeks circuit, this able young divine labored on a promised salary of one hundred dollars for the year, which, however he did not get, and whenever he had a leisure day he worked on the farm, or rather clearing, of his father, to do what he could in helping to support the young and helpless family. The intimacy which grew up between Bascom and Havens, became like that of Jonathan and David. In many respects, they were in genius and character of the same kith and kin, and being of the same high calling, and colleagues in the same work, they became allied to each other by the strong ties of a common interest as well as by those of the higher fellowships.

Bascom's father was a poor man, and in very indifferent health. But having a large family, it was one of the greatest concerns of his noble and eloquent son, to look after its support and prospective interests. Often when Mr. Havens came round to the Bascom neighborhood, he would find his colleague out in a clearing, stripped of his coat and vest, and working among the brush, as if the toils of the woodsman had been his only calling.

It was this noble and self sacrificing spirit which gave Mr. Havens such exalted and abiding confidence in his colleague, and led him through all the after years of his life to speak of him with the highest confidence and praise.

Bascom's style of eloquence was also greatly admired by Mr. Havens, for he saw that it was the bold utterance of a proud and manly nature, and had about it the captivating power of true and genuine eloquence.

It was not a matter of wonder that the hearts of the two became as one, for in many respects they were strikingly similar, both in their personal fearlessness and in their manly independence.

The year was of course a pleasant one, as well as one of great success. At its close the parting of the two itinerants was as the parting of brothers. They had lived long enough together, for each to know the others true manhood—and though they only met casually in subsequent life, until death came to bear the eloquent Bascom to his grave their hearts beat in unison as loyal brothers.

The next year Bascom was sent to Steubenville, and

Mr. Havens was appointed to the Scioto Circuit, with William Simmons as his assistant.

Mr. Havens still retained his old heroic Presiding Elder, Rev. Greensbury R. Jones, whom he had learned to love, as one who might justly be counted among the noblest of his race. Coming to his Circuit once a quarter, where usually he had the entire officiary of the charge—together with hundreds of others— to preach to, this venerable war-veteran would sound his bold trumpet of alarm in the ears of sinners, and expound the deep mysteries of gospel truth to believers in such a manner, and with such sweeping and rhetorical power, as often thrilled his entire congregation. With his Presiding Elder, Mr. Havens had become familiar; for, though he was much his superior, both in office and age, there was still no distinction between them. Both were Methodist preachers, which, of itself, recognized an equality, and this common fraternization, doubtless, gave them additional power among the people. With his colleague, Mr. Havens was also intimate, for he found him both humble and honest, a true yoke-fellow and a good young man. For more than fifty years, Mr. Simmons has continued in the work of the itinerancy, and, at the present writing, he is popularly known as one of the most valuable fathers in the Cincinnati Conference. The life of such a man is well worthy of the highest moral record, for he has stood for the defense of the truth through all the changes and storms of more than a half century. And long after the passing away of nearly every one of his early ministerial associates, he still stands at the head of his Conference, among the third generation of preachers, every one of whom rise up and call him blessed.

While there were many good and noble men, both in the ministry and membership in Ohio, with whom Mr. Havens had formed warm friendships, he now and then, in the discharge of his duties as a Circuit rider, met with a few men of the other sort—men who did but little good themselves, and who seemed to become angry or jealous whenever they saw another trying to do any good to his race. The world has always had its share of this class of "dumb driven cattle," and, while laboring in Ohio, it was Mr. Havens' unfortunate fate to be no little troubled by them.

To defeat such men is not always an easy task, for often they have wealth to back them, and, in some instances, they are sustained by respectable social positions, and often even by the dignity of office. Such, in former years, was perhaps more particularly the case than in the present days.

At one of Mr. Havens' camp meetings, held on the Rocky Fork of Paint Creek, in Highland county, Ohio, where he was assisted by Job M. Baker and Rev G. B. James, both of whom were excellent preachers, as well as sound divines, the latter was appointed to preach the sermon to the large congregation on Sabbath. The crowd was great, and, of course, there were some who were restless, and very little disposed to pay any attention to either the sermon of the preacher or the rules of the meeting.

One gentleman particularly seemed to lead off in

this insubordination, but, as he was a magistrate, he perhaps thought the importance of his office made him a privileged character. He took his stand with others who were following him, on the seats prepared for the ladies. The squire more than any of the gang made a conspicuous figure, as he wore a large red vest. He consequently attracted very general attention. Mr. James kindly and modestly requested the gentlemen to be seated, and suggested the propriety of their occupying their own side of the congregation. To this the magistrate and his associate crowd paid no attention. This of course stirred the blood of Mr. Havens to the point of self protection, at least, and he jumped to his feet and asked the preacher to hold up a minute until he would regulate the congregation.

Mr. James stepped back a pace, when Mr. Havens addressed the assembly.

"I wish to say to this vast assembly that there are a great many things in nature which might be so changed, that they would possess entirely different qualities and properties—but a simple substance, you all know, can never be changed, you may change the mode of its existence, but it will still possess the same nature. I believe, said he, that I will give you an illustration of what I am aiming at. For instance you may make a magistrate out of an ass and attempt to change him into a gentleman by dressing him up in scarlet colors—but all you can do in that way, will affect but little. The color will not hide his nature, or conceal his ears. They will still stick out, and every one who will look at him will see that he is a *bona fide* ass, even in defiance of all his assumed official dignity."

The manner in which this was said, and the significant pointing of his finger toward the red breasted magistrate, as he stood on the seats of the ladies, in contemptuous defiance of all rules, made the township dignitary wilt before the well timed and richly merited excoriation, and in a moment or two, he and his entire gang sloped from the presence of the delighted congregation, and the preacher went on with his sermon as if nothing at all had happened.

Some few weeks after this camp meeting Mr. Havens was passing to an appointment near where this red breasted magistrate resided, when suddenly he pitched out from behind a tree and seizing Mr. Havens' horse by the bridle, he sternly and with great threats demanded satisfaction for the gross insult he claimed to have received at the above meeting. He held a large club in his hands, and seemed ready and determined to strike. He dared the preacher to get down from his horse. This, Mr. Havens did not feel just then disposed to do, as fighting was not in his *role*. Still the squire threatened to strike.

"If you do strike me squire, said Mr. Havens, you had better strike hard enough to disable me, or you may rest assured that a certain *justice of the peace* will get such a whipping as he never dreamed of since he was born." With this declaration, Mr. Havens made a seeming effort to dismount, when the first thing he knew the gallant squire had dropped the reins of his bridle, and was making for the woods as fast as his feet could carry him. It was after such order as this that many of the early pioneer preachers of the West had to contend against flesh and blood of "the baser sort," and it seemed to be necessary, at times, for some of them to show such fellows, to use a western phrase, that "they were not born in the woods to be scared by an owl."

CHAPTER XXII.

HIS INDIANA COTEMPORARIES.

Mr. Havens came to Indiana in the year 1824. Transferred from the Ohio to the Illinois Conference, he removed his family in the fall of that year to this State, with the purpose of settling them on land which he hoped to call his own. The Illinois Conference had been authorized the spring before, and included the State of Indiana, as well as the State whose name it bore. This entire territory contained only a little over six thousand members, and counted only about thirty itinerant preachers. The country was all new, and much of it had never been touched with the ax of the pioneer.

Two of the districts of this large Conference lay in Indiana, and included all of the settled portions of the State. The Madison District was presided over by Rev. John Strange, and the Indiana District by Rev. James Armstrong.

Mr. Havens was appointed to the Connersville Circuit, which included all of the country above Brookville, on the White Water, as far as the settlements extended. It was reported to contain four hundred and five members.

At that period, John Strange was the most distinguished, as he was considered the most eloquent, preacher in the Conference. Impulsive and eccentric, and full of the fire and zeal of his itinerant mission, his success was only equaled by his popularity, and it was not remarkable that he stood at the head of his Conference.

Tall and straight, and possessing only the accomplishments of a Brush College graduate, he yet had about him the power to command promiscuous assemblies in such a manner as no other minister in the State possessed.

Graceful in action, and clear in utterance, his voice itself was eloquent, and, when he elevated it to its highest pitch, it rang out upon his congregations with a commanding majesty, and subduing force, which could only be compared to the storm winds, when the fierceness of the hurricane is on its track.

Many have attempted to describe the style of his peculiar oratory, but we doubt if any one has ever yet succeeded. It could not be said that he imitated any one who ever preceded him, for he never had a master. He held the people with the enchantment of his intonations, and his pulpit performances were like the charm-power of a musical amateur. The people gathered to hear him by thousands, and he made them laugh and cry, as if they had been but titular subjects, incapable of resistance. All loved him with an ardency which knew no limit, and they consequently listened to his preaching, as if he had been an apostle. No man with a purer spirit, or a greater self-sacrificing zeal, has ever been known among the ministers of the State. This world was not his home. Heaven was alone the song of his soul, and the only objective point of all his expectations.

It is said that a friend once presented him with a deed for a quarter section of land, which afterwards became exceedingly valuable; but he did not accept of it. He thought the earthly allurement might harm him, and he returned the deed to the generous donor, and declined his offer. "If I accept your land," said he, "I will never again be able sing:"

> 'No foot of land do I possess,
> Nor cottage in this wilderness,
> A poor way-faring man.'

In those days it was thought that humility and poverty traveled together, and that nothing would rob a preacher of his spirituality and power, sooner or more certainly, than worldly-mindedness. This, at least, was John Strange's idea, and the conception may possibly have a greater amount of Jerusalem philosophy in it than many may willingly admit of at the present day.

The animus of the ministry in those early times was simple and unobtrusive in all worldly things. Yet, in all that involved the interests of the soul, it was bold and fearless, and full of the fire of an invincible divinity.

Among those who may be properly classed as the cotemporaries of Mr. Havens, none were held in higher esteem than John Strange. He was Mr. Havens' first Indiana Presiding Elder, and their hearts ran together like those of Jonathan and David. For eight years they labored together as bonded yokefellows; and when, on the 2d day of December, 1832, Strange laid off his armor in death, Mr. Havens felt and said that "the brighest star of the Conference had fallen." Young in life and in the ministry, he had at forty-four years of age exchanged the cross for the crown, and was followed to his grave by the lamentations of more people than any minister, perhaps, who has ever died in Indiana.

Rev. Allen Wiley, the eminent doctrinal preacher and studious divine, was another of Mr. Havens' cotemporaries, whose sincere and exalted character secured for him the most distinguished consideration of the Conference, which position he continued to maintain up to the day of his death.

As a theologian, Mr. Wiley had the reputation of being the profoundest of his Conference. To this department he had specifically and studiously directed the chief attention of his life, with the happiest results. Church history, ecclesiastical jurisprudence, and polemic divinity, had commanded his patient studies for years. Hence, he was thoroughly informed in all that comprehends the history of theology, as well as with its numerous and technical doctrines. Like his brother associates, he was no collegiate, for his student days began when such institutions were only a myth in the West. The broad recitation rooms of Nature's Institute, known among the Methodist clergy as "Brush College," afforded him ample opportunities for mental application, which he improved with a studious assiduity that ultimately placed him as a divine in the very first rank among western theologians. Without a master, Mr. Wiley took up the Latin and Greek languages, and while traveling large Circuits and Districts, and doing the full labors of a faithful itinerant, he made himself familiar with their structure and idiom. Though uninfluenced by any thought, or hope of literary emolument, his habits of study, even led him as late as 1844, when he was in New York attending the General Conference, to purchase a supply of Hebrew works, the study of which engaged his attention up to the day of his death. Indeed, it may be said that he was *the pioneer student* among the itinerants of the State. He, more than any other man, set the example of study to the younger ministers, and barked the way for the establishment of the college now so well known in our State, as the "Asbury University." Mr. Wiley had not the eloquence of Strange, nor did he possess the practical heroism of Havens; yet, in classical and theological scholarship, he far excelled them both.

The scholarly attainments of Wesley were his *beau ideal* of ministerial accomplishment, and while he diligently mastered all the doctrinal points of Methodist theology, and made himself familiar with all the peculiarities of Methodist discipline, Mr. Wiley aimed "to show himself a minister who needed not be ashamed" before any audience, or in any pulpit.

Of course his services to the Church bore an invaluable stamp, and held him for many years at the head of his Conference—for humble and patient—arduous and true, he gave all the vigor of his years to her upbuilding, and even when he retired—which was an error which the Conference should never have permitted—he acted in view of others, and not of himself.

The example and wisdom of experienced age, is doubtless, essential to the safe guidance of the ministry in all bodies, and it is on this account that such men should be cared for—even aside from a decent gratitude—because they serve as reliable head lights along the tracks of religious civilization, without which progress is often only deterioration, and even advancement, itself, bears but a dubious character.

The names of Strange and Wiley, Havens and Ruter, Armstrong and Locke, Jones and Oglesby, were associated in the primitive records of Indiana Methodism, and the history of any one of them would involve the life incidents of all the rest. For years, these pioneers, and wilderness evangelists, met in their annual convocations, with perhaps as pure fraternal feelings as often falls to the lot of men. They were brethren, and if at any time there were manifestations of an unpleasant character, the weakness was that of nature rather than of principle, for honest and sincere, as well as deeply conscientious, these humble missionaries, were as tender in their emotions, as they were generous and noble, in all of life's higher and purer sensibilities.

It was our privelege to meet them first at the Conference held in the then village of Lafayette, in the month of October, 1835.

Calvin W Ruter, another of Mr. Havens' old compeers particularly attracted our attention at that conference, for he was tall and athletic, and carried in his mien the dignified air of an intelligent Christian gentleman.

For nearly a score of years he had been identified with the itinerancy, and he stood up among his brethren of that Conference, as a leading chief, whose words bore the majesty of law—while his gentle and conservative spirit only tended to increase his power.

The evidence of his goodness was apparent to every one—and through all the years of his laborious and useful life, he steadily and consistently continued to sustain the same high character. Mr. Ruter was, perhaps, the finest looking man of his Conference, and though not equal to Wiley in scholarship, or to Strange in eloquence, or to Havens in bold energy, he was in his general character and qualifications, for the work of the ministry, the full equal of any of them. His commanding appearance in the pulpit, as on the floor of the Conference, gave him the dignified advantage of the orator, while his tender and pathetic spirit always touched the feelings, and held the respectful regards of his audiences. His preaching was consequently effective and popular, and gave him a position in the Conference among the first and foremost of his brethren.

With James Armstrong and George Locke, we were not acquainted. The former died at Laporte on the 12th of September, 1834, and the latter in New Albany on the 15th of July of the same year. Nehemiah B. Griffith, whose name has been so sacredly blended with those of Armstrong and Locke, died in St. Joseph county, on the 22d of August, also in that year. Losing three such valuable co-laborers, so near together, the Conference felt the loss more severely, and their names, on this account, have always been held in sacred association.

Griffith was zealous, Locke was solid, and Armstrong was eloquent. Thus distinguished, they were valued as workmen above the ordinary character; and when within a few months of each other, their deaths were announced, the solemn emotions of the Conference gave evidence that three of their most valued cotemporaries had fallen. The sorrows of regret manifested on the occasion of the deaths of good men is always a tribute to worth and virtue, which reflects well upon the living as well as upon the dead. Virtue, indeed, need ask for no higher monument than to live in the memories of the good, the true and the noble. For then the moral of its power is best preserved, and the honor of its achievements will have an enduring record.

Among the immediate cotemporaries of Mr. Havens, we may also name the Rev. Joseph Oglesby, whose tall and gaunt form, and small but piercing grey eye, indicated his intellectual and nervous character. Possessing a mind somewhat disposed to metaphysical discussions, Dr. Oglesby was at one time thought by some of his brethren to be a little tinctured with Socinian views, and, at the Conference of 1835, there was some complaint made against him on this score. But as nothing definite could be obtained, the venerable Roberts, who presided at the conference, suggested that Dr. Oglesby had better be heard before he was condemned for heresy. That night the Doctor preached a sermon on original sin and human depravity, before the whole Conference, including the Bishop himself. The next morning his character passed, but not until the venerable Roberts had remarked that "if Dr. Oglesby was a herectic, he himself had been preaching heresy all his life."

The style of Dr. Oglesby's preaching was often highly metaphysical; and while his arguments were clear to the minds of well educated thinkers, they were not always comprehended by the ordinary ones.

Being a physician as well as a minister, Dr. Oglesby had thought, as well as read, and it was not, therefore, strange that, in some of his higher discussions, he was misconstrued by the suspicious or the thick-headed and ignorant. It is not always the better fortune for a preacher to get beyond the depths of his hearers, for, in such cases, he will be liable to failure for the want of proper appreciation. This, perhaps, more than anything else, was the case with the venerable Oglesby. His intellectual power, in its depth and fullness, was not as highly appreciated as it really deserved; for he was evidently a minister of culture, and should have carried down to his grave a much brighter theological renown than many gave him.

But Dr. Oglesby will long be remembered for his eminent pioneer zeal, his numerous sacrifices, his personal piety, as well as for his great usefulness and distinguished abilities. He died in the city of Madison, in the year 1850.

Of James Jones and James L. Thompson, we may also make honorable mention in this connection, for both of them were long associated with Mr. Havens in the work of the itinerancy, and were held by him in the highest esteem. They were both true yoke-fellows in the gospel harness, and successful laborers in the great vineyard of Indiana itinerancy.

There were many others who were long associated in the work of the ministry with the venerable Havens, whose characters might be justly sketched up in this brief chapter, but most of them were of a younger class, and, therefore, may be termed associates rather than cotemporaries. Rev. Aaron Wood, D. D., who is still living, and whom we have the honor to claim as our first Presiding Elder, was on the Connersville Circuit in 1823, the year before Mr. Havens, having been admitted on trial in the Ohio Conference in 1822. Dr. Wood, however, was a younger man, and belongs legitimately to a succeeding generation, as is the case also with the eloquent Richard Hargrave. Both of these distinguished Methodist divines are still living, though they, too, are passing rapidly before another generation, who are treading closely upon their heels. The rapidity of the flying decades gives such transitions in the ministerial life as should lead us to remember that "dust we are and unto dust shall we all return."

There is power in everything of a cotemporaneus character, which is apt to make it sacred, and in the holy work of the ministry, and particularly in the old pioneer sacrifices of the Methodist itinerancy, there was found an affinity of brotherhood—a sacred bond of fraternity, which gave to the ministry a purity, and an unselfish dignity, which if it was not legitimately apostolic, was at least divine.

There were then no rich stations for the ambitious to be jealous about, and no fat circuits for the aspiring to ask for. Even the Presiding Elders, who were in those days, the fathers of the Conference—had the hardest fields, and were called upon to make the greatest sacrifices. What is now known as a salary, or even as an allowance, for support, was unknown among these early pioneer itinerants and when they met in their annual Conferences and reported the amount of quarterage received, it was evident to all that sacrifice was the common order of their support.

It was not therefore marvelous, that the friendships of such men were sincere. They knew each other as heroes in a common cause, and the grand success of their battle fields, in connection with their personal and family sufferings, gave them the most implicit confidence in one another.

Their common fortunes made them fraternal while the zeal and spirit of their itinerant chivalry, led them on to victory, often regardless of personal health, and with but few thoughts of who should be the greatest in the Kingdom of Heaven. Such men deserve the honors of a perpetual memory.

CHAPTER XXIII.

HIS LOCAL MINISTRY.

The practical system of theological schools instituted by the Methodists, first in Europe and then in America, of licensing local preachers, was as novel as it was primitive.

It demanded no stately edifice with collegiate endowments, or scholastic Professors to teach young novitiates the lessons of anatomic theology, or to polish them off with the accomplishments of linguistic lore. All such attainments—however highly prized they may be in the present day—would have utterly failed of appreciation among the early settlers of the West.

Sincere, and earnest, and zealous men were the only proper workmen for those early times. Men who held the higher commission, the superior qualifications of being pious, and humble, and self-sacrificing, and fearless, and who cared more to possess the spirit of Christ than they did for any qualifications or greatness mankind could give them, were the only ministers who had success among the people, or who could meet the public will.

Heroic and self taught, and under the conviction that they were called of God to the work of the ministry, they never thought of waiting for "calls," or churches, or salaries. They, indeed, "stood not on the order of their going," anywhere, but having experienced pardon themselves, they felt constrained to publish it to others. It was not human science that they aimed to teach, but the love of Christ. Hence they made no pretensions to human greatness of any sort. They gave themselves alone to the work of the ministry, and were recognized as the instruments of numerous conversions, which in those days, was considered the strongest evangelical evidence of being called of God to the work.

The field was large and the harvest great, and sincere and honest laborers were welcomed everywhere by both preachers and people. Many young men were licensed to preach, whose literary educations were limited to the mere qualification of being able to read in a stammering manner the word of God. Right in heart, because of their baptism by the Holy Spirit, and poorly educated as they were, they carried with them a power which was readily recognized, as it moved all hearts, and often resulted in revivals which worked reform, even in the most hardened neighborhoods.

The principle became a fixed one among the early Methodists, that the power of usefulness was always the best evidence of divine endowments. Hence, it was not a difficult matter for them to believe that he had "a call to preach" who had "gifts, grace and fruits," no matter how deficient he might be in education or general knowledge.

In the economy of the Methodist Episcopal Church, the power to license men to preach has always been invested in the Quarterly Conferences, which are composed of the Presiding Elder of the District—who is ex *officio* President—the preachers of the Circuit, or Station, and the stewards and class leaders. But even they can not license any one to preach, unless he is first recommended by the class of private members to which he belongs.

The fact is, therefore, a patent one, that all Methodist preachers have to come up from among the people, who are the primary judges of their characters, abilities and qualifications, as well as of their future promise. To this peculiar feature of Methodism, we, undoubtedly, may refer the fact, that many have become eminently useful, and others eminently distinguished, who, if they had "tarried at Jericho until their beards were grown," would never have preached a sermon, or have been known in the ministry. Especially would this have been the case with Mr. Havens, for, when he was converted, as he often used to say, "he knew nothing, save that he was a sinner saved by grace." His field of thought and education had been, up to that hour, only the mere privileges of the wilderness. With books and schools he had had no communication; and though he had life and health, and the bold energy of a noble young manhood, the great purposes and aims of his life had never occurred to him, and, indeed, they did not until his heart was moved by the spirit of God to repentance, when his eyes were first opened and he began to see that

" It was not the whole of life to live,"

and that there was a work for him to do which God required at his hands; and though young and ignorant, and without the means to obtain an education, he at once heroically determined to make the best of his poor circumstances, and, come what might, he would give his life to the services of preaching the gospel of the Lord Jesus Christ.

Timid and always confident of his own weakness, his reliance for success was on the arm that was alone almighty. The Holy Bible, was the text book of his life, and he made it the man of his counsel, and the guide of his years. This invaluable treasury of spiritual light and infinite ideas, he read day and night, with a reverence which was as profound and sincere as was his faith. This book of books, in his esteem, was infinitely above all others, and to his high and abiding regard for all its declarations, we may, doubtless, attribute the particular soundness of his theology through all the years of his ministry.

Without a master to teach him, or a school to lead him on, with a self-reliance and perseverance, as noble as they were rare, he by the steady dint of labored thought, forced his way toward the temple of divine knowledge, gathering strength from the richness of his personal experience and from the fields of his practical operations; and possessing, as he did, a voice of commanding power, he had no difficulty in obtaining a congregation whenever he made an appointment.

Having married about the time he was licensed to preach, it became more difficult for him to enter the itinerant field, as there were but few of the circuits in those days that could support more than one married preacher, and where there were two on a circuit one of them was nearly always a single man. Consequently he remained in a local relation to the Church, preaching at such times and places as he was able, and as was the custom in that day with all local preachers, getting nothing for his labors.

But immediately after the Conference of 1818, Rev. John Collins, then Presiding Elder of the Scioto District, finding Mr. Havens among the local preachers of the district, and preceiving, which he quickly did, that he had a tongue of readiness and a good share of what they called in those days "the itinerant fire," he engaged him to travel the Scioto Circuit in the place of Thomas Lowery. Job M. Baker was the preacher in charge of the circuit, who gave him a kind and genial welcome as his assistant, and encouraged him to never think of anything else but to spend his life in the labors of the itinerancy. The manly forbearance and fraternal sympathy of Job M. Baker, Mr. Havens never forgot. Even down to the latest period of his life, he seemed never to think of his first colleague without expressing the kindliest gratitude for the many tokens of his gentle and Christian attentions. He knew he was ignorant, and he felt that he was but a poor preacher at best, and to be treated as an equal and encouraged as a brother, was more than he expected. Had Mr. Baker been the reverse in his character and dealt unkindly with his young assistant, it might have been that Mr. Havens would have given up all his itinerant aspirations and the world and the Church would have lost the fruitful benefits of his long and distinguished labors.

We have known young preachers to be driven from the field of the ministry—yea and even some old ones too—by the indiscreet conduct of ambitious men who as Shakspeare has it—

> "Dressed in a little brief authority,
> Play such fantastic tricks before high heaven,
> As make the angels weep."

Such specimens of the *genus homo* have ever been found in the ministry, and perhaps always will be, whose liberal acquaintance but seldom extends beyond themselves. Like the Indian, they know "big man me," and on him they exhaust all the little store of their selfish partialities. The large and generous feelings of the priestly character they never know, and wherever such ministers are found, like the Indian's gun, "they cost more than they come to."

The following year, Mr. Havens was employed again as a local supply by the same Presiding Elder, but on the Deer Creek Circuit, with Rev. John Brown, in charge.

Mr. Havens had not the indorsement of being an appointee of the Conference. His relation was only that of a local preacher, which, as some measure it, is a sort of an anomalous relationship in the ministry, as it gives the preacher no charge, and, consequently, no pay, and yet it holds him responsible for the exercise of his gifts and office, both as a member of the church and also as a preacher. The economy seems, however, to recognize the relation as a *corps de reserve*, rather than as a distinct and instituted class in the regular ministry. But humble and unpretending as the relationship may be, it has constituted, through all its history, an arm of strength in the wide-spread field of itinerant Methodism, the fidelity and usefulness of which has been acknowledged in every department of the Church. It was to this corps that Mr. Havens properly belonged, though the Presiding Elder had him exercising his gifts and graces in an itinerant capacity. But how well he would succeed he knew not, and with many doubts and fears he had yielded to the solicitations of the venerable Collins to try the work of a "Circuit Rider" another year.

The boundaries of a circuit in the State of Ohio in 1819, usually included the entire territory of three or four counties, and contained preaching places, which were either private dwellings or school houses, and gave an appointment, and sometimes two, for every day in the month.

It required four weeks to go round one of these circuits, and, as the preachers followed each other, the system gave the people preaching regularly every two weeks. The more prominent localities enjoyed the privileges of Sabbath services, while all others had to put up with week day preaching, which, indeed, they were glad to get, as it was their only chance of hearing the gospel at all. Though preaching to thousands in their rounds, these indefatigable gospel pioneers but seldom got more than one or two hundred dollars a year for their services. These figures usually constituted the maximum of their pay, and were only realized on the more popular and wealthier circuits. On most of the circuits, the "quarterage" contributions were but feeble mites, and when divided, as they always were, at the quarterly meetings, between the Presiding Elder and the two "Circuit Riders," the result only made a starving display, a meager remuneration of arduous labors, which demonstrated to the people that they were not sitting under "a sordid ministry."

Several circumstances conspired to make this a year of severe trial to Mr. Havens. His talents were far above his education, and, as a matter of course, in his bold style of declamation, he would sometimes "murder the King's English," and violate the rules of grammar, however strong and vigorous might be his rhetoric. These blunders, though unnoticed among the great masses of his hearers, gave room for certain scholastic upstarts to find fault with and to criticise him. Of course he was sensitive, for he knew and felt his deficiencies, but how to remedy them he knew not, except by the slow process of his own self-teaching.

At the beginning of his labors on this Deer Creek Circuit, one who also sustained the relation of a local preacher, a short time after his first introduction to Mr. Havens, approached him with a scowling and dissocial air, and scanning him from head to foot, broke in upon him about as follows:

"Well, Havens, you look as little like a preacher as anybody I've ever seen. No doubt you think because you wear boots and carry a pair of saddle-bags, that you're somebody. If I had my way I'd send you home, and set you to raising corn."

Such insinuations, coming from a man who was himself a preacher, while they savored heavily of the deepest moral impudence, were not without their painfully mortifying power over the young assistant. He could but feel that it was rather a delicate matter to thus joke on palpable facts. But he well knew that his ignorance was his misfortune, and not his crime, and, therefore, he felt that he was yet on the Lord's side, even if he was a weak instrument in the ministry.

Another of these indiscreet critics, who was also in the local ministry, some time after this took Mr. Havens to one side and seriously advised him "to quit and go home; that he never would make a preacher."

Fortunately for the church, and for the salvation of thousands, these imprudent, not to say impudent advisors, did not succeed in their designs. Mr. Havens had the nerve of the hero as well as the spirit of the ministry, and he well knew that it took something better than good grammar and respectable appearances to convert souls.

His was a mission for the souls of men, and he felt impelled to execute it even at the risk of human ridicule, or the visible insinuations of a pedantic and envious brotherhood. His experience told him that God was his friend, and he saw each round that he made on his circuit that souls were converted through his humble instrumentality. In his convictions such testimony was more than golden, and after passing through such trying ordeals, his heart gathered new fire, as he sang and prayed around his numerous forest altars. When under such clouds he often sang—

> "Fear not, I am with thee; O, be not dismayed,
> For I am thy God, and will still give thee aid;
> I'll strengthen thee, help thee and cause thee to stand,
> Upheld by my righteous, omnipotent hand."

Only some two or three years after this one of these local preachers who had talked so discouragingly to Mr. Havens, met him at a camp meeting where it fell to Mr. Havens' lot to preach to a large congregation at the popular Sunday hour. The occasion was an important one, which the preacher felt more sensibly, perhaps, than any one on the ground. Many other preachers were present, but the Presiding Elder had given him the hour and it only remained for him to meet the emergency, which he did in such a manner and with such a spirit of success and of gospel triumph, as led the repentant local preacher greatly to his honor as well as to his Christian character, to call Mr. Havens out to a private confession after the sermon, when with a heart full of emotion he entreated him to forgive and forget "how he had abused him while he was on the Deer Creek Circuit."

Mr. Havens assured the brother that he had not abused him at all, for said he, "Every word you then said about my ignorance was all true, and I am glad you ever told me of it, for it made me determined to make such efforts to improve as would prevent all others from ever again telling me the same story." From that hour the two were friends, for none ever won on Mr. Havens' friendship more than the man of frankness. He was plain himself—and sometimes even blunt and rough—but being honest in it all, he was disposed to accredit the same honorable motives in others. He well knew that the naked truth often cut keenly, but he loved it the better on that account.

CHAPTER XXIV

HIS CIRCUITS.

The institution of circuit preaching, on the plan of the itinerancy, has opened the way for the exercise of every variety of talent in the ministry. As is well known, lay preachers chiefly occupied this field in the outstart of Methodism, and, when the work extended to America, the same ministerial order was continued until the regular organization of the Methodist Episcopal Church in the year 1784. From that period the preachers have been ordained deacons after two, and elders after four years' service in the itinerancy; while local preachers have been required to serve about twice as long before they could receive ordination.

Having had some two years' experience on circuits, as a local preacher, while employed by Presiding Elders, Mr. Havens was in some sense prepared by experience to take the charge of a work, of which fact the Conference must have been convinced, or he would not have received his first appointment without a colleague. To go to a circuit alone in those early days, was not devoutly wished for among the preachers, for they were generally sent by twos, as it was deemed the better plan, as well as more in accordance with the old Apostolic custom.

Salt Creek was Mr. Havens' first circuit in the Conference; and though it was both a large and rough one, its title, one might think, assured him of his "salt," however meager might be his other supplies.

The hills were steep and rugged, and the stream which designated his field of toil had often to be crossed, and, as its waters were both deep and rapid, the effort, at times, gave the young itinerant good reasons to fear that he might never reach in safety the opposite shore. He had to preach some thirty times every four weeks in making his round on the work; and, as there was not a church, or meeting house, in its bounds, all his religious services were held either in log school houses, or else in the cabin-homes of the people. The rides were long, and often cold as well as dangerous; and the lonely monotony of the dreary travel was only broken by the grandeur of Nature's scenery—or by the stealthy tread of wild animals through the thick and gigantic forests.

The quarterly meetings of the year brought to his society and aid the venerable Samuel West, who was his Presiding Elder, to which periods he always looked with the warmest anticipations. Mr. West was a good preacher, and one of the very best of Christian men, and in each of his visits he cheered the young circuit rider with the happy relations of his own experience, and entertained him with many interesting incidents of his itinerant travels, which did much to spur up his zeal and to lead him to determine not to lay down the cross until he did so to receive his crown.

All around his work the people treated him kindly, and it was only now and then that he met with any who might have been termed "the beasts of Ephesus."

A few of this latter class, of course, stumbled upon him here and there, but the contest was always a short one, as he well knew how to manage them. The old fire of western chivalry had long before taught him never to run from a foe, and no matter who interfered with his religious meetings, he was always ready to stand in his own defense, and if it was forced upon him, he was not wholly averse to give them a lesson in some sort of gymnastics, and in such a way as to make them remember him.

The year 1821, found Mr. Havens on the Straight Creek Circuit, as it was customary in those days to change every preacher at each Conference, and give him a new field. This, it was thought in that day, was the only sure way to keep up the itinerancy. Straight Creek was nearer Mr. Havens' home than Salt Creek, and was as large a circuit, and in many respects was very much like it, and on this representation of it, he went to it with a cheerful determination to do his duty. He had no colleague, which he felt to be his greatest trial, for the whole year would pass away, probably, without his being privileged to see any of his itinerant brethren except his Presiding Elder. In the quarterly visitations of such an Elder as he had this year—Greenbury R. Jones—Mr. Havens realized that his quarterly meetings were seasons of refreshing beyond what he had ever experienced before.

The name of Greenbury R. Jones, was not only a power in the Conference, but also among the people, for as a preacher, he was recognized as one of the most eloquent men of the West. On this circuit Mr. Havens was greatly favored in his work, and met with a success which showed him to be worthy of even a leadership among his brethren. He found 391 members in his circuit and at the close of the Conference year he reported 625. In the zeal of his mission he often preached day and night, and wherever he went, the people gathered in the cabins to hear him with admiring and implicit confidence.

The Conference of 1822, which was held at Marietta, placed Mr. Havens on Brush Creek Circuit, with Henry B. Bascom, as preacher in charge.

Having been admitted into full connection and ordained Deacon by Bishop R. R. Roberts, at this Conference, Mr. Havens was now in full standing among his brethren, and as he had heard his name read out in connection with that of the most eloquent preacher of the Conference it was natural that he should have well grounded fears, that, in comparison with his colleague he would be almost a cipher. He knew that he had only been preaching along the creeks of Ohio, for the past three years, and as he expressed himself, he "did not expect to be able to hold a candle by the side of Bascom."

Brush Creek was a large field of labor, and its mountainous hills made the travel as laborious as the preaching. Within its bounds, however, were many families of intelligence, and the membership numbered nearly one thousand. Bascom's father and mother resided in the lower part of the circuit, where he of course made his home. At this point the two itinerants often met, and the warm and genial brotherhood which grew up between them during the intercourse of the year, made them friends all the rest of their lives.

Generous of heart and always moved by the noblest impulses, Bascom never stood on formalities or held back for a moment when humanity was to be served, for refined and lofty, both in his air and spirit, he scorned the heartless distinctions of the world's pride, and consequently, he had a heart of sympathy, as well as of affinity, for any one who had about him the true ring of a generous humanity. The year's association of these two ministers was never forgotten, but was often referred to by both of them as a bright and cheerful *oasis* in their itinerant histories.

Scioto Circuit was Mr. Havens' third appointment. To this field, on which he had before spent a year, under the Presiding Elder, he was now sent by the Conference, with William Simmons, as his colleague. This was Mr. Simmons' third circuit, and his large heart and generous nature, made him a most agreeable companion, which, with the numerous greetings of old friends, made the year an exceedingly pleasant one for Mr. Havens. Of course society was yet primitive along the Scioto—but the frankness of the old western hospitality made the original cabins appear as palaces, and the inmates, however, rustic, had about them generally much of the nobleness and purity of a sincere religious humanity.

The General Conference of 1824 having made a number of grand divisions among the western Conferences, Mr. Havens attended the Ohio Conference in the Fall of that year, at Zanesville, for the last time. His large and growing family, he knew was unsuited to the privations of the itinerant work, and after mature deliberations, he determined to make Indiana his future home, as well as the field of his subsequent labors, and he therefore took a transfer to the Illinois Conference, which from that period included not only the territory of Illinois but also that of Indiana.

In the month of November, 1824, Mr. Havens removed his family to Spring Hill, Decatur county, Indiana, and the Illinois Conference appointed him to the Connersville Circuit. Rev. John Strange was his Presiding Elder, who was traveling a district which included about one-fourth of the State.

That fall Mr. Havens began his work on the Connersville Circuit with renewed vigor and success, and the following spring, he entered a quarter section of land three miles west of the town of Rushville, on which he and his sons erected a rude log cabin, into which he moved his family even before it was fairly finished. In this humble cabin home, and on this quarter section of land his large family continued to live through a large portion of his itinerant years.

It was perhaps the next season after this cabin was erected, that Mrs. Havens and her sons, in the absence of the husband and father, determined to move it, "turret and foundation," to another part of the quarter section. The resolve was accomplished, while the family was sheltered under an improvised tent, in which they spent several days and nights.

A week or two passed away and Mr. Havens, having a distant appointment on his Circuit, essayed to reach his cabin-home before night fall, but in this he failed, for darkness was around him when he arrived at the spot where he had last seen it. But the cabin was gone; not a log of it was left, and, for a few moments, his feelings were most unenviable.

He dismounted from his horse perfectly unable to comprehend the situation. He stood and looked and wondered what magic power had spirited away his humble dwelling; but a little closer inspection showed him the traces of the logs, as they appeared to have been drawn away to another locality. He followed the trace through the dark forest, when his heart was relieved as he saw the curling smoke ascending from what appeared to be the same identical cabin. Hitching his horse to the limb of a tree, with his saddle-bags on his arm, he knocked at the door, when he was met by his "better half," whom he found alive and well, and with the children happily engaged in cracking hickory nuts.

Mrs. Havens soon explained the circumstances of the situation. She and the boys thought that it would be cheaper to move the cabin to the spring than it would be to move the spring to the cabin, and they had done it all within five days. Such an economist was essential as the wife of an itinerant in those times, for the Connersville Circuit, though extensive in territory, and including several county seats, only yielded him, all told, $56.06¼ for his year's services.

The Conference of 1825 appointed Mr. Havens to the Whitewater Circuit, on which he continued two years. John Strange was his Presiding Elder, and the second year, John T. Johnson was his assistant.

The year 1827, brought him back to the Rushville Circuit, with Allen Wiley as his Presiding Elder.

The Conference of 1828 gave him a supernumerary relation, and returned him to Rushville Circuit, with John Kerns, a young man just admitted into the Conference, as preacher in charge.

The year 1829, he sustained the same relation but was appointed to the Whitewater Circuit, with Lorenzo D. Smith as his assistant.

In 1830, his health was so poor that he had to take a superannuated relation, but in 1831, it was again changed to that of supernumerary. The sudden death of Rev. Benj. C. Stephenson occurring directly after Conference, Mr. Havens was called to fill his place in the Indianapolis station. His appointment to this new field, though he was still in very precarious health, ended the circuit work of his itinerant life. For some twelve years he had been engaged in this class of appointments, and as they required a sermon for almost every day in the year, the continued attacks of fever and ague, in connection with his excessive labors, had so reduced him in health that many feared that his days of usefulness were gone by forever.

What he had done in this circuit work may not now be comprehended by the sermon labors of our present circuits, for most of the fields which he had traveled counted from twenty-five to thirty appointments, and demanded about thirty sermons a month, which, in the year, would make at least three hundred sermons. The circuits of the present day do not, we presume, average over ten sermons a month. But

22

through all this immense labor of traveling and preaching, Mr. Havens had gone for twelve or fifteen years, when he found himself miserably diseased by the foul miasma of the early settlements, and borne down by repeated attacks of fever and ague, he became convinced that he was traveling very near the doors of death.

Some have thought Mr. Havens did not make very great sacrifices for the church, because he did not move his family through most of his circuit days. Such a requisition as that, if it had been made, would have driven him from the work entirely, for his family was large, much larger than usually falls to the lot of men. His children ultimately numbered fifteen, all of whom lived to maturity, not one of them dying until the father had attained his sixty-fourth year.

The humble cabin-home, in which he had placed his family because he was compelled to do so or retire from the work of the itinerancy, was a sacrifice which but few men would make even for the sake of the gospel. But this he did, not because he lacked in love for his wife and children, or because he was indifferent in regard to their proper education, but it was the compulsion of necessity—the demanded sacrifice required at the hands of the early itinerants. Here in Indiana, many brave moral heroes were associated with him, who laid down their lives in the primitive itinerancy of the State. They did not die of age or from any natural diseases; but they heroically fell at their posts, like soldiers on the battle field, with all their armor on. Exposed to long rides, and to liabilities of almost every conceivable character, in eating and sleeping, and often but poorly protected from the inclemency of the weather—riding on horseback through winds and storms of rain and snow—frequently swimming the wildest streams to reach their appointments, many of them have broken down, and in a few brief years sank to untimely graves. A few, who yet linger on the walls of Zion as active laborers, and who had some participating knowledge in these sacrificing and trying circuit labors, will bear their testimony that we are not coloring up tragic stories in the statements we here give of these early itinerants. We do not here allude to them with any purpose of drawing disparaging contrasts between *then* and *now*. This is not our wish or design. We aim only to recount the noble deeds of that heroic faith and labor of love, which laid the foundations of our present "grand temple," and which now give moral shelter to a hundred thousand members, and a hundred thousand Sunday School scholars, besides opening up a beautiful moral pathway of health and substantial support for half a thousand ministerial itinerants.

The invaluable labors of these early pioneers can not well be estimated too highly, and their memories should be embalmed in the hearts of all who have the least respect for any of the grand evangelisms of Indiana.

The work of the moral hero is certainly far above that of the military; for the one gives his life energies to preserve men from death, while the other only marches to the throne of his power and fame over the fallen bodies of his fellow men. Both may be patriots and true to their country, but surely he who has kindled the fires of a renewed life for the benefit of the million is God's noblest workman, and, therefore, should hold the place imperial.

CHAPTER XXV.

HIS STATIONS.

IN 1820, when Mr. Havens was admitted on trial in the Ohio conference, there was no such thing known as a station in the great broad West. Circuits constituted the uniform order of the itinerancy, and such was the universality of this plan of the work that the horse was as essential as the man, to meet the true itinerant conception.

This itinerancy, then, admitted of no invidious, or class distinctions, for every preacher was a "Circuit Rider." The system in its entire simplicity was certainly Apostolic, if it was not also the most successful known to the modern ages, for the development of its zeal and talents, as well as *for the high cast of its* eloquence and oratory. The bold and suggestive majesty, the thrilling and masterly eloquence of the early Methodist preachers, grew into a proverb. Without the knowledge of the classics, many of them were as eloquent as Cicero, and the wild storms of their oratorical declamations often held the mighty multitudes, as if they were chained to their rude seats as with the lightnings of Heaven.

Who that has ever listened to the eloquent and stirring appeals of Waterman or Bascom, Christie or Bigelow, Stamper or Kavenaugh, but will admit that they have never heard many who were their superiors. Or who that has ever attended any of the camp meetings of such itinerants as Finley or Elliott, Strange or Havens, but will yield to them the palm of having been grand marshals on the divine battle field. The style of oratory of such men, had in it the soul of a divinity, which struck fire as the flint, and kindling its consuming flame, it burned as with the power of Omnipotence.

Nature often makes orators far superior to those of the schools, and in this institution of "the higher charter" most of these early Methodist divines received their only diplomas. Having traveled many thousands of miles on horse-back through all seasons, visiting the recitation rooms of nature, and conversing frequently and intimately with all of her learned Professors, the lightnings, the thunders and storms of the night, and with the sun itself through many a long, weary day, these extraordinary men entered the world clothed upon with Heaven's sure artillery. Soldiers of the cross, they were willing to face any danger, and commissioned from Heaven they felt themselves rich without a dollar. Consequently, they made no compromises with the world of gain, but preached what they believed to be the truth, perfectly fearless of all human circumstances.

With endowments of this order, but with shattered health, in the fall of 1831, Mr. Havens, after taking a superannuated relation at the Conference, accepted of a call to the Indianapolis station, to which Rev Benjamin C. Stephenson had been appointed. Mr. Stephenson died some two short months after his marriage to an excellent widow lady in the city of

Madison, in which city he had labored the previous year. Mr. Havens immediately repaired to this new field, and entered upon the labors of a stationed minister at the Capital, with a zeal and power which greatly astonished his old friends. For four years he had served them in the capacity of Presiding Elder, and though he was highly esteemed among them in this relationship, his popular power over them was greatly increased, when his congregation came to hear him twice every Sabbath.

His audiences were large and in them were seen many of the best cultivated minds of the community. The membership of the church then counted two hundred and fifty-five, but his audiences frequently numbered from four to five hundred.

As this was his first station, Mr. Havens made every possible effort to discover the difference between the workings of the station system and that of the circuit. The one he had been familiar with through all his ministerial life—but the other was comparatively a new departure, particularly in Indiana, and though he had, during his Presiding Eldership seen something of its operations, he was not yet fully satisfied that it would prove the more efficient plan.

The older itinerants had witnessed the grand revival success of the old circuit system, and it was not very natural for them to fall in love at once, with the plan of sending one man to preach to the same congregation for one and perhaps two years.

Other denominations were chiefly comfined to this one man station system, and it was argued by the old

Circuit Riders, that it would lead to formality, sermon reading, and to mere sterreotyped devotional usages. They thought it might build up a sort of mechanical Christianity, and if it was generally adopted among the Methodists the preachers might become theological, automatons, instead of being the flaming heralds of a present and free salvation.

Mr. Havens was yet only in the prime of his years, but his health was poor, and he was only kept in the work by the energy of his indomitable will. The universal kindness of his friends made him feel at home in his work, and the large congregations which crowded out to hear him every Sabbath gave him a a full and fair opportunity of doing good on what might be termed a large scale.

His quarterly meetings brought to his aid the heroic and eloquent Strange, who was then making his last rounds on the district work of this lower world, and though sinking gradually under the deceptious flatteries of a pulmonary disease, he stood up in the pulpit before his weeping audiences and "swept the lyre of his song" with a voice as shrill and awakening as when he enjoyed perfect health. The hearts of these two gospel ministers beat in as happy unison as any two itinerants who have ever been known in the State.

Possessing the common genius of a true and natural eloquence, and belonging to the Alumni of the grand old "Brush College," they had drunk of the same clear waters, and washed in the same old fountains, and their hearts were one.

Thus far in life their paths had been in the same direction, and the trumpets of Israel had called them together at "the front" on many a battle field ; and now it was by the mysterious order of Providence that they were spending the last earthly year of their association together.

Strange was a poor man and so was Havens, for up to that period, and, indeed, for many years after, the stipends of Indiana itinerants were only barely sufficient to keep soul and body from forcible divorcement.

The service of their lives had been given to the preaching of the gospel, always subject to annual removals, and without any of the circumstances of a fixed or definite salary.

The quarterage allowance of one hundred dollars for the married preacher, and the same for his wife, and twenty-four dollars for each child over seven and under fourteen, and sixteen dollars for all children under seven, constituted the only disciplinary provision of the Church for the support of her ministry up to the General Conference of 1836, consequently it was under this regime that these two faithful servants had thus far spent their ministry. The moral and spiritual civilization of the people had been their one living pursuit; and in the fulfillment of their duties, and in the accomplishment of this grand object they had found their highest wealth, as well as their most substantial joys.

The fact may not now be readily credited, but several of the old Quarterly Conference journals which we have seen, show that Mr. Strange, as Presiding

Elder, had only received for his share of the quarterage brought up "for the support of the gospel," the meager sums of fifty and seventy-five cents. These contributions, however, were no evidence of the parsimoniousness of the people, for many of them but seldom saw a dollar, and instances have often occurred where men worked out in the harvest field at fifty cents a day, or split rails on the same wages, to get their money to help support the preacher.

The year Mr. Havens spent in the Indianapolis station was, in many respects, a pleasant one, and made him friends who remained such to the latest period of his life.

The only cloud which the close of the year left over him was the declining health of Mr. Strange, who was compelled to take a superannuated relation, as his earthly pilgrimage was evidently about to close.

Mr. Havens was called to take a district when Mr. Strange retired, and was continued in this relation, with the exception of one year when he was agent of the Preachers' Aid Society, until the Conference of 1844, when he was appointed to the Rushville Station, which was his old home where he had preached more sermons than he had in any place of his former labors. But the people received him gladly, and among them he spent one of the happiest years of his life. They knew him well, both as a man and a minister, and they venerated him as one of the Apostles of the Conference.

The next year he asked for a removal, and he was sent to Greensburg, which was a larger field, and in his view opened before him a better opportunity of success.

The general idea of these older itinerants was, a new man and a new field for success, and to this iron rule they sacrificed domestic ease, social power, and the strong ties of long acquaintance without the selfish show of a single regret.

As a stationed preacher, Mr. Havens never sank into the coldness of a lifeless monotony, for he met his congregations from Sabbath to Sabbath with the appeals of a sincere and earnest heart, and in no instance was he ever known to give them what some have termed "cold coffee warmed over."

Rich in the deep thought of his soul, and always carrying with him a zeal kindled by a live coal from off the divine altar, he held his audiences by the enchantment of a power evidently more than human. What he said was said simply and earnestly, without notes or manuscript, and he often bore off his congregations with flights of faith and inspiration such as no pen can well describe.

The duties of a stationed preacher he saw were quite different from those of a Presiding Elder; but, old as he was, he aimed faithfully to perform them. He often met the classes and led the prayer meetings, and visited the members, because he understood these duties to be especially required in all stations.

Though always distinguished for his social qualities, as well as his plain and frank manners, he, in his intercourse among the people, knew well how to preserve the dignity of the minister, and to command respect, which he always did at the hands of all classes of the community. And yet he never pandered to the pride of the rich, or in any way encouraged the building up of a church aristocracy.

The assertion has often been made in regard to him that he knew no distinctions among men, save those made by vice and virtue. The poor and the ignorant found him their friend, and even the wicked realized the fact that he did not feel himself too good "to beard the lion in his den."

In this station Mr. Havens had none to stand to his back, both in counsel and support, with more steady and fraternal consistency than Mr. Silas Stewart and Mr. Ira Grover. They had both been devoted Methodists from their early manhood, and in any church would have served as substantial pillars.

The year closed, and Mr. Havens, true to the old itinerant idea of annual removals, was at the next Conference appointed to the Laurel Station. In this place he had labored in former years, and his name was as "familiar as household words."

Laurel had been laid out by Rev. James Conwell, a local elder in the Methodist Episcopal Church, who was a wealthy farmer, a large pork dealer and merchant, and one of the most zealous and successful local preachers of Eastern Indiana.

As a station, the field was new to Mr. Havens, and he began his work with a full determination to show himself a minister that need not be ashamed. The whole community crowded out to hear him, and his congregations filled the church to overflowing. Within a few months his labors were honored with one of the greatest revivals ever known in the place. Many of the best citizens of the village and vicinity connected themselves with the church, with a large number of young men and women. The work was evidently of the genuine stamp, and the old hero moved among them as if the blood of his youth had returned to him again. He felt that history was repeating itself, and that the spiritual wand of his earlier years was laid upon the people with the hand of the Divine power.

In the midst of these joyful exultations, he was reminded that every cup of earthly bliss is more or less mingled with gall, for one night, while he and his family were absent at meeting, his dwelling took fire, and before the flames could be subdued, his furniture, books and papers, were all consumed; not even leaving him the sacred relic of his earlier years, his well-worn and highly cherished "old-fashioned family Bible."

Of course his loss was largely made up, but the notes of his sermons and many records of value to himself, relating to the history of the past, were all gone, and the dull, dead ashes were all that was left of them.

But nothing daunted or discouraged, he pursued his work with zeal through the year, and when the Conference again met he was induced to return to the charge for a second term.

During this year, as in the past, the work went on, and the interest in his sermons and exhortations never flagged, nor did he let down in any respect in the spirit of his zeal.

From Laurel, Mr, Havens was again called to the work of a district, and for seven or eight years he continued in his old relation as Presiding Elder, until the fall of 1855, when he was admonished by his declining energies and health to accept of the nominal appointment of Conference Missionary.

In 1861, the preacher who was stationed at Strange Chapel, in Indianapolis, accepted of a chaplaincy in the Union army, and a unanimous call was extended by the members of that charge to Father Havens, as he was then universally called. True to the instincts of his earlier ministry, he accepted of the invitation, and as his children were now all married, he and the venerable companion of his life took up their abode in the parsonage of that church, and once more, after an interregnum of some six years, he was again the pastor of a flock. This charge was his last life appointment, and though he was now feeble and well stricken in years, the fires of youth often flashed in his sermons, and the turgid eloquence of his former years was frequently manifested. The venerable cognomen of "the old man eloquent," was kindly applied to him by many who crowded his church to hear the oldest apostle of Indiana Methodism. Not for his own name did he speak, but the same old spirit of his ancient zeal moved him to preach for souls, to call sinners to repentance, and to lead the members of the charge on to still higher victories. This work closed the pastoral services of his long and useful life.

CHAPTER XXVI.

HIS DISTRICTS AND CHARACTER AS PRESIDING ELDER.

The office of Presiding Elder is one of the peculiarities of Methodism which seems to have grown up as a necessity in the itinerancy. The power of stationing the ministers and preachers of the Conferences having been placed in the hands of the Bishops of the Church, it became necessary for these general superintendents to call to their aid some of the older and leading members of each Conference to assist them in making these appointments. This, of course, soon led to the institution of the office of Presiding Elder, and the test of experience, of almost a hundred years, has vindicated it to be a wise and efficient wheel in the itinerant economy. As a part of the general machinery of the Church, this economy has had to pass through the fiery furnace of criticism and protest, of conflict and animadversion, where its practicability has, perhaps, been as severely tried as any other feature of Methodist polity. Some have objected to the mode of appointing Presiding Elders; while others have found fault with the measure of their power. Others, while admitting the necessity of the office, have contended that only the leading and most gifted men of the Conference should be appointed to it; while others, again, have argued that the office should be given in turns to all the experienced men of the Conferences in rotation, and without any partiality. Many, also, have held the opinion that no one should serve as Presiding Elder more than one term at a time, and not a few have advocated the theory that the office should be abolished altogether.

But so far, none of these doubtful improvements have been tried or adopted. Those who have had the power of legislating for the Church have been exceedingly cautious in changing any of its organic laws, and this part of the polity of Methodism exists to-day as it was instituted by the Christmas Conference of 1784, when the Methodist Episcopal Church was first organized.

The full moral power of this office, in the grand workings of the itinerancy, as may be safely said, has never been either fairly weighed or properly estimated. In the exercise of its official and broad influences, many of the strongest men of the Conferences have undoubtedly done more work, and led the Church to greater and more numerous victories in a few years of ministerial labor than they would or could have accomplished even in a long life time in the more ordinary fields of the pastoral work.

The original districts over which these officials presided were large as well as important, and as each Sabbath brought them before new congregations made up of preachers, both traveling and local, stewards, class leaders, and the most intelligent of the laity, besides the general public, who everywhere crowded out to hear them by hundreds and thousands, their opportunities for doing good, for writing upon the minds and hearts of the people the high moral obligations of Christian truth, were as prominent and wide as any class of gospel ministers has ever enjoyed in the land.

In the earlier days it was not uncommon for whole families to travel, ten, twenty, and sometimes even thirty miles, to attend a quarterly meeting to hear the Presiding Elder preach, and to enjoy the revival inspirations of such occasions.

At many of these meetings the congregations were large and oftentimes they were compelled to resort to the woods, where, under the rich protecting shade of the forest trees, they for days partook of the Gospel food, as God's ancient Israel ate of the manna in the wilderness. On many of these occasions the scenes of the day of Pentecost were largely re-enacted, and an impulse was given to the cause of spiritual progress which would sometimes continue to pervade the whole country for months and years.

No other office of Methodism has ever afforded so grand a field for the higher ministerial developments, as that of the Presiding Eldership. He who filled it usually presided over some ten or twelve circuits and stations, which he visited quarterly, where he met the officiary of each charge respectively, and over whom he presided in a Quarterly Conference, in which the interests of the whole work was looked after, including the conduct of the preachers, the support of their families, the licensing of young men for the ministry, and all other matters concerning the welfare of the charge. Then, besides all these duties, he was expected to preach at least two sermons, and to administer the ordinance of the Lord's Supper; and as the congregations were large, attentive and intelligent, it was expected that his sermons would be full of sound doctrine and also abound with the power of the Divine baptism.

The men who filled this office in the earlier days of Methodism in the West, in many instances, won for themselves reputations of the very highest character. The names of such heroes might be given by the score and hundred, for the church was not scarce of such "eminent timber." She had them in her well-trained ranks, full of faith and of the Holy Ghost, and ever ready for the onset; men who counted not their lives dear unto themselves, so they might finish their course with joy and the ministry which they had received of the Lord Jesus.

At the first session of the Indiana Conference, which was held at New Albany, in the fall of 1832, the self-sacrificing and eloquent Strange was voted a superannuated relation, as his health was gone and his tremulous footsteps were just on the verge of Jordan. His retirement from the work of the Presiding Eldership made a vacancy, and Mr. Havens was suggested as a suitable successor, and he was appointed to the Madison district. The field was a large one, reaching from the Ohio river to the Mississinaway making almost one-fourth of the territory of the State. The rides were long and the exposures numerous, but still he met his appointments, notwithstanding his health was imperfect, and at the end of the year he was changed to the Indianapolis district. This work reached from the Capital of the State to Bloomington, in Monroe county, and as there was no other way to reach his appointments except on horse back, this mode of conveyance was his only reliance, and the weary pilgrimage around this large district was thus made four times during the year. On this field, Mr. Havens continued the constitutional term of four years, at the close of which he served one year as agent of the Preachers' Aid Society.

At the Conference of 1838, he was again appointed Presiding Elder, and sent to the Centreville District. The following year he was on the Connersville District, and in 1840 he was again appointed to the Indianapolis District, which relation he continued to occupy for four years, when he was stationed in Rushville, Greensburg and Laurel, and in 1847, he was appointed to the Greensburg District, on which he labored four years, when, in 1851, he was placed for the third time on the Indianapolis District, on which he remained until the fall of 1855, at which time it was thought by many of his friends that the days of his active service were numbered. For eighteen years he had been an active and efficient Presiding Elder, and now that his great work was about finished he had made himself a name which the church could not well forget, and living thousands all over the State were ready to stand up as the monuments of God's grace, who had been led through his preaching to the duties of a religious life.

The travel and labors of almost a score of years, spent in district preaching, had led him over a large portion of the State, and made his name familiar to many thousands of the families of Indiana, among whom he had moved and preached as a master hero in the great moral strife against sin, and in no instance was his name ever associated with a taint of crime or in any way touched with the stigma of a dishonorable deed. Ever earnest as well as sincere in battling for that which was true in doctrine, and for all that was pure in moral principles, the heroism of his positions was always consistently vindicated by the firmness and stability of his own character, and, therefore, he commanded the reverent regards of men of all classes and of every condition in life.

Hon. Oliver H. Smith, in his "Reminiscences of Early Indiana," speaks thus of him:

"James Havens was the Napoleon of the Methodist preachers of Eastern Indiana. I knew him well. He seemed to be made for the very work in which he was engaged. He had a good person, a strong physical formation, expanded lungs, a clear and powerful voice, reaching to the verge of the camp ground, the eye of the eagle, and both a moral and personal courage that never quailed. His powers as a preacher were of a very high order. I never heard but one man that was like him in his meridian days, and that was Father Newton, who visited this country years ago from England, as a delegate to the American General Conference.

"The great characteristic of Mr. Havens, as a preacher, was his good common sense. He could distinguish his audience so as not to throw his pearls before swine. He could feed his babes with the milk of the word, and hurl the terrors of the law against old sinners with fearful power. He seemed to know that old blood never runs in young veins, which so many preachers and presidents of colleges too often forget. Mr. Havens was one of the most powerful preachers I ever heard, and I have no hesitation in saying that the State of Indiana owes him a heavier debt of gratitude for the efforts of his long and valuable life to form society on the basis of *morality, education and religion* than any other man, living or dead."

Though wholly unconscious of the fact that his personal ministry was making some of the most interesting pages in the history of Indiana Methodism, as well as in the advancement of our general civilization, Mr. Havens always seemed to have an eye to the public integrity, as the highest culmination of private virtue. For it was the fixed faith of his heart that religion, pure and undefiled, was the only permanent foundation on which civil society can rest with any respectable safety, and this he taught in his sermons and exhortations with a zeal which knew no restraint save that which was regulated by Christianity itself.

The position which he maintained for so many years as Presiding Elder necessarily constituted him a leader in Israel, as well as an official director in the affairs of his Conference. He, of course, became familiar with the standing of every preacher, as well as with the whims, caprices and prejudices of the people, and in making the appointments for his districts from year to year, he often suffered in mind the most painful agitations, because he could not always meet the wishes of the people, or send the preachers where he would like to, and where he believed they ought to have gone.

The annual changes which were common in most of the Conferences, during the days of his Presiding Elder administration, made the duties of such an officer oftentimes exceedingly unpleasant, particularly when he came to make out the appointments for the coming year. The Presiding Elders of the other districts of the Conference, of course, had their own respective interests to guard; and while the Bishop, as was most generally the case, had no ax to grind, or partialities to show, made no troublesome interferences, still the natural conflicts of equal claims on the part of both preacher and people, rendered the duties especially onerous to men of warm sympathies and honest natures, such as Mr. Havens possessed.

The cabinet of a Bishop, though composed of the best men of the Conference as Presiding Elders, will have its conflicts as well as its official honors. No one need imagine that it is an easy matter to station one or two hundred preachers. The interests of the work must be looked after, and with sensible men this consideration is and should be paramount to all others. As far as is possible, the wants and wishes of the people should be met, and this can ordinarily only be done by appointing the right men to the right places. If this is done, some will think they have been overlooked, or, at least, that they have not been properly appreciated. That there are and have been mistakes made no one acquainted with the work will deny

Infallibility has never yet been claimed in any department of Methodism, and in this of making the appointments from year to year, the good sense and judgment of even the best of Presiding Elders may sometimes fail them.

We have often conversed with Mr. Havens upon this subject, and heard him express himself fully and freely in regard to his own district, his preachers and those of the Conference. His frankness in regard to the disqualifications of some men for certain fields and positions, which they greatly desired, may have sometimes lost him friends, but he had too much sterling honesty about him and too great a regard for the good of the work and the honor of Methodism, to flatter the stupid, or to pander to the preacher whose personal aspirations excelled the measure of his intelligence. Still he was ever lenient toward the sincere, the honest and devoted; and the preacher of misfortune found in him a friend on whom he could rely, as well as an advisor who would give him the counsel of a father.

It was the lot of Mr. Havens several times during the long period of his Presiding Eldership, to have to stand in the official position of prosecutor among some of his brethren, but what he did in this relationship was done conscientiously, as well as fearlessly; and while performing his duty in these specific cases, he never seemed to be impelled by any other motive than that of the honor and purity of the church, for he had no desire to put down or crush any innocent man.

He knew that Methodist preachers could do wrong as well as other men, and his doctrine was that if they did, they should suffer the penalty of that wrong as certainly as any others. This position he was always ready to maintain, no matter who might be the transgressor; and if, in any such instances, he ever lost friends, he considered himself none the poorer, but on the other hand he felt that he had vinicated what he understood to be the cause of God and his own consistency and self-respect.

Both as a man and a Christian, he was too independent and fearless to purchase public favor at the expense of his own moral manhood, and on this account some have spoken of him with but little respect, who otherwise, no doubt, would have been quite sycophantic admirers.

The fact that he several times represented his Annual Conference in the higher counsels of the General Conference, on a majority vote of his brethren, gives assurances of their confidence both in his intelligence and integrity, and also sustains the principle that the uniform adherence of an honest man to the truth and the right, will win for him the respect of the respectable and the confidence of the honorable.

This distinguished confidence he had among the people always in an eminent degree, and wherever he went, he was received by them not only as an apostolic minister, but as a Christian gentleman, who never had any compromises to make with sin, or any fulsome flatteries to pay to sinners.

On one occasion, while on the Greensburg District, he noticed that he had all the lawyers in town in his congregation except Judge Davidson, then of the Supreme Court The Monday following, passing by the Judge's office, and seeing him and Mrs. Davidson sitting by the table, he stepped in the door, and, after saluting them both, he said:

"Judge Davidson, seeing you and your wife here in the office, I just thought I would stop and tell you what I thought of you to your face."

"Well, Mr. Havens," said the Judge, straightening himself up and looking the venerable clergyman eye to eye, "let us hear your judgment."

"Well, Judge," remarked Mr. Havens, "I think you are one of the worst Christians in this town." Then pausing and looking sternly in the face of the Judge, "and yet, after all," he added, "I believe, Judge, you are one of the best citizens of the place."

Judge Davidson but seldom ever attended the church, and he did not make any profession of being a Christian; still all who knew him gave him the credit of being a conscientious and honest man.

It was the purpose of Mr. Havens, no doubt, to draw the Judge's thoughts to the distinction, which he deemed important, between the honesty of a Christian life and that of a good citizen. The one, in Mr. Havens' view, would save in this world, but the other he taught was necessary to save in the world beyond. The honesty of the reproof, however, was characteristic of the man.

CHAPTER XXVII.

MISCONCEPTIONS OF THE MAN.

In our efforts to vindicate the character of Mr. Havens, and to give the true animus of the man, it may be necessary for us to say what he was not as well as to affirm what he was; for though he was, as we have already written, decidedly affirmative in all his movements, he was not possessed, as some have supposed, of that litigious and aggressive spirit which many have so recklessly attributed to him. With him aggression was usually founded upon provocation, and when he made attacks, it was because he felt called upon to do so, either to maintain the principles of truth which he professed himself, or the rights and privileges which belonged to those whom he led.

Under all circumstances, he never seemed to forget that he was a minister of religion, and in this capacity and profession he felt that the obligation was upon him to especially stand by the people. With him such an office was neither a sinecure nor a position of cowardice, even though it was that of the Christian ministry, and, therefore, he did not always deem it his duty to deal in soft or honeyed words with every class of characters. To the rough and insubordinate, he often dealt out their own sort of medicine, and on a few rare occasions he has been known to have used even more than mere moral force to bring them into subjection. Unlike many others of his brethren in the ministry, he was not disposed to take an insult without in some way resenting it. Not that he wished for contention or strife, but because he did not believe in yielding to the impositions of the unprincipled, or of bowing to the onslaughts of the abandoned.

In many instances he felt satisfied that those who were so thoughtless and unlawful as to attempt the interruption of the religious services of the people, whom he was serving as a minister, were cowards at heart, and would soon give way, particularly if any sort of a bold front was presented before them. It was this conviction which sometimes led him to assume positions of danger, where his friends often feared for his personal safety.

The numerous stories which have been told all over the State, of his knocking men down and whipping them, and which, in some instances, have even been given to the press, are for the most part without any foundation in fact, and we presume have been told more to display the powers of writers or to gratify the *Munchausen* genius of narrators, than either to build up the reputation of the minister or to do credit to the real courage of the man.

Many of these incredible stories have been told so often and been repeated by men of such reputed veracity, that it will, perhaps, be difficult to disabuse the public mind and convince it of their utter falsity. Mr. Havens was not a fighter or a bully, for but few men loved peace and friendship more highly than he did, and yet he would not suffer himself or his congregations to be imposed upon. If impudence and ignorance attempted to break in upon the rights or privileges of his people, he believed it to be his duty to read them a lesson in moral reform in some way, and this he often did in words which were understood to "have the bark on."

Many who lived in Indiana forty years ago, were often irregular and disorderly, particularly at camp meetings, who, when at home, would have been ashamed of any such misconduct. This Mr. Havens well knew, and therefore he had no fears of personal injury from them. He believed them to be cowards, and with a little strategic management he often brought them "to their oats," as he used to term it, without much ceremony.

Some in telling of his subjugation of the notorious Buckhart at a camp meeting near Indianapolis, many years ago, have represented that "he knocked the athletic bully down three times, and took from him a large bowie knife, and then handed him to the constable" when the simple facts were as we have already given them in another chapter. He did not strike the man at all, and, besides, Buckhart had no knife about him. His own fearlessness and a little strategy made Buckhart a prisoner without much effort, and the colorings which have been given to this little incident, like many other things told in history, may all be set down to the credit of the too common apocryphal genius of the country.

Mr. Havens' knowledge of his own rights and his indomitable personal courage in maintaining them, made him quite conspicuous before the people as a man of fearless spirit, when he himself laid no claim to anything more than a mere conscientious regard for the rights and privileges of the people. It was this heroic spirit which gave him the reputation of being a somewhat dangerous minister to deal with, and impressed many with the idea that he would not pause long on the edge of a fight unless it was through policy, until he would strike, no matter who the opponent might be. But those who made such inferences really did not know the man; for even when he appeared to be the most positive in his positions, he expected only to conquer a peace by the display of firmness rather than by any coercive measures.

Many persons out of the Church, who did not know him, thought he would fight, particularly in an emergency, and, therefore, they were afraid of him, and it was this conception of his character which gave him such positive rule over them. The religious portion of the people, however, loved and obeyed him through reverence; and through these two antagonistic influences he often swayed the vast camp meeting assemblies which were at times before him, as the trees of the forest are moved in the presence of the storm.

Ordinarily, Mr. Havens was as mild and placid, as kind and social, as any of the ministers of his Conference; and it was only when there was a coming or surrounding storm that the lion was aroused within him. On such occasions he would show a spirit of resolve, a purpose of command, which made the timid tremble. When such circumstances did occur under his jurisdiction the man was sunk in the hero, and the bold preacher looked as if he would, Peter like, cut some fellow's ear off before he was through with the imbroglio. It was this spirit of determination and daring which, doubtless, gave Mr. Havens his chief prominence among his brethren, as most of them, governed as they were by the more conservative obligations of the Christian life, preferred to yield to boisterous opposition rather than to fight it, while he dared to maintain his rights under all circumstances, because he believed that a vigorous vindication of principle was much more pious and honorable than any cowardly yielding could be to the demands of presumptive arrogance, or even to the not less dubious claims of insincere piety.

Prayers and soft words may work reforms among the cultivated and considerate, but it is often the case now, and it was much more so years ago, that men of the baser sort are only held in decent subjection by some positive and visible power. It was this order of government that Mr. Havens was called upon to exercise, and hence many who witnessed his commanding generalship on such occasions, received the impression that he would be as ready to use physical force to accomplish his purposes as that of the higher character.

The ministers of the present day can have but feeble conceptions of what the early preachers had to pass through in the pioneer work of their ministry. Then there were but few churches in which meetings could be held, and on this account they often had to resort to the woods, particularly on popular occasions, where the usual restraints of religious services were but indifferently acknowledged, and it was not an uncommon circumstance that the ministry found that the maintainance of good order was the most difficult task they had to perform. Every one in those days went to meeting, and the gathered crowds presented an appearance as diversified and motley, as our modern county fairs, and the preachers were, representatively, responsible for the good order of the crowd.

On such occasions it was frequently the case, that "Satan appeared there also," in the shape of gamblers, horse racers, whisky peddlers, and scoffers of all religious ceremonies, and the work of regulating and governing such discordant elements, and at the same time conducting the religious services, was certainly no ordinary obligation.

The panoramic display of such religious gatherings, would in these days frighten many of our timid and conservative divines, either into personal flight or moral spasms, for such a school would be as novel to them, as the "chase of the antelope over the plains." But few of them would know what steps to take to still the multitudes, or to feed with the bread of life the sincere and the hungry. Yet these and similar scenes, were familiar to most of our early itinerants, and they were, therefore, in some degree, often compelled to assume the command of the alien, as well as the saint, in the fulfillment of their mission.

To manage such meetings and to conduct them decently and in order, required much more than mere pulpit talents, and the heroic ardor with which they were governed and which made them so grand a success in the moral advancement of our western civilization, should certainly not be overlooked in any biographical sketches we may make of any of our pioneer ministers.

What they did in the reformation of these uncouth and native elements, was like the workmanship of those who lay the foundations of stately edifices. The material was rough and was often "neither oblong nor square," and might have been justly rejected by the builders; but it was not, and the consequence has been that many of our present most intelligent divines, might, if they would, trace their own genealogies back to some of these original, rough foundation stones, which were used in the elementary building of the church in the West.

Mr. Havens was himself a specimen of this class, which he always well remembered, and it was perhaps on this account, he felt it to be his particular personal obligation never to pass by or overlook even the roughest classes of men. He well understood it was natural for men to be sinners, and that if the evil could be taken out of them they would become as good and true and perhaps as prominent in usefulness as they ever had been in vice or immorality.

But his conflicts were not all with the rougher classes. He, in some instances, met men whose positions in society, and whose relationships in the ministry, should have taught them how to treat a brother minister at least, but it seems they had not, for he used to tell a story of one who officiated at a certain Conference, as "the stationed preacher," in assigning the members to their boarding places during its sessions who certainly fell below the mark.

This man of authority had sent him away on the outskirts of the town to put up with a family where there was neither accommodations for man or horse. Of course he felt that it would be an imposition upon the family as well as upon himself to remain, and thanking the wife and mother of the large family, for any trouble he may have given her, he reported himself to the stationed preacher as being without a home. That gentleman being of the class whose own personal interests absorb all of their usual capacity, offered him no relief, and informed him he would have to find a home for himself. Mounting his horse, he rode up to a tavern in the town and hitching his horse to the sign post, he entered the bar room, where he found the landlord. "Landlord," said he, "can you take care of me and my horse during the session of our Conference and take your pay in silver when it is over?"

"Yes, certainly, I can," was the prompt response. His horse was put away, and a nice private room was at once assigned him. The landlord and his wife and daughter treated him with the utmost kindness during the session of the Conference, and at its close refused any remuneration. Mr. Havens felt that he had settled with his kind and generous host, and he thought it might do some good in the future to have some sort of a one with the stationed preacher. Seeing him in the Conference room, he approached and addressed him.

"Brother," said he, "I wish to thank you for the very cool treatment you have shown me during this

Conference. Your conduct has convinced me that your personal devotions are perhaps equal to those of any member of our Conference, and I merely wish to suggest to you that, in the future, it perhaps would be better for you to divide them a little."

But few Methodist preachers could make such frank remarks to a delinquent brother with greater self-possession than Mr. Havens, and though it was not often he was called upon to perform such duty, yet, when he was, he did not hesitate to speak plainly, no matter what might be the personal pretensions of the reproved.

That he sometimes erred in his rebukes, may be acknowledged, without any detriment to his character, for all who knew him well, were fully satisfied that he never aimed to rebuke or wound any one wantonly. It is true, in his frank independence, he sometimes said severe things, but he said them because he believed them to be true, and because their frank utterance was called for by the demands of virtue, and by the requisitions of honesty and the public welfare. It was this candor and personal independence which doubtless led many to believe he was iron willed and overbearing. They saw him perhaps only when he moved upon the great line of his ministerial purposes, or it may have been when he had taken his stand antagonistic to some moral delinquency. On such occasions it was not characteristic of him to either shrink from responsibility, for fear of the popular favor, or to hesitate in his prosecutions of the guilty from any false pride or sympathy.

For generous as he was impulsive, and brave as he was honorable, he scorned to become an accessory in wrong by preaching cowardly indulgences. His faith was that God would stand by the innocent and would bring him out in the end the conqueror. "If you are innocent," we once heard him say to a brother in an hour which seemed as dark as death itself—"God will bring you through your troubles as safely as he did the three Hebrew children from the fiery furnace." This same brother, after passing through an ordeal of trial such as no minister in Indiana ever realized before or since, holds his relationship in the Conference, and stands "redeemed, regenerated and disenthralled." In this case Mr. Havens was a prophet as well as a comforter.

Mr. Havens' confidence in the equity of the divine government led him to the faith that honesty was the best policy in peace as well as in war, and therefore, he was not disposed to swerve from it either to accommodate a friend or to prosecute an enemy.

That some men hated him we do not doubt, and that some yet living may greatly underrate his claims upon the public gratitude, now that he is dead, is perhaps equally as probable. But all such men have none of the elements of greatness in themselves, and on this account it is difficult for them to see them in others. This "dog in the manger" spirit is sometimes seen even in the ministry; but we have always noticed, no matter what department of life they officiate in, they are never willing to accord the meed of superiority, or of greatness, to any who are or who have been their own immediate associates. Their jealousy overtops the liberality of their sentiments, and consequently they open not their lips to give utterance to eulogy, particularly if the subject has been one of their own competitors.

If the world had been full of such men, Father Havens would have gone down to his grave without a monument, and the pen of his biographer would have rested in silence forever for the want of a theme.

CHAPTER XXVIII.

ITINERANT REVIEW.

The preaching of the gospel to the poor is Heaven's best recognition of the true mission of the Church. This, in fact, is its primary object, and always its highest obligation, and, therefore, where the poor are left out in its services, God himself is undoubtedly ignored in the same proportion. Even humanity looks after the suffering, and the higher Divinity certainly can not fall below this standard.

What the Church does for the rich is paid for "dollar for dollar," and, therefore, what she does for the poor constitutes her only credit. Human greatness may crown her with honors, but true spiritual sympathy for the poor, the fallen, and the guilty, can alone give evidence of her inspiration.

Indeed, it may be said that the Church makes Infidels of men when she serves only the rich, for they become her governors, as well as the chief samples of her piety, and the consequent reflection makes but a poor comment on both her zeal and character. Good men have seen these results, and have often mourned over them. Many have sought to remedy such evils by substituting new orders of benevolence, and by inculcating a higher missionary zeal. But in defiance of their efforts the Church has grown richer, and her clergy more selfish and aristocratic, while the poor, by the million, have been left to wander uncared for on the mountains of desolation.

When Mr. John Wesley began the work of his itinerancy in England, though it was thought to be irregular by the Church, many were made hopeful that a brighter era was about to dawn upon the world. True, many in the higher walks of life looked upon his itinerant scheme of spreading the gospel as being both visionary and fanatical, but "the poor of England" hailed it almost everywhere as a millenial issue. They gave audience to his preaching in gathered thousands, and many became his followers. Organization ensued, as a forced consequence, and the simple "societies" of Mr. Wesley grew in a few years to be the most efficient body of religious workmen in the kingdom.

It was the grand result of his plan of itinerancy in connection with his employment of men in the ministry, who were uneducated. Personal and moral qualifications were made the chief and essential requisites for the work, and the old evangelism became the rule of their characters—"by their fruits ye shall know them."

This peculiar feature of Methodism has done more to advance the moral civilization of the people of Europe and America, than many are willing to admit of. Even the facts of history sustain the assertion that the civilized world has everywhere felt its power.

However irregular it may have been deemed, or however its ignorance may have been laughed at, it has kindled the flame of Christian love in the hearts of millions, and made the world better through the grand efficiency of its itinerant ministry

Men have been employed to preach who had never

seen a college, and if they did not understand the "dead languages," they made good use of the living one, as well as "full proof of their ministry."

The mission of this scriptural evangelism among the people of our own country just at the period when they were about to lay the foundations of a new empire, was both opportune and fortunate. The people were poor and the country thinly settled, and the itinerant plan of spreading the gospel alone could meet the emergency.

Like the men who bore the stars and stripes in defense of the liberties of the people and the independence of the Republic, the primitive Methodist preachers, gave themselves to the work without pay and for the cause alone. The heroism of their services equaled the soldiers' valor, and the fervency of their zeal gave them as numerous and complete victories.

But what Methodism has done in the East is not our theme. We only wish, in a brief way, to here speak of its introduction into the West, where its field, which but a few years ago was a wilderness, has now become a magnificent and prosperous empire.

With others, we feel that we owe a debt of remembrance and gratitude to the early ministers of the West, of all churches, which we will never be able to pay. Those ministers of the wilderness are now all dead, and we can only rescue them from oblivion by the patient investigations of unwritten history. Working for eternity rather than for time, but few of them made any record of their deeds or doings and consequently many of them have gone down to their graves the unmerited victims of a dreamless obscurity

With most of them the struggles of life were among the undeveloped resources of the wilderness, where fame had never yet built a temple, and where the conventional rules of church etiquette were as yet a dead letter.

Of the mission of Methodism, of which we wish to speak more particularly, we may state that its introduction among the western pioneers was attended with personal exposures and numerous sacrifices, such as the pen of the historian may now never describe.

The entire country was a wilderness, and the smoke of the red man's wigwam was often the only evidence that it was occupied by a human inhabitant. The sparse settlements of the white man who had come as a pioneer to take up his home in the West, made the only preaching places of the brave missionary.

At his own expense and personal risk, with no company but that of his favorite horse, he passed from settlement to settlement hunting up "the lost sheep of the house of Israel," and faring with the humble inhabitants on the wild game of the forests.

In most instances they were welcomed with the most sincere cheerfulness, and the best their log cabins could afford was kindly set before them. The settlers recognized them as God's messengers, and consequently treated them with respect and reverence. Of course there were occasional exceptions to these rules in their travels, but even when they did occur, in most instances the preacher maintained his ground long enough to tell the story of his mission.

Preaching in these primitive wilderness temples, the preacher read his hymns and lessons by the light that came down the chimney, or else the door of the cabin was left open to give the necessary light to the whole congregation. It was not true in the West that

"The groves were God's first temples,"

for they were only resorted to in emergencies when the congregations became too large to be crowded into cabins. For years many of the cabins and better dwellings of the western pioneers were the only meeting houses of religious worship known to the itinerant. He preached, ate and slept all in the same room, and not unfrequently the father and mother of the family, with a half dozen or more children, enjoyed with him the same accommodations. Necessity made families liberal in those early times, as well as devout and reverential towards the ministers of religion. Many gave up their dwellings for religious meetings from two to four days in a month, and often after the services were over, nearly the whole congregation, on invitation of the generous housekeeper, would stop and take dinner with the preacher.

Such hospitality is in striking contrast with that which has obtained in some of our fine steepled, organ-choired and rich aristocratic churches of the present day, where the strange preacher, after delivering his sermon to an "intelligent audience," is coldly left to hunt up his own dinner. To sustain us in this rather sarcastic reflection, we will here remark that a number of ministers, whose experience has been their tutor, have assured us that "such facts of history" can not well be gainsayed.

Hospitality was a distinguished trait of the early pioneers. They had but little, but they well understood the laws of reciprocity, and when a stranger came to their doors, they gave him the welcome of the western hunter, that was "to eat once what they had to live on all the time if they could relish it."

In such homes as these the early itinerant found his congregations, and his resting places, and his greatest difficulty, was to go from neighborhood to neighborhood without being drowned, or frozen to death, or swamped in some quagmire. In such cases his favorite charger was his main reliance, and often he had such confidence in the superior intelligence of his horse that he would trust to his decisions when he would not have done so even to a Bishop.

Indian paths and sometimes notched roads were the usual lines of his travel, though now and then, he was compelled to take to the woods to reach his preaching place, where his only guide were the points of the compass.

Swollen creeks and rivers had to be crossed, which he often did by swimming his horse, at the risk of life, and in some instances the clothes on his body would be frozen stiff before he could reach a habitation.

One of Mr. Havens' colleagues, Henry B. Bascom, once swam his horse with himself on his back across a river of this kind on a cold winter's day, and having to ride five miles after he had crossed, it was with great difficulty he could get his clothes from his body when he arrived at his cabin destination.

It was of such stuff as this that many of the early Methodist preachers were made. They were dauntless in the presence of any obstacle, and their daring intripidity but seldom quailed in their attempt to overcome it. The physical courage of many of these unpretending itinerants was fully equal to their moral heroism, and though neither learned nor eloquent as may be said of many of them, they did a work of moral achievement which the glory of a thousand battle fields can not eclipse, and which no human honors can ever properly reward.

Fifty years ago, the itinerancy, though somewhat improved, had still about it much of the exposure and danger of wild adventure. The same creeks and rivers were to ford, for there were still but few ferries or bridges, and though appointments were not so distant, they were much more numerous, and still far enough apart, to give the preacher long rides almost every day in the year besides preaching and "leading class" some thirty times a month.

But few of the people of the present period have any just conceptions of what these early Methodist preachers and their families were called upon to endure. Even the ministers of to-day who, in most instances, are so happily situated, have but limited ideas of what "the fathers" had to pass through. For what circuits were then, and what they are now, may only be known by the law of extreme contrasts. Then, what is called a parsonage was unknown, and when the preacher arrived in his work with his family, he was subjected to whatever hospitality might be offered him, and until, he "with the advice and counsel" of frequently very indifferent "stewards," could hunt up a house of some sort, he and his family were adrift on the kindness, whatever it might be, of the people.

Even in this State, it has often occurred that preachers were thrown by their annual appointments from one side of the State to the other, and in such cases the preacher realized the great advantage of that happy apothegm, "Blessed is the preacher who has nothing, for he can be moved to any distance."

These frequent and long removals from one circuit to another constituted, perhaps, the hardest trials of many of these old itinerants. For just as they were getting comfortably fixed in their parsonage homes, and becoming acquainted with the people of their charges, the Conference has called upon them to go to another field where, perhaps, they were total strangers, and where it was more than probable there would be no provision whatever made for their reception.

Still it would not answer for them to complain or murmur, or find fault with the appointing power, for the die was cast for that year, and if they backed out, or refused to accept the appointment given them, the days of their itinerancy were perhaps ended. At this very point many hundreds have given up the itinerancy, and though they have afterwards filled useful positions in the local ranks, their names have only been subject to merely local recognitions.

Though the local ministry of our American Methodism has always been respectable, it has not had any of the usual advantages of emolument or distinction which have belonged *ex officio* to the itinerancy. Their position has not been looked upon as being as sacred or as sacrificing as that of the itinerancy, and, therefore, it has been thought that their claims upon the Church entitled them to no particular distinctions. Such, as least, has been the usual order of the administration of the Church, and we presume the reason for it has been that the itinerancy could alone give and preserve to the church its high and aggressive character.

In the earlier days, however, but few preachers were local in their labors of any rank, for even those who did not belong to the itinerancy were nevertheless itinerant. On the Sabbath they went everywhere preaching the word, and many of them whom we have known have deserved monuments of renown far above others who have even lived and died in the itinerant work.

It takes something more than mere station in life to give some men character, while there are others who will push their way up to celebrity in any position. They do not seek it, but it seeks them. They are true to themselves and stand to their positions. Hence, honors come upon them, because their fidelity equals their integrity and character is awarded them because they have in their place proven themselves ready and sufficient for any emergency.

It is on this basis that character above the ordinary

rank was so largely accorded to Father Havens. The people knew him as a man and as a Christian, and as an itinerant Methodist preacher. As such they loved him, had confidence in him, and reverenced him. Among Methodist preachers he was their hero, and as such they felt that they could trust him for advice and counsel whether living or dying.

The itinerancy was the field of his life's activity, and in its toils and labors he spent his years as faithfully and honorably and with as much regard for the church of God and the salvation of souls as any minister, perhaps, who has ever been known in the State.

The wide fields which he has occupied and the distinctive part he has taken in the work of the ministry made him better known to the people than any minister who has been connected with the Indiana itinerancy.

For nearly fifty years he was engaged in the work and though he never made pretensions of being a great man he was nevertheless styled such by many of the greatest and best men of his day.

Among the last public services of Father Havens' life was the preaching of a sermon on the funeral occasion of the late Hon. Samuel W Parker, of Connersville. They had long been ardent and mutual friends and though Mr. Parker was much the youngest man, he died first, and his old war-worn friend was invited by the family to officiate on the solemn occasion.

To hold the confidence of such a man as Mr. Parker was a compliment in itself, of the very highest character. For he was no ordinary man either in thought or judgment. A consumate reader of character, he had full confidence in Father Havens' sincerity and integrity as a Christian and minister, and it was his dying wish that he should attend his funeral.

It was thus he saw one after another of his old and tried friends with whom he had formed acquaintance while he was in the active itinerant field, passing away, and he could but feel sad at the rapid changes which time was making around him. The good and the excellent of his earlier years were passing in swift succession before him and he began to feel that he too was standing on the brink of the mysterious river and that the very next boat perhaps would carry him over.

The spirit of his hope was on the wing, and his thoughts, which had been so long on the itinerancy of men, began to feed on the greater glories of the itinerancy of the angels.

His hopes were, that he should never locate, for he remembered with gladness the interrogation of St. Paul, "Are they not all ministering spirits sent forth to minister for them who shall be heirs of salvation?" This he hoped would continue his itinerancy forever.

CHAPTER XXIX.

SUPERANNUATED YEARS.

The regular active labors of Mr. Havens in the itinerancy ended at the September Conference of 1855, when his third full term of four years was closed on the Indianapolis District. He was then only in his sixty-fifth year, which should not be considered as an advanced or superannuated age in the ministry; for at this period of life many have their ripest thoughts of wisdom, and often carry with them still their life's richest influences. Physically, Mr. Havens was not the man he had been, and it may be that his mental powers were more or less abated because of his nervous debility, but still he yet retained his faculties of thought in evident manhood, and had about him much of the touching and venerable fire of his earlier years.

The over-weening and evident haste which is sometimes manifested by some of the Conferences to place their old men on the superannuated list, to say the least of it, will not always bear the most charitable construction; and though it may be truthfully recorded on the minutes, "superannuated at his own request," yet even this does not say that it should have been done, for it is frequently the case that the old and venerable minister, who has fought through the exciting campaigns of more than two score of years, finds it one of the hardest battles of his life to quit the field, and more especially is this true if he gets the impression that his younger brethren want him out of the way.

The sensitive tenderness of the aged should certainly always be most carefully guarded, paticularly where they have endured the noble sacrifices of the pioneer, and made such a record of personal sufferings as the present advancements of our civilization prohibit their successors from ever following in their footsteps, or of giving themselves any similar honors.

Father Havens was one of the heroes of Indiana Methodism, and with the earlier ministers he had been identified as a brother, and with them he had fought the battles of Israel when the wilderness bounded every side of his circuits, and the horse and the saddle-bags were his daily companions. The humble cabins of the pioneer settlers were the only temples of his devotions, and the rattling of cow bells gave him the best assurances that he was nearing his preaching places. Often pumpkins and cow fodder were the best feed he could obtain for his favorite charger, while his own entertainment consisted of fare of the most unpretending character.

The brave old soldier never forgets his hardest campaigns, and often in memory, at least, he fights over his most terrific battles. What and all he has gone through in fire and flood, in sufferings and hardships, in companionships, and life toils, come up before him afresh, and he can not but feel sad when he comes to lay off his armor and retire for the rest of his years to the inoperative shades of private life.

To quit the field of active labor, and retire to that of a superannuated relation, requires more passive philosophy than most men imagine, and, on this account, we have often thought that those who fall on the field of battle, though they seemingly die prematurely, may be classed among the fortunates, for they certainly escape the ordeal of a trying retirement, which, in some respects, nearly always casts unpleasant shadows along down the valley of declining years.

To grow old gracefully, even in the ministry, is the lot, of only the few, for men often think themselves able still to do battle in the vineyard when they are not, while not unfrequently, they fear that their successors will not prove true and faithful to the ancient land-marks. They forget, or appear not to know, that each successive generation has its own peculiar idiosyncrasies, and that the laws of age, which are gradually bearing them on to the tomb, are in accordance with the philosophy of all true developments, as well as of all substantial progress. Rapid succession is the order of nature, and what one generation has accomplished may never be counted a success, unless the next takes it up and carries it forward to its progressive and legitimate issues. Principles may not change, and yet their full power is never seen under any one monotonous order. It is this necessity which demands the changes continually seen in successive generations.

With these laws of progress Father Havens had some acquaintance, and when he saw, as he did in his superannuated years, the introduction of choirs and organs in the Methodist congregations of the country, and of extended notes and written sermons in the pulpits, he made no efforts to forestall them, further than to say that he had his fears that they would ultimately lead to a formality very different from that of old fashioned Methodism. But still, he did not argue that it would necessarily be the case, for he was well aware that such things had been common among other respectable and highly useful denominations, even for many years.

In agreement with the education of his life, he of course preferred the plain services of the earlier years, and when he preached in any of the churches, as he sometimes did, where these changes had been already introduced, he made no allusions to them in his sermons. What he had to say was usually uttered to brethren in private, and even then he said but little, for he had too much good sense to suppose that he could beat back the tide of such a rapidly growing power.

Indeed it was not his custom, even in his active days, to waste his amunition on the mere forms of religious services. Its spirit and principle, he well knew were the chief and essential points to be looked after, and these he hoped would be maintained as long as the church lasted.

The old spirit of revival power, where it issued in sound conversions, and introduced into the church, true and faithful members, held his devotions above all the glittering displays of forms and ceremonies, of ecclesiastical pride, or pageantry. He had seen Methodism grow up in the West, from the insignificant position of wide spread and disintegrated societies in the wilderness, to a church dignity fully equal to that of any other in the United States, and while he beheld it all, his great wish was that it would never lose its old fashioned and grand reformatory energies.

Though he had retired to his humble home in the town of Rushville, where he had been residing for some years, he still kept his eye on the work and he often felt that if some light field was given him, he could yet do something for his master.

For some six years, he had held a superannuated relation, when a vacancy occurred in the Strange Chapel, charge of Indianapolis, and he was unanimously invited by that congregation to supply its pulpit for the rest of the year.

Accepting the call he brought his aged companion with him to the station, and in the old style of the itinerancy, they went to house keeping in the parsonage.

In that church he found many to whom he had been preaching for more than thirty years. They knew him as a venerable Father in Israel, and during the year, they listened to his preaching with the very highest respect and reverence. Though bordering on seventy in the years of his pilgrimage, he frequently evinced in his pulpit efforts the fires of his more youthful years, crowds came to hear him, and many who did not belong to the charge, for no minister of the city was held in higher esteem, and but few had greater power over their audiences.

In this field he exercised his last official functions, as a minister, in charge of a congregation, and as it bore the honored name of his old companion in the gospel ministry, Rev. John Strange, he was by a peculiar providence closing his public labors in Indiana, as he had begun them in intimate connection with the honored name of the illustrious Strange.

No Methodist preacher he had ever known held a holier place in his heart's best memories, and he looked forward to Heaven itself for the renewal of their old fraternity, with a fondness of hope and a confidence of recognition, which no pen can well describe. Though thirty years had passed away since his beloved confrere had crossed the cold waters, Father Havens still talked about him as if the separation had been of but recent occurrence.

Finishing his labors in this temporary charge, he returned again to his old home, where he continued to preach as opportunity would permit him, and on several occasions he visited distant parts of the State, where he had been invited by his old friends, who wished once more to hear his voice before he went hence to be seen no more among men.

On such occasions he was honored among the people with much more than the usual reverence. Every class of Christians called upon him, and the most distinguished citizens of the country gave him their attention and respect, because they saw that the time of his departure was near at hand, that he had fought a good fight, that he had honorably kept the faith as one of the pioneer heroes of Indiana Methodism and therefore they felt that to honor him, was an honor to themselves, and they gathered around him in his visitations as if he had been their own father.

The pale features of the good old minister, in connection with the almost snow-whiteness of his head, gave to many the conviction that he was much older than he really was. General John W Rose, formerly of Union county, but now residing in the town of Wabash, who is one of the oldest Master Masons in Indiana, and also a very warm and zealous Methodist, said to us the year before Father Havens died:

"I met father Havens the other day on the cars. At first I scarcely knew him, and I went up to him and asked:

"Is not this Father Havens?"

"Yes," said the old gentleman; "they call me Father Havens."

"Well," said I to him, "Father Havens, you must be getting to be quite an old man, for they have been calling you Father Havens ever since I can remember. How old are you?" I asked.

"Well, General," said he, "I am just seventy-three years of age."

"Why, is that all?" I asked.

"That is my age, sir," said he.

"You astonish me, Father Havens," said I.

"Why," he asked.

"Why," said I to him, "they have been calling you Father Havens as far back as I can remember, and yet I am three years older than you are."

The good old General, like many others who had known Father Havens all their lives, judged from his looks that he was much older than he really was.

But this misjudgment was not strange, for the abundant labors of the man, and the great wear on his nervous system, had given him the appearance of premature age, and if he had not possessed a strong iron constitution, he would not have been the last to die of the early race of Indiana Methodist preachers.

We remember, some twenty years before Father Havens' death, a speculating conversation which we had with the then vigorous Allen Wiley, in regard to the probable length of the lives of Calvin W Ruter, James Havens, and that of his own. We both then thought that Father Havens would not live ten years, and that Mr. Ruter would not be long after him.

Appearances were then greatly in favor of the longevity of Mr. Wiley, as he was temperate and healthy, and as active as a boy in his teens. But the venerable Wiley died in 1848, when he was only fifty-eight years of age, and a superannuated preacher, and the lamented Ruter passed away suddenly in the year 1859, while Father Havens did not die until 1864.

During most of Father Havens' superannuated years he stood alone. The hand of death had broken off all the old ministerial fraternities of his earlier years, and he was left in the Conference, the last relic of his class.

He made it his duty notwithstanding, to attend each session of the Conference in which he held his membership. In these annual convocations he had found, for many years, his dearest and warmest ministerial affiliations. His younger brethren, who had been taught to reverence him in his former official relation of Presiding Elder, greeted him with manifestations of kindness and respect, and not a few of them looked up to him as their father in the ministry. They venerated him for what he then was, and honored him for what he had been. The oldest member of the Conference, and the most distinguished of the body, there was none to envy him, or to do him dishonor. All felt that he had made his record, and that the roll of the Conference bore no name more worthy of respect. He had carried the banner of the cross when most of them were in their cradles, and now that his life story was about all told, the tongues of eulogistic gratitude could alone do justice to his virtues.

But it is not always the case, even in annual Conferences of Methodist preachers, that full justice is done to the memory of a long life of sacrifices. Many appear to think that the reward of faithfulness is in the divine hands, and therefore they seem to forget that respectful veneration for valuable services rendered in the cause of Christ and humanity, is among the nobler virtues of the Christian life.

But in these regards Father Havens, perhaps, had as little cause of complaint, as most any of his departed compeers, for being the last of his age to die, his junior brethren felt it to be a privilege to honor him, which they did with the tenderest sensibilities.

The position of superannuation, however, in the Methodist ministry is always rather anomalus, for it gives to its holder the relation of a dead man, while he is yet still living. With no field in which to act, and no responsibilities to keep him in life, he has nothing to live for, in the way of public duty, and consequently, all that remains for him is to take leave of the world and to lie down and die.

As many of his brethren will remember, no relationship which the Church ever gave him was so trying to Father Havens as this. It was much like burying him before he was dead, and it was not at all strange that he sometimes complained of his coffin. It did not fit him, because he was not yet ready for the grave.

As we have already stated, at sixty-five this relation was given him, and though there was some of the "old man" recognized about him, yet the sound vigor of his venerable wisdom was still as strong in him as ever.

The people knew him everywhere, and no preacher in the State excelled him in maintaining the public confidence, or in the length and breadth of his personal influence, for he was everywhere known as a "moral hero of a thousand battles," as one of the last relics of the old Indiana itinerant pioneers.

But his heels were trod upon by the coming tramp of a younger race of itinerants, who were full of life and ready for the battle, and it only remained for him to retire from the work to give place to "illustrious successors."

CHAPTER XXX.

CHARACTER AND DEATH OF HIS WIFE.

To the mothers of distinguished men, biography has often given much more than the usual praise, for to their maternal wisdom and prudence may be traced the formation of early character, the vitality of a healthy ambition, and the distinguished purity of subsequent history. Nature gives them the power of making first impressions, and filial regards not unfrequently render them continuous and lasting. The acknowledgment of such power should always be made with gratitude, and the maternal source of it should ever be faithfully honored.

But what shall we say of the equally sacred relationship—the holy life-tie that gives to man his dearest bosom friend,—who, if she is true to herself, is his hearth-counsellor, his guiding star, and the crowning glory of his life's history!

The work of the wife and mother, in the sustenance and success of any public service the husband has rendered, is but seldom known, for what she is and what she has done may not well be measured. Her children may rise up and call her blessed, and, in them the world may read something of her power, but what her influence over her husband has been, and to what extent she has contributed to his life's success, is too often only an unwritten chapter, which if the world knew at her death, her grave would doubtless be honored equally with that of her husband's and the chaplets of fame bequeathed to the one would be as freely and as honorably bestowed upon the other.

It is no doubt frequently the case that the public voice gives that praise to the man, the husband, for his virtuous integrity and personal success in life, which might be largely traced back to his home and hearth, where the wife has ruled in her gentleness and love, and where the mild sceptre of her influence has brought order out of confusion, and directed the steps of moral timidity in the highest paths of usefulnes and honor.

It is not wealth or education, or fashionable accomplishments, that make the good and prudential wife. It is the sound common sense, the virtuous purity and well governed disposition, which constitute her highest home and household endowments, and make her the inspiring source of her husband's prosperity.

She perhaps became his bride when he knew not the world, and the world knew nothing of him. The grass of spring was growing under his feet when their union began, and through all the changes and responsibilities of the seasons of life, she has been his bosom companion, and the most intimate partner of his joys and sorrows.

The wife of Mr. Havens, to whom we wish here to pay a passing tribute of respect, was a pattern of plainness, as well as of simplicity. The artlessness of nature was always observable in her spirit, while her quiet manners and striking common sense constituted the most prominent features of her character.

Honored as she only was with a mere domestic education, Mrs. Havens gave her whole life to her home and her children; and according to her best convictions, she aimed to fulfill the obligations of a wife and mother. These were the relations of life which she felt to be chiefly binding upon her. The kindly sympathies of neighborship, and of humanity, were instinctive with her, and to the needy and the wayfaring, she was always ready to extend her hand in the ministrations of aid and kindness.

To the world, the life of such a woman may seem to be obscure, and the vicissitudes of her history be deemed unimportant, but to the honest and the thoughtful, there is a lesson of wisdom in the simplicity of such a character, and in the usefulness of such toils, from which prudence may gather the instructions of wisdom, and even the most pretending might profit if they would, in the simplicity of her experience.

Civilization always errs, when the expectations of life are based only upon the gifts of wealth, and where happiness is counted on, because of mere educational attainment and polish. The one, it is true, may impart the comforts of palatial splendor, and the other give to the social circle many of the appearances of a fashionable ecstasy, but after all, the simple dominion of nature is always princely, and the beauty of her manners is much more apt to hold the heart to its steadiest loyalty.

The frivolous fastidiousness of fashionable life is continually making blunders, and its wild conceptions often find their only relief in fancied delusions; and when disappointment comes, as come it will, the blame is not unfrequently placed upon nature, as if the divinity had made our race only to be miserable.

The simple life which was led by the early pioneers in their humble primitive cabins in the West, had in it, perhaps, as much pure happiness as any other portion of the world has ever enjoyed.

The eccentric tanner-poet, of our State, Mr. John Finley, has thus delineated cabin life, and those who have seen it give him full credit for its truthfulness—

> "The emigrant so soon located,
> In Hoosier life initiated;
> Erects a cabin in the woods,
> Wherein he stows his household goods,
> At first round logs and clapboard roof,
> With puncheon floor, quite carpet proof,
> And paper windows, oiled and neat,
> His edifice is then complete,
> Ensconced in this, let those who can,
> Find out a truly happier man.
> The little youngsters rise around him,
> So numerous they quite astound him;
> Each with an ax, or wheel in hand,
> And instinct to subdue the land."

It was in such a cabin as this, that Mrs. Havens spent many of the years of her life. Surrounded by her children, which, as we have stated, were numerous, and busy with the cares of her maternal obligations, it may not reasonably be supposed that she was often lonesome. Though the tall forest trees towered around her, casting their dense shadows over her humble dwelling place, the dancing sun-light cheered her spirit with a love of life, while the songsters of nature gave her free concerts, such as even connosieurs would have admired with more than the usual professional devotion. But while she was thus occupying this cabin home in the woods, her itinerant husband was much of his time away on his circuits and districts, and consequently it became her duty to look after the interests of their little farm, as well as the cares of her numerous family. She of course trained her children to work, for their labor was necessary to support them, as the "quarterage" salary of Mr. Havens would not much more than pay his personal expenses.

In the discharge of all these responsibilities, she made no complaints, but patiently gave her strength to the onerous task, as if nature and providence had designed her the destiny. She always submissively and reverently honored the ministry of her husband, and endeavored to so manage the affairs of home, that he might never miss an appointment. No one was more cognizant of these facts than Mr. Havens himself, and he faithfully reciprocated her thoughtful tenderness with an affection and gratitude which ceased only when he closed his own earthly life.

Actuated by the true spirit of religious obligations, Mrs. Havens appeared never to wish to live for herself. Her thoughts and her labors were for others, and while she studied the laws of domestic economy with her most serious thoughts, she made it the great object of her earthly toils, to do "what she could" to honor the ministry of her companion and to bring up her children in the ways of truth and honesty

The services of such women in the Methodist itinerancy, particularly in the earlier years, was certainly no ordinary sacrifice. What they did in the great work, though only or chiefly seen in the more public labors of their husbands, certainly gave them claims upon the gratitude of the church which none should ignore, and which entitles their memories to a record of honor as enduring as that of their husbands themselves.

With the wives of many of the old pioneer preachers we had some acquaintance, and we feel proud to bear our humble and sincere testimony to their many virtues. Full of the faith of honorable Christain women, and ardently devoted to the cause of their master, they gave themselves to the sacrifices and privations of an itinerant life because their husbands believed they had been called to such a field of labor.

Many of the perplexities of annual removals were however, largely avoided by Mr. Havens, by settling his family in the very commencement of his Indiana itinerancy in their humble country cabin, for with him, as well as with others of that day, such economy was a necessity, for the alternative, if they had not done so would have been to have retired from the itinerancy altogether.

His family being a large one, he made the best possible arrangements in his power for his continuance in the itinerant field, and after doing this to a great extent, his good wife and children made their own support, while he gave himself up wholly to the ministry.

It was the assumption of this great responsibility, which gave to this good woman the profoundest respect of all who knew her. They over-looked the defects of her worldly accomplishments, and lack of general knowledge, in their admiration of her good sense and simplicity of character and the many excellencies of her domestic servitude.

Wholly unpretending as she always was, the plain and beautiful simplicity of her life, gave her the recognition of "a Mother in Israel." "Mother Havens" and "Aunt Anna," were the usual appellations given her among all her acquaintances, and no one could be found so poor as to refuse to do her reverence.

All knew that her life had been a plain one, and that the care of her children had given her arduous obligations, yet in her later years, when her children had grown to maturity, her life was crowned with as many respectful attentions as perhaps any other matron of the country.

In one of her visits to the capital of the State, she was invited to the magnificent mansion of an old-time friend who had once lived in an humble cabin, as poor as she had ever been herself. Wealth and education and modern fashions had, however, wrought wonderful changes in the family, and these great changes of style were particularly noticed by the plain and venerable matron, who would probably have let everything pass without a remark, if it had not been she saw there was some visible aristocratic exaltation from then until now, which, as was natural, she thought to check a little.

After a brief reception in the drawing-room, the mother said to the daughter:

"Bettie, dear, hadn't you better give Aunt Anna a little music before she goes?"

Of course consent was readily given, as the young Miss, no doubt, felt somewhat proud of her musical accomplishments, and they all passed into the finely furnished parlor, where the spacious and costly damask-covered rocking chair was given to their venerable guest, who seated herself, while the grand piano was being opened.

Aunt Anna looked round over the room as our old style women are apt to do, and observing the paintings and furniture, the carpets and piano, together with the rich curtains adorning the windows, she said to the lady of the house: "I see, sister, a great change between this fine parlor and the old log cabin where I first saw you."

Here the piano was opened and the daughter made her fingers dance over the keys, by which she drew out such music as Aunt Anna had never heard before. Several of our modern waltzes were played, when the young Miss ceased.

"Well, I suppose," said Mrs. Havens "that is what you call piano music, but for my part, I would just about as *lief hear a cat squall as one of your pianos.*"

This left handed compliment, of course, was only intended as a playful sarcasm, by the old lady, but still, she doubtless spoke the truth, as it regarded her appreciation of the fashionable pretensions of the age. The put-on airs of our American aristocracy can have but limited attractions among the women whose musical culture was amid the hummings of the spinning wheel. The songs of the cradle, and the old household melodies, comprised all the musical studies of Mother Havens' life, and a fish would certainly not be less at home out of water, than such persons usually are, amidst the piano performances of many of our modern belles. The lessons of labor, of practical industry, were more highly prized by these old time people than any of our modern accomplishments, and in their view, the young lady who did not understand the general routine of domestic duties, of household obligations, was only suitable for a show window, or to make some man a fashionable slave for the mere honor of being married.

Mrs. Havens had so educated herself to industry that she often knit her childrens' stockings when she walked into town, as she frequently did in preference to riding. A story is authentically told of her, that in one of these trips she dropped her ball of yarn out of her pocket, and traveled on unwinding the yarn while the ball danced on the road behind her. One of her neighbors coming on horseback saw the ball nearly a quarter of a mile before he overtook her, and dismounting from his horse, he picked it up and began the operation of winding it. Looking away ahead, he saw the old lady moving slowly along, and with all his efforts, it was some time before he could wind up to her. He had a hearty laugh at her expense, particularly when she said:

"I thought I felt something jerking; but I did n't dream that it was my ball of yarn."

The last few years of Mrs. Havens' life were spent

in Rushville, where they had a comfortable little home and where she had seen her youngest daughter married. With them life had made many changes, but yet amidst them all they had abundant reasons for gratefulness to the Almighty Giver of all good, for the tenderness of his providences and for his bounteous mercies. Her children were still all living, but three. Daniel, David and Conwell, had died after they had grown to manhood, one of whom, David, was a traveling minister in the Iowa Conference at the time of his death. Two other sons, George and Landy, had been in the itinerant ministry for years. The rest were all settled around her, in married life, and the venerable parents were once more left alone. But the sun of their natural lives was evidently sinking low in the west, and the time was rapidly approaching when the silver cords would be loosed and the golden bowl be broken, for it was written of them as of others:

"Then shall the dust return to the earth as it was, and the spirit shall return unto God who gave it."

The death of a mother is always a sad calamity in any family, for her scepter of rule and government in most all cases, is that of love. It is this power which the good mother learns to be her strongest hold, and she cultivates it ordinarily in proportion to her endowments of sense and virtue. This power Mother Havens had exercised over her family through all the long years of her experience, and now that she had grown old, she still felt the same spirit moving her to send her daily prayers after them. The innocence of her life, and the gentleness of her spirit, gave her much of the disposition of the child, so that when her death sickness came upon her, she resigned her life without a sigh or a groan.

Supported by her simple faith in Christ, she felt assured that all was well, and bidding her children to trust in the same Savior, she retired from this mortal life on the 23d of March, 1864, aged seventy-five years. Thus passed from the earth one of the humblest and most sincere mothers of our Indiana itinerancy, and though she had seen more than her three score years and ten, her death was lamented as though she had died in her teens. To Father Havens especially, her demise was the darkest cloud of his years. He seemed not to know how to live without her. She had been so long the true wife of his heart and had so often kindled the fires of his gratitude by the numerous kindnesses of her deeds, that when she was gone and hid away in the grave, the lonely and venerable pioneer felt, that his very life star had set, that no other earthly charm remained to him, and the sacred place where they buried her out of his sight became from thenceforth, until within a few days of his own death, the only seeming altar of his acceptable sacrifice.

CHAPTER XXXI.

HIS OWN DEMISE.

The death of a good man is never an ordinary event. The loss we are aware is not often acknowledged, because society but seldom appreciates such a character. But felt or not, recognized or ignored, the moral nerve of humanity is weakened by such an affliction, and the vaccum created in the ranks of reform and of personal heroism which the death of such a one has made, will never again be filled by another. For each human being, either good or bad, fills his own *niche* in the temple of the universe, and when by death a vacancy is created in this outer court of mortal life the vaccum is never filled again, others may survive who may represent the departed, but the vital character of the dead has been taken with him, and his individual identity and personal power thenceforth belong to the scenes and responsibilities of his eternal mission.

It is in this respect only that death is our enemy. His inflictions bereave us, leave us in orphanage and carry away from our sides and presence life's strongest props, and earth's brightest stars. On those moral supports we can never lean again, and the cheerful glitterings of those stars are seen by us no more.

Why it is thus in our worldly relationships the philosophy of Christianity alone explains. Mortal life has its missions as well as the immortal, and the one fits us for the other as thought kindles thought, as association creates affection, as home makes life, and as aspiration feeds upon the hopes of an immortal destiny.

The fact is well recognized, as well as universal, that earthly experiences and aspirations all fail to satisfy the longings of mind. Even honor, fame and wealth, the three great divinities of the present life fall short of any permanent human gratification, and the hearts of the million turn away from them with disgust and satiety.

Beautiful as this world may be, it was never intended as our lasting abiding place. It is only the garden of our origin and of our mortal trial. The earth receives us as temporary citizens, on the agreement that our mortal lives shall be regulated by its laws. Therefore, what we are physically is always fixed by this submission, while what we are intellectually and morally is in proportion to the efforts of our cultivation and of our obedience to moral principles.

All men, it seems, believe in some sort of an eternal future, but what it is and what will be its personal and relative responsibilities, they appear not to comprehend. They do not think as they ought to, that such specific revelations as they would wish for are not now necessary. "We now see through a glass darkly, but then face to face. We now know in part, but then shall we know even as we are known." This is Heaven's order, and the economy is certainly a wise one, for if any other philosophy was taught us, the very cowardice of men would force them to an exit from the earth regardless of their whole mortal mission, in view merely of freeing themselves from worldly trial and responsibility.

Life has its requisitions as well as death, and if law is observed, the latter must wait on the former until life's mission is duly finished and the clay house of its earthly dwelling falls to pieces with its own years. This is Christianity's simplest lesson, and men should study it because it is practical as well as philosophical.

What we are here is life's great concern, as it is also the living burden of our religious philosophy. The present is a reality, a personal responsibility and demands our sincerest devotions, and whatever lot falls to our destiny, the path of faithful duty is always the road to an honorable destiny.

Then, when a good man dies we can confidently believe that "our loss is his infinite gain." Nature may be robbed of a citizen, and we who survive may be bereaved, but life itself is nothing the loser. The thought of mind, once freed from the clay tenement, goes on to a higher destination of being, where beneficent employments absorb its powers, and the work of angelic ministration becomes its eternal life, as a part and portion of the immortal agencies in the divine beneficence.

Hence, it may be said, in agreement with the very genius of Christian truth, that death never triumphs over life. It possesses no such conquering powers. Its highest attributes only give to it the endowment of an earthly gate-way to the spirit land, where truth holds universal empire, and love and beneficence measure the boundaries and capacity of every living soul. Earthly duties and earthly relationships may hold us here with hooks of steel, but when the good man, at any age, feels that his work is done, eternity has no terrors which can throw a storm-cloud over the hopes of his soul, and death itself comes to him only as gentle slumbers come to a child.

For many long years, such thoughts as these influenced and governed the mind and heart of our departed hero, Father Havens. And when the years of his life had numbered over three score and ten, he could but look around him in expectation of the speedy coming of death to give him his release from the feebleness of age, and to restore him to the relationships of "the loved and the lost," who had gone before him to the better land.

To him the world had lost most of its charms. The wife of his youth and the companion of his years, had but a few months before passed away, and the loneliness of life had seemingly become to him as the "valley of the shadow of death."

All of his old pioneer companions in the ministry of Indiana, had gone the way of their fathers, and he felt that he was left alone. He saw in the dim vision of his age, that his sun of life was casting its long shadows very near his feet, and he felt that the time of his departure from the earth was near at hand.

Solemn as the conviction was, the thought of dying now became intermingled with his dearest hopes, for he well knew that the shores of reunion could only be reached through the gates of death and therefore he was not afraid to die. The grave of his wife had become earth's dearest spot to his spirit, and he made his pilgrimages to the cemetry's sacred enclosure with a devotion of love to her memory such as we have never known in any other instance. His affection for his wife seemed to have been doubled by her death. The bright visage of her simple and unostentatious virtues lived in his heart, as if its impress had been fastened there by the infinite fingers. The wife of his bosom and the mother of his children, she had been the divinity of his domestic joys, and now that she was gone from him, he could but mourn as one who had been left behind amidst the desolations of a wilderness. On her grave he would go and bow his knees in prayer to the Father of all life, and there he claimed to receive richer assurances of their speedy reunion among the immortal ones, than he could or did anywhere else.

In family bereavements Father Havens may be said to have been more than usually favored. The father of so many children, there was never a death among them until he had reached his sixty-fourth year. With him the lessons of life had been far greater than those of death. Through many gathering years the sunlight along his earthly pathway had been without a mortal cloud. The gentle providence was fully recognized by him, and he often said, that in this respect he had been the most highly favored of men. When at a late period in his life, this cloud did gather over him, he could but feel that it was all right, for he well knew that it was "appointed unto man once to die," and he did not dare to murmur when the day of darkness eventually came upon his own hearth.

He had often witnessed the ravages of death in families around him, and with the best words of his heart he had endeavored to speak to the sorrowing the consolations of the Christian faith. Twice, just a few weeks before his death, was he called to the Capital of the State to officiate at the burial services of two of his old and particular friends.

One of these was Morris Morris, one of the oldest citizens of the city. For more than forty years the hospitable dwelling of Mr. Morris had been one of Father Havens' most intimate homes, and when the venerable old pioneer was about to die, he expressed the wish that Father Havens should attend and preach a funeral discourse at his burial.

A compliance with this request gave him his last opportunity of officiating in Indianapolis. Of course, the ceremonies attending this funeral led the venerable minister to look back upon the past as well as forward upon the future. The changes around him were great, for the wilderness had become the thronged city, and but few who had worshiped with him in their first rude meeting house were left to witness the solemn valedictory services of this funeral occasion.

Returning to his Rushville home, after seeing his old friend, "Pa Morris," laid away in his grave, Divine Providence, as if about to make him familiar with death, in view of his own speedy demise, called him suddenly to the bedside of his daughter, Emily Hitt, then residing in Kokomo. As yet, the venerable Apostle had never lost a daughter, and though old and stricken in years, he was prompt to obey the call, and taking the cars, in a few hours he was by her bedside, with all the kindly sympathies of a devoted and loving father.

The case, he saw, was an intricate one, and admitted but little hope of recovery, and he bid her put her trust in God, no matter what might be the issue.

Day and night he watched over her, doing and directing what he could for her relief and comfort, and when he saw that she must die, he bowed in prayer by her bedside and surrendered her back to her Maker with all that solemn and deep feeling, so characteristic of his strong and affectionate nature.

In a few moments his beloved daughter was dead. A wife and a mother, she had been called away early in life, but with the full hope of a glorious immortality beyond.

When her mortal remains were decently put away in the grave, feeling as he had never felt before that his own end was not far off, he turned his face once more homeward, that he might die in his own bed and among his own kindred. His Conference being in session at Shelbyville, he stopped, though feeling greatly fatigued from his recent exposures, that he might once more look in upon his brethren and bid them God speed in their great work of evangelization. A single appearance in the Conference room was all he could make for he was too feeble to render any service, and without a word of ceremony, he left the Conference, and taking the cars for Rushville, he was once more under his own roof.

Like the soldier from the battle field—though his friends did not know it—he had come home to die. Nature, with him, had made her chief life struggles, and now that her once proud vessel was about to sink, he was confident his soul would ride the storm.

It was while he was in this frail condition of physical debility that he learned from a friend and neighbor, who had called upon him, that it was the day of the October election. His friend asked him if he would like to vote?

"If I thought I could stand it to get there, I would be glad to do so," said he, and he then added, "I have always loved my country, and I have always tried to vote for the right, and as this is perhaps my last opportunity, if I can be taken in a carriage, I think I can stand it." In a couple of hours, a carriage was brought to his door, and with some assistance, he was enabled to get into it, when he was driven to the polls. A ticket was handed him, and he took out his glasses and placed them on his face, in order to examine it. He got out of the carriage with the assistance of friends who had gathered around him and handing his ballot to the judges, he said, "This, gentlemen, I presume, is my last vote." Then being assisted into the carriage again, the crowd seemingly looking upon him as if they thought it was the last time and as most of them had known him for many years they could but reverence him, and a number came forward and shook hands with him.

Excited by the crowd and the scene before him, and feeling that it was his last opportunity, he said, "Gentlemen, some of you may think me imprudent in coming out in my present feeble state of health to vote to-day. It may be that I have been, but I felt it to be my duty to come and vote. For years I have had a deep concern for my country, and I have even been afraid that it would not stand. The dreadful war now raging, for what I know, may give it to the flames of destruction, but I hope it will not. You, gentlemen, will live to see the end of this fearful struggle, but I will not; my days, I feel, are about numbered, and I wish to say to you all, be true to your country, constitution and laws, and never sacrifice to party ambition the welfare of the government."

The old fire of the venerable patriot was still burning in his bosom, and in thus performing his last public duty as a citizen, he showed the living earnestness of his spirit, and the bold and determined patriotism of his life. Returning to his room and bed, he laid himself upon his couch trusting that in the hands of a kind and merciful Providence that all would be well.

To his children and friends who visited him from day to day, he bore strong testimony to his faith in God, and he assured them that in Christ his Saviour his salvation would be complete.

To his son, Rev. George Havens, he said: "I have no fears of death. Christ the Lord is my salvation both living and dying, and I feel that I shall soon be at rest."

Implicit confidence in his heavenly Father appeared to be his most distinguishing dying trait, and though he talked but little, what he said satisfied his children and neighbors that his passage to the shades of death was calm and placid. He felt that his life-work was finished and the light of his lamp went out gently and sweetly—

"Like the stars,
Which sink not behind the darkened West,
But melt away into the light of Heaven."

On the morning of the 4th of November, 1864, the sad news was told through the streets of the town that Father Havens was dead. To every heart the tidings were mournful, for all felt that they had lost a good man from among them, that a venerable and worthy patriarch was dead. For nearly seventy-four years, he had been a pilgrim of earth, and at this good old age he was gathered to his fathers. Though advanced in life and unable longer to go out as a gospel messenger among men, the thousands of his friends felt loth to believe him gone even after they knew he had been placed in his grave.

CHAPTER XXXII.

FUNERAL OBSEQUIES.

When the sad tidings was told that Father Havens was dead, the hearts of thousands lamented his departure. For forty years he had claimed a citizenship in the county of Rush, and during all that period the definite trumpet tones of his warnings had been familiar among the people. He had stood in the gate guarding the citadel of reform against popular evils, and always fearless of the public censure. Every one knew him. His character was understood, and but few could justly speak evil of him. The flag that he bore had been but seldom furled, and in the moral conflicts of the country, he had always been seen in the front of the battle.

Thus known, good men loved him, and even bad men reverenced him, because they knew he would stand up for the right though the very heavens fell. Such a man and minister could not well die without drawing around his bier the sincere regrets and mournful sympathies of many thousands.

The building up of the moral fortunes of the people had been the sole objective labors of his life, and when it was told that "Father Havens" (as all called him) was dead, multitudes felt that the loss was theirs much more than it was his. He had stood before them as an apostle of truth and right through so many years, with all the fearless independence and moral firmness of a man of God, and a minister of righteousness, that when they knew he was no more, they could but ask, "Who will ever fill his place?"

What he was, dead and in his coffin, did not affect them so much as what they all felt they had lost in the heroism of his life and in the manliness of his ministry. Surrounded by numerous moral dangers, as they knew they all were, they could but fear for their own future welfare, as there was no one recognized by them to take his place. Missed by the Church, as well as by the world, the vacuum created by his death, was felt to be much more than an ordinary one, and many remarked very truly "His exact likeness, will never be seen among us again."

In his own house, in the town of Rushville, he had died, and there he lay in state, plainly and humbly, as a true and faithful Methodist preacher. He was only this and nothing more. He had never indeed made pretensions to anything else. This was enough, and as he had often expressed himself, "It was even much more than he could well honor as he wished."

By the side of his wife, he had appeared for months, anxious to rest, and there they now prepared his grave, that they might lay him away in that consecrated "God's acre," where his dust might sleep until the Savior of man comes to make up his jewels.

The full funeral ceremonies which his friends all felt were so justly due to his memory and virtues, were postponed to accommodate the wide circle of his kindred and brethren, and after proper religious services, conducted by Rev. John W Mellender, who was the pastor of the Rushville Station, his body was deposited in its last resting place.

The funeral cortege was a large one, and the dust of the grave which rattled upon his coffin was watched with deep emotion by the gathered circle, for the solemn conviction was upon them all, that a hero had perished, that a Prince in Israel had fallen!

Nature itself demands a tribute of respect when a good man is put away in his grave, but on the occasion of Father Havens' burial the marked solemnity of the scene gave evidence of the deepest reverence. Well stricken in years, as he was, and though they all knew that he had lived out the measure of a long and honorable life, they were still not prepared for his exit.

To die thus amid the regrets of thousands is a destiny allotted only to the few. Love may shed its tears of warm affection over the graves of youth and infancy but when the aged die the reverence of universal regret becomes the higest attestation both of virtue and character. No higher eulogy can be given to departed greatness, and no richer chaplet can wreath the monument of worth and goodness. An embalment in the hearts of the people when one is dead is the highest inheritance of human life. Nothing in honor or fame can equal it, and the contrast between such an immortality and that of the penury-bound millionare, or the mere worldly schemer, however respectable he may be, is as wide as the distance of the poles. Millions of such earth travelers perish and go down to the dust without anything more than a mere passing thought and their existences here might be set down as palpable moral abortions. The lives of all such selfish, worldly drivelers contradict in every particular the philosophy of humanity, and even put to shame the modesty of the commonest charity.

Of the good, the honest hearted always love to speak in praise, and in all such cases the language of eulogy becomes their vernacular, and the justness of their verdicts is seen in the reformatory power of their subjects long after they are dead.

With such a man as Father Havens had been, his kindred and friends did not think it would be doing proper justice to his memory to bury him away in the grave with the mere ordinary ceremonies of a funeral occasion. They claimed what was true, that both as a man and a minister, he was above the common order and, therefore, it was determined to appoint a day when his friends might gather and give to the memory of his virtues and life, that becoming tribute of respect and reverence which so many declared was due to such a grand old Methodist hero.

The first Sunday in June, 1865, was appointed for the gathering of his friends and kindred to pay this tribute, and when the day arrived they came from far and near by the thousands—so that the vast assembly was supposed to number between three and four thousand.

The churches of the town were all closed and their congregations united in the solemn ceremonies with as much sincere regard for the memory of the venerable dead as if he had been their own father or brother.

By an agreement made several years before Father Havens' death, the honor of preaching his funeral was conceded to one of his sons in the ministry, Rev. John W. T. McMullen. With this young Methodist preacher Father Havens had long been intimate. The one was old and the other young, but the simplicity of honest hearts made them congenial, and the warmth of their friendship without abatement continued until it was severed by the hand of death.

By many, this selection was thought to be a strange one, particularly as Mr. McMullen was a young man, while in different parts of the State there were a number of able and venerable ministers who had long been identified with Father Havens in episcopal counsels and through many social years.

But those who had any such thoughts did not call to mind the peculiar independence of character which Father Havens always possessed. He never could be flattered, and he cared as little for compliments as any minister we have known. Living or dead, he did not wish for any fulsome praise. We once heard him say "that he would as lief have an exhorter to preach his funeral, if he was dead, as a bishop." His intimate friends all knew that while he had a high appreciation of the abilities and characters of others, he was not the man ever to yield to any eulogies of himself.

If the selection of the preacher was an error, it was in no sense intended to be malignant or even partial, but was simply agreed to in conformity with the long well known attachment between the father and the son.

We are aware of the fact that even in the churches it is not often the case that the people are disposed to worship setting suns. Youthful fires are supposed to send forth the brighter blaze, while dying embers are only supposed to give the feeble emblems of energies well spent.

In this peculiar idiosyncrasy of the age, but few men were better posted than Father Havens himself, and even to his latest days he detested it as "a mark of the beast" which would dishonor any church or people. Reverence for the integrity and wisdom of age was certainly one of his virtues. But while this fact is affirmed, the other assertion may be made, that he was never disposed to turn his back upon youthful simplicity, or to think less of sincerity because it was found in the bosom of youth. He was always the friend of the young man, and especially of the young minister, and if he sometimes spoke to him in the language of rebuke, he was impelled to it by a sincere and ardent wish that the reproof might work a reform, that the young man might be cured of his malady.

The medicine which he gave to others he was always willing to take himself, and therefore, even in view of his own death, he had no desire to have one word said of him when he was gone, unless it was fully sustained by the facts of history. He had indeed so charged his young companion when the proposition was made that he should preach his funeral. Truthful frankness was his beau ideal of an honest funeral sermon, and he had no wish that his own case should be an exception.

The large congregation which met to participate in

the final obsequies of Father Havens could not be accommodated in any church of the town, and preparations for their accommodation were made in the beautiful grove of the court house campus where a stand had been erected for the ministers, and where all could comfortably hear the officiating speaker.

Having been personally invited to be present on this mournful occasion, we arrived on Sunday morning just in time to witness the assembling of the people and the commencement of the religious services. We saw there was no pompous programme or formal paegantry. The people came as was their custom to worship, and taking their seats in general order, the services were begun with singing by the whole congregation, when devout prayer was offered by Rev. D. M. Stewart, of the Presbyterian Church, who for nearly twenty years had been the neighbor of Father Havens as well as an associate brother minister.

Mr. Stewart had known the departed dead through a majority of his ministerial years, and his prayer, while it was humble and contrite before God, savored of his high appreciation of the venerated Father, and gave strong assurances of his abiding faith that the spirit of the good man whose death they all mourned, was safely housed. " where the wicked cease from troubling and the weary are at rest."

When several appropriate passages of scripture had been read, and another hymn was sung by the congregation, Brother McMullen arose and read his text: "And I saw a new heaven and a new earth; for the first heaven and the first earth were passed away; and there was no more sea," etc., etc. Rev. xxi, 1.

To give any definite outline of this lengthy and elaborate sermon transcends our present privilege, and as we have never seen the manuscript since the day it was read to that large and attentive congregation of sympathizing friends, it would be impossible for us to do it justice in any report we might here make of it.

The subject of "the new creation" was the theme of the speaker, which he handled with much more than the ordinary ability. The effort might have been styled a grand one, for its exhibition was "a wilderness of words and ideas," and the visions of its general theory, whether probable or tangible, were as beautiful as the gardens of Paradise. The day was as lovely as summer, and the aroma of the flowers of June threw around us the inspirations of the present life, and we found it difficult to follow the winged messengers of the sermonic thought from this creation to any other. However beautiful the celestial theory, or grand and graphic the rhetoric of the speaker's happy expressions, our thoughts were of and with the lamented dead. The wings of fancied theories were not ours on the occasion, and ever and anon we had to let the eloquent orator fly where he might or could, independent of our accompaniment.

It is strange, and yet it is true, the solemnities of death admit only of the eloquence and music of love. All other aggrandisements lose their power in its presence.

In thought and memory that holy day had been consecrated by that whole assembly to the sacred reminiscences of Father Havens' life and history. The dust of his grave still held them to the earth, and they could only mount the chariot of fire, where his spirit was presumed to be one of the company. All admitted that the effort of Mr. McMullen was both able and eloquent. No one could censure him for not being elaborately prepared for the occasion. But the misfortune was, he had not anticipated the still powerful dominion of the lamented dead. Just then a simple narrative of the thoughts and feelings, the hopes and fears, with brief sketches of the character and life of Father Havens, to that audience, would have been appreciated far beyond the grandest speculative theories of the future life theologians have ever invented.

We had traveled a long distance to pay a reverential tribute to the memory of the man and minister whom we had looked upon as being the ablest of our Indiana pioneer Methodist preachers, and our own thoughts were in unison with those of the congregation. The specific purpose of the day and the object of its funeral consecration was the life and character of Father Havens as the original premises. Hence, our line of thought, like those of the people, was on the track of the venerable hero who had so recently left us, and on this account, we doubtless failed to appreciate, as we should have done, the very learned and eloquent sermon of the orator preacher.

In a few pages which Brother McMullen devoted to

the virtues and character of his beloved Father in the Ministry, he informed us that " he had known him, as a Methodist preacher, from his earliest childhood days.

"He had gone with his own father, when he himself was but a little boy, to hear Father Havens preach, and in the innocency of his youth, he had listened to him with as much reverence as if he had been a minister plenipotentiary direct from Heaven.

"I have never known," said he, "a more simple or purer minded man. A very child in the tenderness of his affections, his thoughts were as just as they were pure. Though he might have erred through the excitement of impulse, he never did by any wanton violation of principle.

"With him truth was inviolate and the sacredness of integrity was to be maintained even at the risk of life itself. To live an honest life as well as a useful one, was his great ambition; and although he was sometimes censured for being too frank and too severe, he did not aim to be impertinent, but only to speak the words of truth and soberness. Full of the kindliest sympathy, his hand was ever ready to help the unfortunate, and where guilt was not attached, his great soul would lead him to dare even danger and death to help a suffering fellow mortal.

"But the man and the Christian hero is dead. Our venerable father has gone from us to return no more in the flesh. The silent grave may hold his inanimate dust, but, thank God, his spirit is in no such narrow prison house. The enchantments of the celestial city with its freedom, its happy associations and angelic missions are now his through the blood of the new and everlasting covenant.

"Therefore let us all join in the sublime doxology: 'Now unto the King eternal, invisible, the only wise God, our father, be glory, through Jesus Christ, forever and ever, Amen.' "

CHAPTER XXXIII.

HIS MONUMENT.

The cemetery of Rushville, in which the mortal remains of our Methodist hero, Father Havens, was buried, is located on a beautiful bluff of Flat Rock, about half a mile east of the town.

The location presents to the passer by, perhaps, as quiet and picturesque a place in which to bury the dead as may be found in the State.

The lot for his grave and that of his wife, had been selected years before by Father Havens himself. Conscious as he was that the solemn change of death was not far off, and would inevitably come, he wisely and with good grace and faith chose this spot as their last resting place, where his children and friends might come and call them up in their memories when the outside world had forgotten them.

Humble and obscure as this sacred inclosure may be and far away as it is from the bustle and stir of busy life, the musical chorals of nature's songsters, with the melancholy dirges of the surrounding forest winds, give the locality the solemn appropriateness of a cemetery for the dead.

Here in this quiet burial place is the narrow house of the old itinerant pioneer where he now sleeps well. The spot is pointed out with more than the usual respect and reverence, for the pride of public sentiment which was ever partial to him while living has followed him down to his grave.

The years seem not to have obscured the remembrance of his virtues or to have swept away any of the broad influences of his character. Though most of his associates have gone with him to the grave, the present generation appears to remember him as if he was still cotemporary with themselves.

To this sacred spot, this rural burying place of the dead, is now given a higher character than ever before. Good men were buried in it in other years, but Father Havens now sleeps there and all feel that this fact gives it a still greater distinction; for the place where worth and virtue are buried always becomes holy ground, and marks the particular spot of earth with a sacred richness which nothing else that is mortal can ever equal, for—

> "That dust which forms the winding sheet
> Of good men's bones gives life to death;
> It throws a mantle oe'r their frames,
> And keeps them young as in their birth."

Where the brain of thought and the heart of love decay is consecrated ground. Hence the spot where our fathers sleep in the quiet repose of death becomes hallowed in memory as the buried loves of the soul. Their spirits have gone from us, but the dust they have left behind them and which is so sacredly treasured, is henceforth the attracting neucleus of a thousand pilgrimages.

"In the cave of the field of Macpelah before Mamre, Abraham buried Sarah his wife. And the field and the cave that is therein were made sure unto Abraham for a possession of a burying place by the sons of Heth."

Thus we may see, that even antiquity had its cemetery veneration, as well as our modern ages. Indeed it may be asserted that the regards paid to the dead are the distinguishing marks of our civilization, as well as a delicate evidence of our intelligent Christian refinements. It is not enough to merely hide them away in the dust, but as Gray in his "Church Yard Elegy" has so beautifully told it:

> "Yet e'en these bones from insult to protect,
> Some frail memorial still erected nigh,
> With uncouth rhymes and shapeless sculpture decked,
> Implores the passing tribute of a sigh.
> Their names, their years, spelt by the unlettered muse,
> The place of fame and elegy supply;
> And many a holy text around she strews,
> To teach the rustic moralist to die."

The simple affection for the man and the sincere reverence for the minister which was so universally manifested in the case of Father Havens, led many to say when he was dead that his grave should be marked by a monument such as would justly and properly represent him, and in some respects be commensurate with his life and character.

They thought that, as his services and itinerant fame had extended over the whole State, the four Indiana Conferences would, if the matter was properly presented to them, move in the line of a monument, such as might fully meet the exigency.

But more mature reflection convinced them that this plan was impracticable, for it would have been both partial and invidious, as many other good ministers had died whose graves were only marked by plain monumental tablets, while some were without even a grave stone of any kind. Therefore, all public effort was abandoned, and the beautiful spire which marks his grave is alone the gift of his own children.

Soon after his death, the Administrators of his estate, Rev. George Havens and John Dixon, Esq., contracted for the erection of a marble monument at a cost of $2,500, which it was supposed would fully meet the wishes of his friends, and serve as an appropriate memorial of the distinguished itinerant.

The stately and beautiful mausoleum is certainly creditable to the family and to the hero whose memory it perpetuates. It is composed of the finest grained Italian marble and exhibits fine mechanical skill and workmanship, and ornamented as it is with a striking bust in *bas relief* of "the brave old man," the presentation is as complete as it is beautiful and appropriate. Some, indeed, may think the display an extravagance, but nothing less would have done justice to the man or the minister, or have given to the present or coming generations any fair conceptions of his worth and virtues.

William Wirt tells us that "no memorial, no slab even raised by *the hand of national gratitude*, points to the grave of Patrick Henry or tells where sleeps the ashes of the patriot and sage," and he has well and beautifully added: "Had his lot been cast in the Republics of Greece or Rome, his name would have been enrolled by some immortal pen among the expellers of tyrants and the champions of liberty; the proudest monuments of national gratitude would have risen to his honor and handed down his memory to future generations." Such reflections are as eloquent of reply as they are justly regardful of the worth of departed greatness and we place them here to vindicate our own position.

On the beautiful Sabbath afternoon of the funeral ceremonies in memory of Father Havens, several hundred of the kindred and friends assembled around his grave to look upon the structure of his monument and to listen to some short addresses commemorative of his life and character. The thought was but a simple one, for it was not expected that the speakers would indulge in any fulsome eulogies or empty panegyrics of the dead, but would only call up some of the old fires of affection which so many desired should live in their heart of hearts while life itself should last. It wsa, in short, a meeting to pay a last sad tribute to one—

> Whose life was brave, but gentle; and the elements
> So mixed in him, that nature might stand up
> And say to all the world—*This is a man.*

The verdant grass and surrounding evergreens, the numerous monuments of the dead, and the tall forest trees, casting their long shadows over us, with the mild complacency of the sun far down in the west, gave to the scene a thoughtful and sombre character which doubtless impressed every one present.

An appropriate him was sung and prayer was offered, when the first speaker addressed us:

"My friends," said he, "the shadows which play

around us here this lovely summer evening, are enough to awaken within us living thoughts of the spirit land. Standing as I do, in the presence of the grave and monument of the greatest Methodist hero the State of Indiana has ever had, I can not but acknowledge the lingering presence of his personal power. I feel as if Father Havens was still here; that he 'is not dead but yet speaketh.'

"What he was we have all known, and what he is here in his grave we all see. But where he is in his spirit's activity and life, we know not, for this is beyond our privilege to discern.

"His history in this life is all we have of him. We can look back upon that, here and now, as the only inheritance we have of the man. Death has stripped him of mortal life and we have laid his body in this charnel house before us, to await the second act in life's immortal programme. With him the first act is past, and his mortal trial is over. But we may add,

' Death makes no conquest of this conqueror,
For now he lives in fame though not in life.'

"His work on earth is done, and it was well done. But few have ever done it better. His indomitable will and unwearied faithfulness, enabled him to fullfil his mission with honor. And may we not now still ask:

'Can he be dead,
Whose spirit influence yet is on his kind?
May we not hear him still from speaking dust,
Like angel whispers from the spirit land?'

"It is indeed, my friends, a most difficult task to recognize that Father Havens is dead. I still seem to see him and hear him speak. His presence appears to be with me in my soul's recognitions, almost as fully visible as when he was yet living. His words of thought and his lessons of wisdom are still heard in their echoes, and I can not forget them, for they always weighed with me as silver, as I well knew they came from the mint of an honest heart. Frank and brave, sincere and benignant, no one ever dared to charge him with treachery, or accuse him of forsaking a friend in order to take the better care of himself.

"I have traveled a hundred miles to attend the solemnities of his funeral, and standing as I do, with you, amidst the august pageantry of this burial place of the dead, I feel that it is good to be here, because it is my privilege and honor to be among the throng who are paying a simple but just tribute to one who was morally illustrious in life, and in death is worthy of our most regretful memories."

Judge J. D. Logan, of the Rushville bar, was next called out, and spoke as follows:

"You must excuse me ladies and gentlemen from attempting anything more on this solemn occasion than a few casual remarks.

"I knew Father Havens, and I may say I knew him well for many years. He was a good citizen and a true man; and I am justified in saying he was worthy of being ranked among the ablest ministers of the State. Gentle and kind, affable and polite, his manners were always those of a gentleman, and yet no man I have ever known excelled him in his devotions to what he deemed to be the right. He was ever as firm in his principles as he was independent in his spirit. Nature had made him a nobleman, as I doubt not but grace had made him a Christian.

"It has often been my privilege to sit under his preaching, and I have had many long conversations with him, for he was my friend, and as such I was always proud of him. I may say of him, that he was a man who never trimmed his sails to shun a storm of responsibility, or catered in the least degree to any of the corruptions of society. He always appeared to know that he was set for the defense of the gospel, and he maintained this position to the end of his life. Though his profession was very different from mine, I presume there will be nothing improper in my saying that he was the most heroic preacher Indiana has ever had. He preached to men's hearts and consciences, and no minister was truer than he was in telling his congregations of their sins. Of him I may say, as was once said of another,

'This Cardinal
Though from an humble stock, undoubtedly
Was fashioned to much honor. From his cradle
He was a scholar, and a ripe, and good one:
Exceeding wise, fair spoken and persuading;
Lofty and firm—though some there doubtless
            Were, who loved him not.'

"But I may here remark that if any hated Father Havens they surely showed but little love for themselves. For honest in his purposes and always well meaning, his actions were regulated by the laws of truth and right, and if he erred the mantle of charity might well be thrown over his errors, for they were the results of human frailty and not those of any moral intention.

"I turn, I confess, with great personal gratification to the magnificent monument before me, which his children have placed over his grave, and as I look upon it and think of the venerable minister, the brave hero, the genuine Christian and kind father, I can not but say the man was well worthy of such a testimonial, for he was one of the first in the Church of which he was a minister, and he was also an honor to our own community in which he lived and died. His children, and children's children, may well be proud of such a father, for he has left behind him the savor of a name which time will not obscure, nor the ages blot out, for

'He was a man, take him for all in all,
I shall not look upon his like again.'"

Rev. John W T. McMullen, next addressed the assembly. He said:

"My Christain friends. Though I have had your patient attention to day, through a long discourse, if my heart could speak now I would have volumes yet to say of my beloved and lamented father, whose perishing body sleeps beneath that pile of splendid marble. You all know that I loved him, loved him as a son loves a father, for I never had but one father in the ministry, and that was Father Havens.

"When I learned that he was dead, I felt that I was an orphan in the ministry. For years he had been my counselor, my confident and guide, and I had trusted in his judgment with the simplicity of a child.

"Though I was often with him, I never presumed to be his equal in the heroic purity of his christian life, or in any of the grand apostolic endowments of his ministry. Indeed, I may say he had but few equals in these respects anywhere, for nature had graduated him to the first honors of his class, and grace had ennobled him and placed him among the very tallest and mightiest of our ministry. But God has taken him to himself, taken him from us all. But our loss is his infinite gain. He has gone from us like the ripe fruit when it is gathered into the garner, and the grand ecstasies of the immortal world are now his inheritance forevermore."

Such were the last funeral offerings paid to the memory of Father Havens. The tribute may be deemed a simple one, but it was sincere. None left the sacred spot who had not felt it was good to be there. The place, the hour and the man had called up in every mind a train of thought which appeared to have a celestial connection, and the communion had in it, and about it some of the touches of the more beautiful and higher life.

The philosophy was demonstrated, "Let him who will be the greatest among you be the servant of all." This is the Bible theory of greatness, and we know of no other. This is the principle, indeed, of the divine greatness. No other can ever impart anything better than mere empty show.

The truculency of servility may crown some men with an airy and temporary distinction, which the winds will whistle away, and the throws of a brainless ambition may confer upon others the brief empire of a flattering rule, but the laws of an immutable equity must continue to bound the limitations of all human ambition, for—

> There are distinctions that will live in Heaven,
> When time is a forgotten circumstance;
> The elevated brow of kings will lose
> The impress of regalia, and the slave
> Will wear his immortality as free
> Beside the crystal waters; but the depth
> Of glory in the attributes of God,
> Will measure the capacities of mind;
> And as the angels differ, will the ken
> Of gifted spirits glorify him more.

FINIS.

www.ingramcontent.com/pod-product-compliance
Lightning Source LLC
Chambersburg PA
CBHW030308240426
43673CB00040B/1104